From Plato to Postmodernism

FROM PLATO
TO
POSTMODERNISM

The Story of Western Culture
through Philosophy,
Literature and Art

CHRISTOPHER WATKIN

Bristol Classical Press

First published in 2011 by
Bristol Classical Press
an imprint of
Bloomsbury Academic
Bloomsbury Publishing Plc
50 Bedford Square
London WC1B 3DP

CIP records for this book are available from the
British Library and the Library of Congress

ISBN 978-0-7156-3828-6

Typeset by Ray Davies
Printed and bound in Great Britain by
CPI Group Ltd, Croydon, Surrey

www.bloomsburyacademic.com

Contents

Acknowledgements

The seed that grew into this project was planted in Pwllheli, Wales, in 1999 at the *Word Alive* Christian conference by Gavin McGrath, in a series of seminars on 'worldview'. It was watered in Cambridge by Martin Crowley, for whom I taught a critical theory course in the academic year 2006-07, by Nick Hammond, who provided timely encouragement in the publishing process, and by Tom Piercy, who lent me Kenneth Clark's magnificent *Civilisation* DVD series over the summer of 2008.

A project of this scope cannot be completed without the very generous help of many kind friends and colleagues who let themselves be badgered by my questions and who improved this book immeasurably by thoughtfully reading and commenting on various drafts. In alphabetical order, I would like to thank Eline van Asperen, Denis Alexander, John Coffey, Ian Cooper, Joseph Crawford, Michael and Jennifer Dodson, Elizabeth Drayson, Raphael Lyne, Ranald Macaulay, Leo Mellor, David Parry, Tom Piercy, Greg Pritchard, Julian Rivers, Peter Sanlon, Amber Thomas, Dominic and Diane Vincent, Alison Watkin and Kenneth Watkin. If I have omitted to mention anyone here, please accept my sincere apologies; this book will still bear your fingerprints as testimony to your contribution.

The students who attended the Western Culture Seminars at Jesus, Magdalene, Clare and Murray Edwards Colleges in Cambridge also deserve rich thanks for your interest, your questions and the sometimes heated debates the seminars provoked. Many of you will be able to find your comments and questions taken up in the pages that follow; I hope you had as much fun participating as I had leading. I would also like to thank the Master and Fellows of Magdalene College, Cambridge, and the President and Fellows of Murray Edwards College, Cambridge, for providing me with the opportunity to undertake the research for this book. Very sincere thanks go to Deborah Blake at Bloomsbury for her encouragement and guidance for the project over nearly four years.

Very dear and special thanks and admiration are reserved for Alison, who not only provided incisive comments on draft versions of the book but stoked my enthusiasm for the project and kept me going through its writing, encouraging and challenging me to flourish as a whole person, not just as a scholar. It has been a humbling process to spend time contemplating 'the glory and honour of the nations' (Revelation 21:26).

C.W.

Introduction
To the Man with a Hammer ...

human beings are not born once and for all on the day their mothers give
birth to them, but [...] life obliges them over and over again to give birth to
themselves.

Gabriel García Márquez (born 1928)

Picture this scene in your head. Try to imagine that it's really happening
to you right now, and see it with your mind's eye. In a moment I will ask
you three questions about it.

You fall ill in an unfamiliar town. You arrive at the doctor's surgery
in the middle of the afternoon. The doctor's receptionist takes your
details and asks you to sit down. A whole half an hour later the
doctor appears, calls your name, and your consultation begins. After
a brief conversation with the doctor, the nurse comes to take a blood
sample.

Here are the three questions. As you pictured the scene in your head, (1)
What gender was the receptionist? (2) What gender was the doctor? (3)
What gender was the nurse? I'm less interested in what your answer is
in each case than in the fact that you had to make a choice. You had to
picture the receptionist, the doctor and the nurse either as a man or as a
woman. Why did you choose one way rather than another? And can you
be sure that the reason you think you chose one way is the real reason?

We will all make the choices we do for a whole host of reasons that have
a lot to do with our upbringing, our education, our personal experience,
the society in which we live and what we think the exercise is all about.
We necessarily make assumptions all the time, filling in all sorts of
gaps without always realising that is what we are doing. Some of these
assumptions are reasoned, some are unthinking. Some are trivial, like
looking for the keys first in the place you usually leave them. Some are
of great importance, like trusting someone when they say 'I love you'
or thinking that a job is worth leaving if you find it unfulfilling. These
assumptions colour the way we understand everything (including what
'understanding' itself means), and every book we read, every painting we
look at and every piece of music we listen to will come with its own set of
assumptions and understandings.

Philosophy, literature, music and art can be much more deeply understood and much more richly enjoyed by someone who knows a little about the assumptions and ideas that were around when a work was made, just as we can better savour and appreciate a fine wine if we know a little about its provenance. Why does this philosopher think that way? Why does he paint like that? Why is it important that she wrote in that style? Our enjoyment of texts, paintings and philosophical ideas can often be frustrated because we are unaware of the big picture of Western cultural history within which those ideas and texts make glorious sense, but apart from which they can seem faintly ridiculous. The aim of this book is to provide the reader with just such a big picture, a map of Western culture that will help make sense of individual composers, authors, artists and philosophers. Visitors to Paris who travel up the one hundred and eight storeys to the top viewing gallery of the Eiffel Tower suddenly see the whole city in a different light. Museums, shops, streets and districts they had previously visited only individually can now be appreciated as part of a complex and interconnected whole stretching out as far as the eye can see. It is my hope that this book will provide just that sort of one hundred and eight storey overview, allowing the reader to take in the bird's eye view of how ideas and movements link together and flow into each other, before descending back to ground level to explore them in more detail with a new enthusiasm and appreciation.

This book is not simply structured as a chronological survey of high points in Western thought, literature, art and music. First of all, it is written in two parts. The first six chapters paint a big picture of Western cultural history from Abraham (end of the third millennium BC) to nineteenth-century Romanticism, and the final three chapters follow three paths through the jungle of the late nineteenth, twentieth and twenty-first centuries. The reason for spending so much time in the last hundred years or so is that it allows space to explore how recent developments in Western culture can be better understood when viewed in the context of the big picture of Western history. Twentieth-century thought and culture, though closest to us, is also the period which often leaves us most confused, and so one of my aims in writing this book is to help readers understand how 'postmodern' art and philosophy make sense in terms of the Western story of which they are part.

Sooner or later a book like this will have to nail its colours to the mast on the question of what the 'West' is, and now is as good a time as any. By the 'West' I mean the geographical and cultural civilisation formed primarily by the two great influences of Greco-Roman and Judaeo-Christian antiquity, wherever that culture finds its changing frontiers (for example, the North American continent becomes part of the West during the seventeenth century). It is not a perfect definition, but there is no perfect definition. To be sure, the roots of Western civilisation can be traced back to long before the ancient Greek city states began to flourish in the eighth century BC. Crop planting and animal husbandry began in the late stone age around 10,000 BC, and any number of ancient civilisations pre-date the Greek city states of around 800 BC. Nevertheless, it is still helpful if not exhaustive to begin an investigation of the West with Greece and Rome, the first great civilisations to emerge in the modern geographic Western world.

If the West is difficult to pinpoint, then it is child's play compared to attempting a definition of 'culture'. For Abbott Lawrence Lowell (1856-1943), President of Harvard University from 1909 to 1933, 'an attempt to encompass [culture's] meaning in words is like trying to seize the air in the hand, when one finds it is everywhere except within one's hand'. From the Latin *cultura* (cultivation, tillage, care bestowed on plants), 'culture' is not simply the opposite of 'nature', but it is helpful to understand it as a contrast to nature. Nature is the world around us as it exists without our express intervention. It includes the uncultivated natural world, the sun's rising and setting, and our own anatomy. Culture, by contrast, is the world around us insofar as it is the product of our express presence or intervention. It includes a ploughed field, architecture, language, the meaning we give to the sun rising, science, technology, art, literature and song. It is important to stress that by this definition both the sciences and the arts are cultural endeavours, seeking to change and appreciate the world around us and producing knowledge and enjoyment.

Having thought a little about the West and about culture, our next question is this: How shall we describe what it is like to be part of a particular culture? Some writers like to use the term 'worldview' to capture a person's culture. According to the *Oxford English Dictionary*, a worldview is 'a set of fundamental beliefs, values, etc., determining or constituting a comprehensive outlook on the world; a perspective on life'. That is pretty good, but sometimes people use the word more narrowly, focussing predominantly on ideas at the expense of rituals and habits, as if all there is to human life is a set of philosophical notions. In this book I have found 'ethos' and 'sensibility' to be more useful terms in capturing what it is like to be part of a particular historical culture. From the Greek *ethos* (nature, disposition), an ethos is a way of holding oneself in the world, the web of assumptions, behaviours, ideas, aspirations, rituals, thought-forms and 'characteristic spirit' (*OED*) typical of an individual or of an age. It is a difference in ethos that accounts for how an ancient Greek warrior, a medieval peasant and a Romantic poet can all look upon the same grove of trees and see three very different things.

We also need to issue a health warning about historical periods. Dividing history into segments as if it were a string of sausages necessarily flattens out nuances and overlaps. The medieval period did not end the day before the Renaissance started, and people did not wake up in the fourteenth century, draw back the curtains and grumble that it was still fifty years before the Renaissance would finally arrive (unless they happened to be called Petrarch, but more about him later). It is hard to talk meaningfully without using such labels at all, but if they are good servants then they are bad masters, and we should be suspicious of the artificial neatness they can imply.

In this book we will approach the development of Western literature and music through the lens of genre. While a dictionary may tell us that a genre is a category of artistic composition, such a sweetly unassuming definition belies the importance of generic concerns. Genre can be literary (epic, tragedy, detective novel), artistic (landscape, crucifixion painting, installation), or musical (symphony, fugue, minuet), and in each case every genre brings with it a set of expectations that can either be fulfilled or frustrated to varying degrees. It is only in broad terms then, that we can talk of genre as an unproblematic 'category'. Differences in genre are not simply a question of form, but a question of world. The conventions of a tragedy, for example, reflect a particular ethos and a particular understanding of reality, causing a particular world to unfold with its own values, concerns and limits. If something is said differently, something different is said: just ask the worker who has been sacked by text message rather than face to face. The relation between a text and a genre is a dialogue, not a dictat, and so it is necessary to have some familiarity with the conventions and expectations of a genre in order to understand how a given work is challenging or affirming them. We shall see that the prevalent genres at any given period reveal a great deal about the values and outlook of the society in which they flourish, and that any period re-writes the rules and re-draws the categories of genre in its own image. Generic expectations act as a counterpoint with which the melody of a work can resonate and contrast. In the chapters that follow, titles of non-English literary texts, artistic works and musical compositions are given in translation, except where the work is commonly referred to in English by its original foreign language title.

In a book of this size, as with travelling to the top of the Eiffel Tower, any gain in the breadth of the view we can take in must inevitably be at the cost of a loss of detail. Every reader of this book will no doubt find themselves throwing up their hands at some or other inexplicable or unpardonable omission. Why is there a great deal more about ancient Greece than ancient Rome, and a great deal more about Christianity than Judaism? Why is there only a word on jazz? Where is the history of colonialism? Can there really be nothing on Islam? How can you not discuss film? What has happened to the women writers? To each reader exasperated at my lacunae, I beg pardon and contrive no excuse other than the constraints imposed by a book of this size. My hope is that each reader will move on to fill in more detail on the map of Western culture that this book sketches. Readers will also be able to find exceptions to many of the assertions made in these pages, and may take exception to the threads I follow. Isn't the history rather Whig? Isn't the philosophy rather 'Continental'? Aren't there exceptions to what you are saying? There are indeed exceptions, and I shall be mentioning some of them as we go along, but there can be no exceptions at all if there is nothing for them to be exceptions to. A view which is all exception and no general rule is partial and tendentious, and it is only with a clear grasp of the generalities that we can begin to make sense of the exceptions as exceptions and the nuances as nuances. All models and approaches are selective and reductive and if we are looking for a perfect generalisation we will not find one. As Norbert Wiener puts it in his *Philosophy of Science* (1945), 'The best material model of a cat is another, or preferably the same, cat'.

I would be delighted if this book could sound a note for education, where education is understood as more than training. The tradition of a liberal education (Latin: *educare*, to rear, closely related to *educere*, to lead forth) is more than a course of training that prepares the individual with specific skills to be a specific cog in a specific machine. Mortimer Adler puts the case well (and provocatively) in an essay on education in his *Syntopicon* (1952):

> The traditional meaning of the word 'liberal' as applied to education entails a distinction between free men and slaves. Slaves, like domesticated animals, are trained to perform special functions. They are not treated as ends, but as means, and so they are not educated for their own good, but the use to which they are put.

There is nothing wrong with training to perform special functions. We need hairdressers, lawyers, plumbers, doctors, bricklayers and even the odd university professor. Such training is good and necessary, but it is emphatically not everything there is to education. We do not learn simply in order to perform a particular function better, to climb the employment ladder higher, or to get a good job. Education literally 'leads forth'; it sets out without knowing where it is going, questioning its world and itself in the process. Education asks questions to which there are (as yet) no definitive answers, for which there are no cash prises, which don't immediately help to perform a special function. Education explores what it means to be a human being in ways that will never make you rich, but that lead to deeper and different ways of understanding what it means to be rich or poor. If training instructs us how to hammer a nail more efficiently, education asks what we are hammering for, why we find the finished product beautiful, and what our hammering says about us and our way of life. In other words, education forces us to think about the 'why', not simply about the 'how'. Practically as well as etymologically, a liberal education is a free education. I would be delighted if readers of *From Plato to Postmodernism* found the book a help to their formal or informal education, and a provocation to think. 'To a man with a hammer', said Mark Twain, 'everything looks like a nail.' As we survey the cultural history of the West, this book is an invitation to examine our own assumptions, our own ethos, our own hammer.

1

The Roots of Western Culture:
Greece and Rome

It is the year 323 BC. A warrior king lies dying in Babylon, 1,500 miles from his native Macedonia as the crow flies. The dying man is only thirty-two years old, and soon a rumour will begin to spread that he was poisoned by one of his close friends. During the onset of his illness he continues to plan the conquest of southern Arabia, carry out his ritual religious duties from his bed and issue orders to his officers, but after ten days of increasingly high fever he finally passes away, leaving an empire that spans around nine-tenths of the known world. At his death, Macedonia is already peppered with temples honouring him as a god. During his reign (336-323 BC) king Megas Alexandros – or Alexander the Great – travelled more than 20,000 miles on expedition and conquered an empire stretching east through the Khyber Pass as far as Multan in modern-day Pakistan, south as far as the Indian Ocean and Persian Gulf, west into Egypt, and north as far as the Danube in modern-day Romania.

In his own lifetime, the story of Alexander had already become a seamless fabric of fact and myth. His father Philip II of Macedon (382-336 BC) received news of Alexander's birth at the same time that he learned of the victory of his chariots in the Olympic games, and this was to be the first portent of the remarkable set of myths encrusting Alexander's life like dazzling jewels. The Greek historian Plutarch (*c.* 46-*c.* 120 AD) tells how as a youth Alexander entertained Persian ambassadors in Philip's absence, impressing them by the maturity of his questions about their land and battle-readiness. Another legendary story tells how, gazing out onto the Indian Ocean, Alexander wept because he had no more worlds to conquer. What Plutarch in fact records is that 'When Alexander heard [...] of the infinite number of worlds, he wept, and when his friends asked him what was the matter, he replied, "Is it not a matter for tears that, when the number of worlds is infinite, I have not conquered one?"'

Modesty was not a trait for which Alexander was renowned, but on this occasion he understates his case. Although he claims not to have conquered even one world, his multiple conquests did help spread the civilisation of the newly united Greek city states throughout the known world, and the legacy that this civilisation has left to the West is wide-ranging and profound. The Greeks gave the West the basis of the alphabet still used today ('alpha' and 'beta' are the first two letters of the Greek alphabet). The philosopher Aristotle, who was summoned to serve as Alexander's personal tutor when the king was thirteen years old, established many of the assumptions and conventions of logic that undergird Western thinking. The Greeks helped shape the West's early literary genres and develop a Western style of painting and sculpture, and Alexander's conquests established Greek as the international language in which the documents of the Christian New Testament would be written and into which the Hebrew scriptures (the Christian Old Testament) were translated. Alexander's military successes also provided the pattern and inspiration for the later Roman and Byzantine empires. In this chapter we explore the Greek culture in which Alexander lived, and touch briefly on the other great ancient empire of Rome that owes so much to the Greeks its armies conquered. It is impossible to imagine today's politics, literature, art or philosophy apart from the influence of Greco-Roman ideas and practices. Art and literature in the West have regularly returned to Greco-Roman roots in order to measure themselves against the achievements of the ancient world and be inspired to new heights. The Romance languages of modern-day Europe owe a profound debt to Greek and Latin not simply for much of their vocabulary (around 60% of words in educated English usage are borrowed directly or indirectly from Greek and Latin roots) but also for much of their grammar.

Homer (eighth century BC)

Our story starts three centuries before Alexander's birth, with the origins of Western literature. Pisistratus (died 527/8 BC) is ruler of Athens, one of the small independent city-states that flourished from around 750 to 300 BC. Pisistratus is remembered today chiefly for his initiative to conserve the literary traditions of the Athenians, and in particular to standardise the text of the *Iliad* and the *Odyssey*, Homer's two great epics (from *epos*, meaning 'word' or 'tale'). Most scholars today would date written Homer no earlier than 725 BC. No one knows who he was; some have suggested that he was blind ('Homer' sounds like the Greek for 'blind'), some have argued that he was a woman, and many scholars today hold that the epics were the work of many individuals contributing to an oral tradition that developed over a long period. Whoever Homer was, it is the two epics themselves that are of first importance for any understanding of Western literature.

Both the *Iliad* and the *Odyssey* are twenty-four books long, the length of a book being dictated by what could be written on one papyrus scroll. They each tell of events relating to the Trojan War, thought to have taken place in the thirteenth or twelfth century BC. As Homer tells it, the conflict is unleashed when the Trojan prince Paris kidnaps the beautiful Helen, wife of the Spartan king Menelaus. The outraged Menelaus lays siege to the impregnable Troy along with his brother Agamemnon, king of Mycenae. The two brothers finally sack Troy through the ruse of seeming to withdraw and leaving the Trojans the peace offering of a large wooden horse, inside which are hidden thirty of their best warriors (hence the phrase: 'beware of Greeks bearing gifts'!). The *Iliad*, set in the last year of the Trojan War, tells of how the heroic but broody Greek warrior Achilles refuses to join the battle until the death of his comrade Patroclus provokes him to seek revenge by slaying Hector, eldest son of the Trojan king Priam. The *Odyssey*, set after the Trojan War, relates the ten-year wanderings of the Greek Odysseus (or Ulysses), veteran of the Trojan campaign, and his struggle with both gods and mortals on the way back home to his wife Penelope and son Telemachus at his native island of Ithaca.

Homer's epics do not merely present us with stories that have gripped the Western imagination and inspired Western poets and artists for millennia. They also portray for us a particular ethos, a particular way of understanding, living and acting in the world. Central to this ethos is the value of *aretê,* usually translated 'excellence'. Achilles shows *aretê* in his unmatched skill as a warrior and the spoils it brings him, but he lacks *aretê* when in rage he dishonours the body of the dead Hector by dragging it behind his chariot back to the Greek camp. In addition to his physical exploits, Odysseus' *aretê* is also in the cunning and wiliness of the schemes by virtue of which he arrives back home to Ithaca, escaping from the blinded Cyclops by clinging to the underside of a sheep as it is counted out of the Cyclops' cave, and plugging his men's ears with wax to stop them being enchanted by the seductive but deadly Sirens.

For the ancient Greeks *aretê* was shown primarily on the battlefield, but as Greek society developed it was increasingly applied in addition to the public assembly or the field of athletics. As a central principle in Greek education it comes to stand for a full-orbed excellence of body, mind and character, an ethic of doing one's best and being self-disciplined in the pursuit of the best; in the words of the poet Hesiod (active between 750 and 650 BC) the gods have ordained that sweat should come before *aretê*. Elements of the *aretê* ethic remain strong in the modern West, encapsulated in the famous 'Man in the Arena' speech that former US president Theodore Roosevelt gave in Paris, 1910:

> The credit belongs to the man who is actually in the arena, whose face is marred by dust and sweat and blood, who strives valiantly, who errs and comes up short again and again, because there is no effort without error or shortcoming, but who knows the great enthusiasms, the great devotions, who spends himself for a worthy cause; who, at the best, knows, in the end, the triumph of high achievement, and who, at the worst, if he fails, at least he fails while daring greatly, so that his place shall never be with those cold and timid souls who knew neither victory nor defeat.

Reciting Homer from memory was considered an important part of classical Greek education, and the two epics remain today the narratives with the longest history of continuous readership in the world. As to its generic nature, Homeric epic is an 'omnibus genre', incorporating within itself any number of fragments from other genres: laments, prayers, proverbial sayings, ecphrases and catalogues. A typical characteristic is its vivid use of repeated epithets: 'swift-footed Achilles', the 'rose-fingered dawn' or the 'wine-dark sea' upon which Odysseus sails back to Ithaca. No doubt these epithets were an aid to oral recitation, but their repetition also serves to underline the sense of coherence and reliable stability of the world that epic unfolds for us. Part of this stability is provided by the presence of gods and goddesses, and both Homer's epics begin with an appeal to the muse, a goddess of poetic inspiration, for divine help in telling the story that is to follow:

> Sing, O goddess, the anger of Achilles son of Peleus, that brought countless ills upon the Achaeans. (*Iliad*)

> Tell me, O muse, of that ingenious hero who travelled far and wide after he had sacked the famous town of Troy. (*Odyssey*)

Such prologues serve both to frame the action that follows and to establish a continuity between the epic's performance and the events of which it tells.

Homer's undivided world

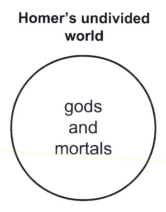

Figure 1.1.

In addition, this appeal to the muse highlights another very important feature of Homer's world. Though the Greek gods and goddesses are immortal and dwell on the heights of Mount Olympus (at 2900 metres the highest peak in modern-day Greece), they live in the same world as human beings (Figure 1.1) and they interact with human beings in many ways. Gods and mortals converse with each other, seek to outwit each other, fight battles against each other and even on occasion produce offspring together. Just like human beings, Homer's gods can be capricious, spiteful, generous, imperfect (Hephaestus is born lame), obstinate and antagonistic towards each other and towards mortals. Furthermore, not even the most powerful Greek gods enjoy omnipotence. Zeus, the Father of the gods, is seduced by Hera in book 14 of the *Iliad* and is unable to outwit destiny. This intimate involvement of the gods in the lives of mortals is an aspect of the Homeric world which many poets living in later times were to look back on with nostalgia and longing, not least because the presence and intervention of the Greek divinities gives a very immediate meaning to Homer's world. The action of gods and goddesses explains why some battles are won and others lost, why some men are heroes and others vanquished. In other words, it is in large part the gods who make Homer's world a cosmos, a world of meaning and order, rather than a chaos. This is echoed particularly strongly in the circular structure of the *Odyssey*: after his long and perilous journey Odysseus finally returns home to Ithaca where household order is restored, justice is done, and the meaning of human existence is re-affirmed.

If we compare the Greek and Roman gods and goddesses, it is conspicuous that the Romans largely carried over the Greek deities into their own mythology, with the minor concession of giving them Latin names. Indeed, the Romans had a policy of appropriating the deities of all the peoples they conquered, as a way of assimilating vanquished nations into the cultural fabric of the Roman empire. The twelve Greek 'Olympians' (Figure 1.2) were the twelve principal gods and goddesses of Greek myth, and they are also those most commonly described, depicted or evoked in the Western tradition. Precisely which gods appeared among the twelve varied from source to source, sometimes according to geographical location and sometimes according to cultic context.

In addition to the twelve Olympians, the Greeks and Romans recognised other gods and goddesses who epitomise certain human traits, moods or beliefs: Eros (Latin: Cupid) god of love, and Psykhe (Psyche), mortal-born goddess of the soul. The way in which the gods and goddesses embody certain traits (beauty), moods (celebration) or occupations (warfare) has ensured their continued potency as symbols in art and literature long after the death of the civilisations that worshipped them. From this literary point of view it can even be argued that the gods and goddesses are truer – that is, they capture an aspect of the human condition more perfectly – than life itself, precisely because they are not caught up in all the nuance, mundanity and ambiguity of life. For an example of how something imagined can be 'more real' than something actually existing, think of a triangle. The idea of a triangle is perfect: it has three perfectly straight sides and its angles add up exactly to 180°. But any actually existing triangle will have tiny imperfections, even if it is just a case of one atom being out of place. So the idea is a purer triangle than the imperfect existing triangle. In the same way, a deity can be for a poet or artist a pure and perfect embodiment of love, or power, or jealousy, in a way that it would be impossible to achieve in the messiness and ambiguity of 'real life'. 'Real' people can undergo this purifying process as well, and Homer is a good case in point. The West's view of Homer as the archetypal poet is in a way similar to his own purified deities.

Pre-Socratic philosophers

Philosophy in the West came into being with Thales of Miletus (sixth century BC), some two centuries after the Homeric epics were written

Greek name	Roman name	Associations
Aphrodite	Venus	Goddess of love, beauty and sexual desire. Daughter of Zeus, wife of Hephaestus.
Apollo	Apollo	God of light, truth, prophecy, poetry and the arts, healing and archery. Son of Zeus.
Ares	Mars	God of War and violence. Son of Zeus.
Artemis	Diana	Goddess of hunting, animals and virginity. Daughter of Zeus.
(Pallas) Athena	Minerva	Goddess of craft, warfare, and wisdom. In the *Odyssey*, instructs Odysseus and aids his passage home. Daughter of Zeus.
Demeter	Ceres	Goddess of the harvest and fertility of the earth. Sister of Zeus.
Dionysus	Bacchus	God of wine and celebration. Son of Zeus.
Hephaestus	Vulcan	God of fire; blacksmith of the gods. Son of Zeus, husband of Aphrodite. Thrown from Olympus and lands on the island of Lemnos.
Hera	Juno	Goddess of marriage, motherhood and childbirth. Queen of the gods. Wife and sister of Zeus.
Hermes	Mercury	Messenger of the gods; protector of travellers, thieves, and merchants. Son of Zeus. Father of Pan, the god of nature.
Poseidon	Neptune	God of the sea, horses and earthquakes. Brother of Zeus and Hades (God of the underworld). Father of the Cyclops; causes Odysseus to be shipwrecked.
Zeus	Jupiter	Father of the gods. God of thunder and sky. Husband and brother of Hera.

Figure 1.2. The twelve Olympians.

down, and was originally a lively mixture of what we would only later divide into physics, chemistry, biology, astronomy, theology and philosophy. We can say with our tongue just a little in our cheek that Western philosophy was born at 6.13 pm on 28 May 585 BC, when Thales used Egyptian astronomical chronicles to predict correctly an eclipse of the sun. According to a story told by Aristotle, Thales put his knowledge to good use:

> The story goes that when they found fault with him for his poverty, supposing that philosophy is useless, he learned from his astronomy that there would be a large crop of olives. Then, while it was still winter, he obtained a little money and made deposits on all the olive presses both in Miletus and in Chios. Since no one bid against him, he rented them cheaply.

When the right time came, suddenly many tried to get the presses all at once, and he rented them out on whatever terms he wished, and so made a great deal of money. In this way he proved that philosophers can easily be wealthy if they desire, but this is not what they are interested in.

Quite right too, Aristotle; it is always good to hear an argument for the usefulness of philosophy, though let's not question too closely how the astronomer knew there would be a bumper olive harvest. Precisely what led the first philosophers – or 'investigators of Nature' as Aristotle calls them – to explore the cosmos in this way may remain a mystery, but the birth of philosophy is marked by the use of reason as a tool to probe the world, along with the rejection of explanations relying exclusively on the intervention of the gods. One important set of assumptions was central to Thales' philosophical (and financial) success, namely that the universe has an order to it, that we can know this order, and that the order does not simply obey divine caprice but is predictable and regular. Thus the first great Greek philosophical contribution to Western culture and civilisation is that the cosmos can be understood, and its phenomena predicted.

Thales was the first of the so-called pre-Socratic philosophers, meaning simply the ones who come before Socrates. For these first Western philosophers, investigating the cosmos starts in an attitude of *thaumazein*, a wondrous and astonished perplexity when faced with inexplicable or contradictory observations. It is *thaumazein* that causes the philosopher to seek the principles or regularities that govern the world. The pre-Socratics pursued their quest for order by seeking after the *archê*, the one unifying element out of which everything, they thought, was made. Thales thought that the *archê* was water; for Anaximenes (died *c*. 528 BC) everything was air, at different degrees of density, whereas for Anaximander (*c*. 610-*c*. 545 BC) it was none of the familiar elements (earth, air, fire and water), but an undefined, unlimited substance called the *apeiron* underlying earth, air, fire and water. Together, Thales, Anaximander and Anaximenes are called the Milesians, after the island of Miletus, in modern day Turkey.

For Heraclitus of Ephesus (*c*. 540-*c*. 475 BC) the *archê* was fire. Heraclitus' writing remains only in fragments, and in fragment 91 we find his famous idea that we cannot step into the same river twice, because a river is a unity of stability (the river runs along the same course from one moment to the next) and flux (the river never contains exactly the same water in the same place from one moment to the next). The principle that unity consists of opposites (stability and flux), that a river will lose its constancy if it ceases to flow, was called by Heraclitus the *logos*, a term that we shall follow through the whole of our journey through Western culture. As we shall see, *logos* will be used by many other philosophers and theologians in different contexts to evoke the principle of coherence of the cosmos, the cosmic 'glue' that holds everything together and gives the world meaning.

Pythagoras (*c.* 570-*c.* 495 BC)

Pythagoras of Samos stands in stark contrast to the nature philosophy of the Milesians and Heraclitus. If for Thales 'all is water', and for Anaximenes 'all is air', then for Pythagoras 'all is number'. Through a mixture of fervent religion and careful mathematics, Pythagoras takes *logos*, the principle of order, to a new pitch. He elaborates a philosophy of harmony: ultimate reality is a matter of abstract relations and proportions, generated from the sacred numbers 1, 2, 3 and 4. Pythagoras' interest in proportion extended to music, and he is usually credited as being the first Western theorist of musical harmony, arguing that musical harmonies are sensible manifestations of the divine relationships between numbers. He also sought harmony and proportion in the heavens, claiming that each planet or constellation moves round the stationary earth in a perfect sphere, each sphere producing a different musical note according to its size. Together, the different notes form the 'music of the spheres', a cosmic harmony that is too pure to apprehend with the human ear. Some of Pythagoras' followers thought that he alone had an ear fine enough to hear this heavenly music.

Pythagoras' search for regularity, harmony and proportion also led him to geometry and to the famous theorem that the square of the hypotenuse of a triangle is equal to the sum of the square of the other two sides ($a^2 + b^2 = c^2$), as every good schoolchild knows. What is not taught at school, however, is the scandal caused by the Pythagorean discovery that the side of a square cannot be expressed as a simple proportion of its diagonal. This horrific disharmony certainly did not fit the cosmic proportions that the Pythagoreans were expecting to discover in a universe divinely ordered by mathematics. Pythagoras, it is said, was so scandalised when his pupil Hippasus showed that the square root of 2 is an irrational number that he condemned him to death by drowning. The Pythagoreans named such irrational proportions *alogon* (from the negating prefix *a* + *logos*), meaning 'unutterable' or 'irrational'. We must remember that for a Pythagorean understanding of the cosmos the existence of such irrational proportions calls into question the whole notion that the world is ordered and comprehensible, a particularly worrying discovery if we also bear in mind that the Greeks had no mathematical expression of infinity to help them deal with non-harmonic proportions. Pythagoras founded a community in southern Italy whose adherents had to renounce all property and eat a largely vegetarian diet, but the story goes that when the Pythagoreans were caught scandalously dabbling in irrational numbers and the *alogon*, their school was closed and all its members put to death.

Plato (*c.* 429-*c.* 347 BC)

As the name 'pre-Socratic' suggests, the earliest Greek philosophers are overshadowed by the towering Athenian figure of Socrates (*c.* 469-*c.* 399

BC), who along with Plato and Aristotle (384-322 BC) makes up the great Athenian philosophical trinity. Chronologically, the first of these three greats is Socrates, but if Socrates himself did ever write anything we do not have it today. What we know of him comes to us through the writing of Plato and, to a lesser extent, Xenophon (*c.* 430-*c.* 354 BC). In some ways Plato's Socrates reaffirms Homer's universe, but in other important ways he marks the end of the view of the world in which gods and mortals exist in the same space. Plato reaffirms Homer because he does have a place for the great principles of existence, the 'behind the scenes' forces that were embodied in Homer's gods. But with Plato the single world inhabited by both gods and mortals has split in two (Figure 1.3).

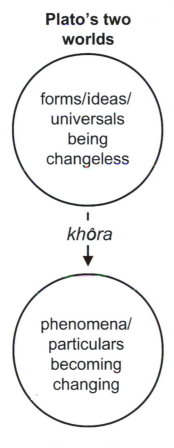

Figure 1.3.

The great difference between Plato and Homer, and philosophy's great split with the pre-philosophical world of myth, is to think that human beings, along with everything else, exist in two different worlds: the world accessible to our senses and a higher world that, as for Pythagoras, is harmonious and mathematically perfect. For Plato, things that we can touch, see, hear, taste and smell exist in the imperfect everyday world of change and decay, but there is also another world, standing above the miserable world of decay as the Olympian deities tower over the mortals they rule. This is the world of what Plato called the 'Forms', (or sometimes 'Ideas' or 'Archetypes'). The Forms are 'universals', meaning that they can be exemplified or instantiated in any number of 'particular' things. So for example 'human being' is a universal, because there can be lots of particular things that are all human beings, whereas you, the reader of this book, are a particular: there is only one thing that can be called you. Redness and the sphere are universals; this red ball on my desk is a particular.

The Forms are perfect models for the objects in the visible world, but those objects themselves are imperfect copies of the Forms. So every table in the world is an imperfect copy of the Form of a table; every particular tree is an imperfect copy of the Form of tree, every dog an imperfect copy of the Form of dog, and so on. Whereas the Form of 'table' is perfect and unchanging, every table that exists in this world is imperfect and subject to flux, change and decay: it fades, chips and stains, and has any number of small imperfections in its craftsmanship. For Plato, this imperfection is introduced by the *khôra* (literally 'interval' or 'space') between the world of the Forms and the world of particulars. For these reasons, only the Forms really exist in the full sense of the word, eternally and perfectly, whereas in this world there is only a constant becoming, decaying and passing away.

Importantly for Plato – and for us in subsequent chapters – Forms give not only the shape of particulars but their meaning as well. Everything that exists participates in the supreme Form, the Form of the Good, and everything that exists has its purpose, what it is 'good for'. The imperfection of this world drives the philosopher to want to ascend to the perfect world of the Forms, and indeed for Plato this ascent is the true goal of human existence. It is to be attained not by exercising the senses, which apprehend only the imperfect and changing, but through the use of the intellect, which can apprehend the Forms. The privileging of the intellect over the sensory and the material world in some of Plato's dialogues is in part responsible for a persistent stream of 'Platonic dualism' in Western thought, where the body is thought of as base and the mind or Spirit as quasi-divine.

The philosopher's access to the Forms through the intellect is vividly portrayed in Plato's allegory of the cave, in book 7 of *The Republic*. The unfortunate inhabitants of Plato's cave are chained facing the cave wall, with a fire blazing behind them. As objects pass in front of the fire behind the prisoners' heads, the objects cast shadows on the cave wall in front of them and the chained inhabitants, knowing no better, take these shadows for the objects themselves. It is only when one prisoner leaves the cave for the dazzling sunlight outside (i.e. when, by means of the intellect, he leaves the world of appearances in order to apprehend the intelligible world illuminated by the Form of the Good) that he becomes aware that the shadows are not real objects. However, when the escaped prisoner returns to the cave and tries to share his knowledge, the other prisoners think him merely blinded by the light outside the cave.

It might sound absurd to mistake shadows for real things, but remember that the prisoners have never seen anything but shadows. If we dismiss the allegory as silly, for Plato we are falling into the same self-certain short-sightedness as the prisoners who dismiss the man returning with news of the outside, assuming that the 'reality' we have thus far experienced is all there is for anyone to experience. The idea of the existence of Forms still divides thinkers today. For example: do numbers exist? We might have two oranges or three apples, but do 'two' and 'three' exist by themselves? Or what about beauty? We might swoon at a beautiful person or be enraptured by a beautiful sunset, but does 'beauty' itself exist, apart from beautiful things? Or Justice, or Goodness, or Red, or Green ...? The controversy over the Forms continues.

Most of Plato's writing is in dialogue form (technically a 'dialectic' or argument), usually a dialogue between Socrates and another philosopher or citizen of Athens. Does that matter for our understanding of Plato? It certainly does, but it took until the nineteenth century for the theologian and philosopher Friedrich Schleiermacher (1768-1834) to show just how important the dialogue genre is. Schleiermacher argued that dialogue is much more than simply the husk that can be discarded once Plato's philosophy has been harvested from it. Dialogue for Schleiermacher is Plato's art form, and he drew the study of Plato back to the fundamental point that 'form and content are inseparable, and each sentence is rightly understood only in its own place, and within the connections and restrictions that Plato established for it'. Furthermore, the plurality of speakers in a dialogue poses its own problems: given that Plato has no speaking part himself, how (if such a thing is even desirable) are we to reconstruct what Plato himself thought, as opposed to what Socrates says in the dialogues? With his own position remaining ambiguous, of course, Plato leaves himself free to probe, develop and frame Socrates' teaching without telling his reader what to think, and reconstructs of 'Plato's philosophy' like the one we have attempted above will always be open to the accusation of disregarding the genre of dialogue. With the example of Plato we see that genre is no less a concern for philosophical writing than for literary, and if Plato is an artist in writing the dialogues, then the interpreter must also be an artist in reading them.

The dialogue form also makes Plato's writing a lot of fun to read. Some of the dialogues are hilariously one-sided, with Socrates' hapless interlocutor merely providing the occasional 'Yes indeed' or 'You are certainly right' to Socrates' long explanations and arguments, once in a while being allowed a slightly longer 'I had never realised that before, Socrates'. Plato's dialogues exemplify what has come to be called the 'Socratic method', the interrogation of an interlocutor with a series of probing questions that cause him to doubt his original assumptions until his starting position has been undermined. The related term 'Socratic irony' is a feigned position of ignorance intended to draw the interlocutor to make statements that are then challenged.

The Socrates of Plato's dialogues is guided by the twin precepts 'know thyself' (words said to have been inscribed in the forecourt of the Temple of Apollo at Delphi) and 'the unexamined life is not worth living'.

Condemned by the Athenian authorities for encouraging disbelief in the gods and thereby corrupting the city's youth, Socrates finally dies by his own hand. His sentence is to drink poisonous hemlock, which he does while gently reprimanding his despondent followers: 'The hour of departure has arrived, and we go our ways – I to die, and you to live. Which is better God only knows.'

Aristotle (384-322 BC)

Logic, biology, literary criticism, political theory, ethics, meteorology ...: many of the disciplines that define Western knowledge and education today were first established by Aristotle, and it is doubtful that anyone can lay claim to a similar number of original contributions to Western learning. Aristotle was a pupil of Plato (rarely can a teacher have had a greater pupil and his pupil a greater teacher!), and like Plato his philosophy has a place for universals. Nevertheless, the Western tradition has often understood itself in terms of an opposition between two attitudes to universals, characterised by Plato and Aristotle respectively. Plato came to stand for what was later called rationalism, a view according to which knowledge arises primarily from the exercise of reason and the intellect, whereas Aristotle came to be identified with what was later called empiricism, which emphasises the primacy of sense experience and observation of the world in gaining knowledge. For Plato access to reality was through the intellect, but for Aristotle things could not be more different. At birth the human mind is a blank slate, a *tabula rasa*, and the knowledge we have is gained through the senses over time. Indeed, the famous opening of Aristotle's *Metaphysics* launches a manifesto for the acquisition of knowledge through the senses:

> All men by nature desire to know. An example is the delight we take in our senses. For even quite apart from their usefulness, they are loved for their own sake, and none more than the sense of sight. [...] The reason is that this, most of all the senses, makes us know and brings to light many differences between things.

In some matters, however, Aristotle seems to have adhered rather loosely to his empirical principles, as Bertrand Russell notes in *A History of Western Philosophy* (1945):

> Aristotle maintained that women have fewer teeth than men; although he was twice married, it never occurred to him to verify this statement by examining his wives' mouths. He said also that children would be healthier if conceived when the wind is in the north. One gathers that the two Mrs Aristotles both had to run out and look at the weathercock every evening before going to bed.

In his *Metaphysics* Aristotle attacks Plato's understanding of the Forms, arguing that 'all other things cannot come from the Forms in any of

18

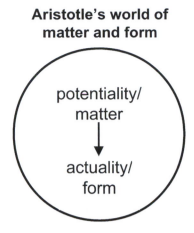

**Aristotle's world of
matter and form**

Figure 1.4.

the usual senses of "from". To say that they are patterns and the other things share in them is to use empty words and poetical metaphors.' Nevertheless, Aristotle does not jettison the notion of Forms completely. In his own thinking, the universal is to be found not separate from things, as a Form (capital F) existing in another world, but always in particular things. In his theory of form, matter and substance, a brass sphere is made by bringing the form (that is, the sphere) into the matter (that is, the brass) to make the substance (that is, the brass sphere). Just as there is no brass apart from the lumps of brass we might encounter in the world, so there is no sphere apart from the spherical objects we might encounter in the world. Furthermore, unformed matter (the lump of brass) has the potentiality to become the form (the brass sphere), which is itself called the actuality (Figure 1.4). So, crucially, whereas for Plato the world of Forms was the real world, of which the sensory world is only a shadow, for Aristotle this world, the one we sense right here and right now, is the fully real world.

The difference between Plato and Aristotle is perhaps most iconically captured in Raphael's *School of Athens*, a fresco painted on the wall of the *Stanza della Segnatura* in the Vatican's Apostolic Palace between 1510 and 1511 (Figure 1.5). It should be clear by now which of the two central figures is Plato, and which is Aristotle. The older Plato, on the left, is directing our intellectual attention upwards, to the world of the Forms, while the younger Aristotle on the right is pointing down to the observable world.

Aristotle was also the first thinker systematically to formalise the rules of logic. 'Aristotelian logic' includes the law of non-contradiction ('a thing cannot be both itself and its opposite at the same time and in the same way', sometimes written 'A ≠ non-A'), and the law of excluded middle ('there is nothing between asserting and denying', or, in a more recent formulation, 'every proposition is either true or false'). We also have Aristotle to thank for the syllogism, a way of formalising an argument with a major premise, a minor premise and conclusion such that, if both the major and minor premises are true and the argument itself valid, then the conclusion is also true. Here is the classic example of a syllogism:

Figure 1.5. Raphael, *The School of Athens* (*c.* 1511), detail of Plato and Socrates. Stanza della Segnatura, Vatican, Rome.

Major premise: All men are mortal.
Minor premise: Socrates is a man.
Conclusion: Socrates is mortal.

This formalisation of logic has exerted an incalculably great influence on our society in everything from the Western conception of the soul to modern technology, and much of twentieth-century thought was concerned with questioning (and some would say misunderstanding) the limits of this sort of logic.

The problem of the planets

Despite their differences on the nature of forms, both Plato and Aristotle understood the cosmos in terms of two very distinct realms: the earth and everything as far as the moon (called the sublunary realm) and everything beyond the moon (called the superlunary realm). The world, unmoving at the centre of the cosmos, is subject to decay, imperfection and change, whereas in the superlunary realm the planets and stars are set in Pythagorean crystal spheres, perfectly formed and perfect in their motion. Aristotle also posits that the superlunary world is made of a different, imperishable kind of matter from terrestrial bodies. Aristotle's god, the 'Prime Mover' who set the spheres in motion, is beyond the farthest sphere.

This sub-/superlunary split was to become the dominant conception informing the West's philosophical, religious, and scientific vision for most of the subsequent fifteen centuries. From the beginning however it was realised that there were some problems with the notion of superlunary perfection, namely that certain heavenly objects did not in fact seem to move in perfect spheres at all. This embarrassing discrepancy between the order expected of the universe and the lack of order observed will be a recurring theme in our story of the West. Imagine the confusion posed for this Platonic-Aristotelian understanding by the observation that, though the stars seemed to be perfectly spherical in their movement across the heavens, the planets move erratically, or wander, across the night sky. Indeed, the Greek term for planets, *asteres planetai*, means 'wandering stars'. Like Pythagoras, Plato believed in a perfectly ordered heavens, and considered it blasphemous to call any celestial bodies 'wanderers'. The task of the astronomer, according to Plato, was therefore to 'save the phenomena', to rescue the apparent disorder of the heavenly bodies as they are observed by explaining how, though the planets *seem* to move erratically, their movement can be shown to be *in fact* perfectly regular and mathematical. The West would have to wait until Johannes Kepler (1571-1630) for the answer to this conundrum.

Other major philosophies

Greek and Roman philosophy at the time of Aristotle and after falls into a number of more or less coherent schools.

Cynics

The Cynic school is commonly thought to have been founded by Antisthenes (*c.* 445-*c.* 360 BC), and is epitomised by Diogenes (*c.* 404-*c.* 323 BC), the bad boy of ancient philosophy whom Plato described as 'Socrates gone mad'. 'Cynic' literally means 'doggish', referring not only to the Cynics' often unkempt appearance (Diogenes is the half-undressed figure lounging in the middle of Raphael's *School of Athens*, see Figure 4.9) but also to their decision to 'play the dog', calling into question the supposed hierarchical division between humanity and the animal kingdom and challenging many practices and beliefs widely held in Greek civilisation. The cynics scorned convention and material goods, seeking to live a 'natural' life of virtue free from possessions. Apocryphal anecdotes abound concerning the unconventional Diogenes. One of them tells how, disgusted by the opulence of Plato's house, Diogenes wiped his feet on Plato's fine floor-covering with the words 'Thus do I trample on the pride of Plato.' His disgruntled host simply replied, 'Yes, Diogenes, with pride of another sort.' Another story tells how Diogenes, having previously owned a cup, cloak and sack, threw away his cup when he saw a boy drinking from cupped hands. When Alexander the Great approached Diogenes and, standing over him, asked what he might do for the philosopher, Diogenes is said to have replied that the king might kindly step out of his light. Finally, in a somewhat misguided attempt to prove that cooking is unnatural he is said to have died from eating a raw octopus. Cynic philosophy flourished in the third century BC, seeing something of a revival in the first century AD and standing as an important precursor to Epicureanism and Stoicism.

Epicureans

In 306 BC Epicurus (*c.* 341-270 BC) established a school just outside the city walls of Athens. He was an empiricist and held the doctrine first formulated by Democritus (*c.* 460-*c.* 370 BC) that all reality, including the mind, is exclusively material, composed of atoms (*atomos* means that which cannot be divided) and void. The gods exist, Epicurus held, but are far off and human beings have nothing either to hope or fear from them, nor need we fear death for it is merely the peaceful end of conscious existence and is followed by no afterlife. The goal of Epicurean philosophy is the maximisation of worldly happiness, to be achieved through a mind free from anxiety or disturbance, and a body free from pain. Epicureanism counsels a life withdrawn from the world of commerce and politics, lived with like-minded people in kindness and community, and teaches the moderation of appetite on the principle that those who require the least are the most happy. Much of the school's teaching is summed up in the precept 'live unnoticed'. The modern sense of 'Epicurean' as a *bon viveur* fond of good food, fine wine and high living dates only from the seventeenth century, when John Milton (1608-1674) rather deliciously upbraids the clergy of his day for 'warming their Palace Kitchins, and from thence their unctuous, and epicurean paunches'. Epicurus was a decisive influence on the Roman atomist Lucretius (*c.* 99-*c.* 55 BC) who wrote the most influential of all Epicurean texts *De rerum natura* (*On the Nature of Things*), a 7,500-line poem describing and extolling Epicurus' atomism. Once more, genre is not an incidental concern for Lucretius' poem; through 'sweet poetic honey' he aims to attract the reader to a philosophy that may from a distance appear uninviting.

Stoics

The Stoic school was founded by Zeno of Citium (*c.* 334-*c.* 262 BC) around the same time as the Epicureans, but in contrast to Epicurean withdrawal from public life the Stoics engaged in political participation and debate. The name 'Stoic' itself comes from the *stoa poikile*, the 'painted porch' in Athens where the group met. Like the Epicureans, the Stoics were materialists: everything (including the gods) is made out of matter. Zeno himself was the disciple of Crates (*c*. 365-*c*. 285 BC), a cynic philosopher with Diogenes' taste for the unconventional. Crates sought to cure Zeno of his modesty by making him carry a bowl of lentil soup through the streets of Athens, a shameful action that would cause him to lose his inhibitions. When Zeno sought to hide the bowl from view under his cloak, Crates broke it with his staff and the modest Zeno fled with soup dripping down his legs. A further apocryphal tale is told of how it was only Zeno's sense of modesty and the use of his large cloak that saved a crowd of onlookers from the spectacle of Crates consummating his marriage with Hipparchia in public.

For the Stoics there are two first principles of the cosmos, the *archê* of matter and the *archê* of divine *logos*: the reason or designing fire that is within all things and structures them according to its plan. Given this divinely pre-planned cosmos, even calamitous circumstances must be for the best and are therefore to be accepted, for only through such acceptance can a person be truly free. Stoicism took over from Epicureanism in the first century AD as the fashionable philosophy of the Roman intelligentsia.

Sceptics

Pyrrho of Elis (*c*. 365-*c*. 270 BC) gave his name to Pyrrhonism, the most widespread form of ancient scepticism. According to his disciple Timon of Philus (*c*. 320-*c*. 230 BC), Pyrrho declared that all things are uncertain and therefore we should suspend judgment about them. This was supposed to lead to tranquillity of mind as the sceptic renounced true knowledge and resolved to live by the appearance of things. It comes down to us through the writings of the Roman Sextus Empiricus (*c*. 160-210 AD) that Pyrrho needed day-to-day help from his friends to save him from natural dangers, notably falling down holes or over precipices and getting burned in fires. Sceptic, literally meaning 'inquirer', was adopted as one of the self-designations of the Pyrrhonist school.

The arts in the ancient world

Having examined some of the most important philosophical ideas that developed and moved away from Homer's view of the undivided universe, we will now consider how the ancient genres of lyric poetry, elegy and tragedy reflected the ethos of ancient Greece, and begin to see how this period established literary forms that would echo down the corridors of history to our own day.

Ancient tragedy

The performance of Greek tragedy developed in the late sixth and early fifth centuries BC in Athens. Previously, public theatrical performances had comprised only a chorus, a group of fifteen to twenty-four actors (all adult men) who would speak or sing in unison. The word 'chorus' comes from a Greek word meaning 'dance', and the chorus would accompany its declamation or singing with movement, the precise nature of which remains a mystery. According to Horace's (65-8 BC) *Ars Poetica* (*Art of Poetry*), Thespis gave the first individual tragic performance in 534 BC, when he separated a speaking actor from the chorus of a choral hymn. We still celebrate Thespis' innovation today in the word 'thespian'.

Tragedies in ancient Athens were performed at the annual City Dionysia, a festival dedicated to Dionysus, the god of wine, festivity and celebration. The festival took the form of a competition. Three playwrights would each submit three tragedies and one satyr play (a short burlesque performance) into the competition, and it was down to a panel of judges to award first, second and third prizes, the winner being decorated with an ivy wreath. Each play would be performed only once, to an open-air audience of up to 15,000 people. The cast always comprised three actors, with any one actor playing two or three different roles, each of which required a different *persona* or mask. In addition to the three actors there was a chorus of twelve or fifteen members, usually representing a marginalised group such as old men, slaves or women. The material of the plays would be taken from myth, and thus would normally be familiar to the audience.

The three great Greek tragedians, and the founders of the Western understanding of theatre, are Aeschylus, Sophocles and Euripides. The influence of the Greek theatre which they helped build can still be seen in any theatre performance today, in the appearance on stage of individual actors who speak (it seems obvious now but its first occurrence in the West was in Greece), in the theatrical genres of tragedy and comedy, and in the division of a play into acts.

Aeschylus (c. 525-c. 456 BC)

Aeschylus won either thirteen or twenty-eight victories at the City Dionysia (sources differ as to the precise number), and though we have the titles of eighty-two of his ninety plays, only one complete trilogy survives: the *Oresteia*. This trilogy, comprising the *Agamemnon*, *Choephoroe* (or *Libation Bearers*), and *Eumenides* (or *Furies*), was performed in 458 BC and tells of the murder of Agamemnon (commander of the Greek army in the Trojan War) by his wife Clytemnestra, and the vengeance of their son Orestes. The level of violence builds as one play progresses to the next, climaxing in the *Eumenides* when the Furies, goddesses embodying the anger and vengeance of the dead, dance around Orestes as he clings to a statue of the goddess Athena. A rather fanciful report tells how the appearance of the Furies at the first performance terrified children in the audience and caused pregnant women to miscarry. In the final play, the goddess Athena presides over a court in Athens, where Orestes is tried and acquitted. Thus the trilogy charts the progress from a regime of blood vengeance to the civic justice of the Athenian state. Aeschylus himself, as legend has it, was not as fortunate as Orestes and his own demise more resembles a farce than a tragedy. He is said to have died when an eagle dropped a tortoise on his head, mistaking it for a stone on which to crack open the animal's shell.

Sophocles (c. 496-406 BC)

Sophocles is by many counts the most successful of the three ancient tragedians, winning the city Dionysia no less than eighteen times, including at his first attempt in 468 BC. Out of Sophocles' one hundred and twenty-three known plays, only seven have survived, the most famous among which are *Oedipus Rex* and *Antigone. Oedipus Rex*, perhaps the most well-known and frequently performed Greek tragedy of all, begins when Oedipus is king of Thebes but relies on an elaborate mythical back-story. The back-story is that Oedipus is abandoned as a baby by his parents Laius and Jocasta, and raised in the court of king Polybus in Corinth. Curious about his origins, Oedipus inquires of the Delphic oracle who prophesies that he is doomed to marry his own mother and kill his own father. On the road to Thebes he encounters a traveller coming the other way and, in an early case of road rage, murders him in a dispute over right of way. The traveller, it turns out, was none other than his own father Laius. Later, Oedipus solves the riddle of the Sphinx: 'What is the creature that walks on four legs in the morning, two legs at noon, and three in the evening?' The answer of course is 'man', who crawls as a baby and walks with a stick when old. When her riddle is solved, the Sphinx kills herself. As a reward, Oedipus gets to marry the queen who is ... his mother Jocasta.

So much for the back-story. Sophocles' play begins with a plague in Thebes, thought to be inflicted because the murderer of Laius has not been punished. Oedipus vows to search for his father's murderer, still unaware that he himself is the culprit. His investigations lead to Jocasta surmising who Oedipus is, and she flees. A messenger finally confirms the truth and, finding Jocasta hanged, Oedipus puts out his own eyes with the gold broaches of her dress. The play ends with Oedipus in exile. In common with almost all the protagonists of ancient Greek tragedy, Oedipus is propelled to his destiny by fate, an impersonal force to which gods and mortals alike must bend. The force is personified in the three Fates, who together decide the length of each person's life as a length of thread: Clotho spins the thread, Lachesis measures it, and Atropos cuts it. The idea that human existence is governed by an inexorable fate flows deeply through much Greek and Roman thought, and subsequent Western conceptions of an impersonal force governing human destiny find their roots here.

In *Antigone* the eponymous heroine, child of Oedipus, is caught between two absolute demands on her loyalty. When king Creon kills Antigone's brother Polyneices, decreeing that he should not receive a proper burial, Antigone must decide between obedience to the king's command and obedience to the unwritten law of family loyalty. She chooses to defy the king and bury her brother, for which she herself is buried alive in a cave by the angry Creon. Warned by the blind prophet Teiresias that the gods do not approve of what he has done, Creon repents and prepares to bury Polyneices and free Antigone, only to find that she has already taken her own life in the cave. Creon finishes the play a broken man. The tragedy dramatises the dilemma of loyalty: should Antigone obey the law of the king, or the unwritten law of family loyalty? By contrast with Aeschylus and Euripides, Sophocles' tragedies are conspicuous for the remoteness of the gods. Athena is the only god to appear in any of his surviving plays, and she does nothing remotely so useful as her inauguration of a system of civic justice at the end of Aeschylus' *Eumenides*.

Euripides (480-c. 406 BC)

Euripides was not, it seems, the critics' choice, taking home the prize at the city Dionysia on only three occasions. Of his ninety plays, eighteen tragedies and one satyr play survive. It is striking that the gods in Euripides' tragedies appear as petty and vengeful. In his *Hippolytus*, Euripides takes up the mythical story of Phaedra, a woman consumed with lust for her step-son Hippolytus who, when he rebuffs her, takes vengeance on him. In Euripides' hands this story is turned into the tale of a good woman struggling heroically against an affliction given her by the vengeful goddess Aphrodite in order to punish Hippolytus.

Aristotle's theory of tragedy

It was Aristotle who first codified and attempted to explain the genre of tragedy, and his description in the *Poetics* has remained influential ever since, especially in its enigmatic emphasis on 'catharsis' and completeness, which we shall explore below. Aristotle is known to have considered Sophocles' *Oedipus Rex* to be the perfect tragic play, and therefore it should not be a great surprise to us that this play fits his definition of tragedy most closely. Aristotle writes:

> Tragedy, then, is an imitation of an action that is serious, complete, and of a certain magnitude; in language embellished with each kind of artistic ornament, the several kinds being found in separate parts of the play; in the form of action, not of narrative; with incidents arousing pity and fear, wherewith to accomplish its *katharsis* of such emotions.

Let us highlight four aspects of this definition. First of all, tragedy is imitation (Greek: *mimesis*). What is represented in the play should imitate an action from life outside the theatre. Secondly, tragedy should arouse pity and fear in the audience. These two words are notoriously difficult to interpret. It may be that, while feeling pity for the plight of the tragic hero, the audience also fears that the same tragic fate could await others, even perhaps themselves. Thirdly, the arousal of pity and fear should lead to catharsis. Once more, two thousand years of commentary have not brought clarity to this term. The word can be translated as 'purgation' or 'cleansing', and it is reasonable to suppose that Aristotle is drawing on an image from the medicine of the day, of purging away excess fluids in the body. Fourthly, the plot, which Aristotle understands to be the 'arrangement of incidents', must form what has been called a 'well-wrought story', one having a beginning, a middle and an end. The plot must introduce complications or knots, which are then unravelled and resolved by the end of the play, not left open-ended.

Aristotle's prescription for tragedy has exerted a great influence, some would say too great an influence, on the subsequent course of Western theatre and culture. Neo-classical playwrights like Jean Racine (1639-1699) at the court of Louis XIV of France would seek to adhere scrupulously to Aristotle's strictures, more scrupulously at times than the ancient Greek tragedians themselves. In order to appreciate how Aristotle's *Poetics* has influenced Western storytelling, watch a Hollywood film – say: *Star Wars* (1977) – and then a Western-influenced Japanese film – say: the delightful animation *Spirited Away* (2001). This juxtaposition highlights the extent to which the well-wrought story with its careful knotting and final unravelling has sculpted a Western understanding of storytelling. Notice that in the non-Western influenced film characters and events are introduced without much explanation and the end does not bring a resolution of all the plot elements.

Lyric and elegiac poetry

In addition to epic poetry, of which Homer is the pre-eminent Greek exponent, ancient Western culture developed the genres of lyric and elegiac. The difference was originally one of performance: lyric poetry was to be sung to the accompaniment of a lyre, and elegiac poetry was sung to a flute. Lyric poetry emerged in the seventh century BC, was generally much shorter than epic and emphasised personal concerns rather than sweeping heroic adventures. Elegiac poetry often deals with issues of loss and mourning. Whereas epic poets would not speak of themselves, lyric and elegiac poetry is often in the first person.

Sappho (born *c.* 630 BC) is, by reputation at least, the most eminent Greek lyric poet, so revered that she became known as the 'tenth muse'. Although there were nine books of her poetry in the library in ancient Alexandria, only one complete poem (usually called the 'Hymn to Aphrodite') remains, along with a number of fragments. In the Hymn, Sappho begs the goddess to come to her aid. We quote here the first three strophes, in which the personal nature of the writing and the tone of anguished pleading force themselves upon the reader:

Throned in splendour, immortal Aphrodite!
Child of Zeus, Enchantress, I implore thee
Slay me not in this distress and anguish,
Lady of beauty.

Hither come as once before thou camest,
When from afar thou heard'st my voice lamenting,
Heard'st and camest, leaving thy glorious father's Palace golden,

Yoking thy chariot. Fair the doves that bore thee;
Swift to the darksome earth their course directing,
Waving their thick wings from the highest heaven
Down through the ether.

When it comes to elegy, it is the Latin poets Catullus (*c.* 84-*c.* 54 BC) and Ovid (43 BC-17/18 AD) who have made the deepest impression on Western poetic practice. Catullus' love elegies portray the poet in thrall to the cruel mistress Lesbia, and helped elevate the elegy to one of the foremost poetic genres. The two-line elegy 'Odi et amo' (I hate and I love), in which Catullus wrestles with his conflicting feelings for Lesbia, achieves its burning intensity through stripping away all nouns and adjectives:

Odi et amo. Quare id faciam, fortasse requiris?
Nescio, sed fieri sentio et excrucior.

I hate and love. Perhaps you ask why I do it.
I know not, but I feel it, and I am in torment.

Athenian democracy and Roman law

Athens was host to the first democracy in the West, a democracy – literally the power (*kratos*) of the people (*demos*) – characterised not by regular elections of representatives like modern-day parliamentary democracies, but by the direct deliberation and voting of the assembly of Athenian citizens, comprising all free males over twenty years of age, amounting to around six thousand men or 20% of the population of the city. To protect against tyranny each year the assembly could vote for one person to be banished from Athens for ten years. This ostracism (from *ostraka*, the shards of pottery used in the voting process) required a minimum of six thousand votes, leading to the banishment of the individual whose name was scratched on most pottery *ostraka*. The story is told of how, at one assembly in 482 BC, the statesman Aristeides was approached by an illiterate farmer who asked him to write a name on his *ostrakon*. When Aristeides asked the farmer whose name he wanted written, the reply was 'Aristeides'. The reason? Because he was always called 'Aristeides the Just'. Living up to this epithet, Aristeides duly inscribed his own name, and was indeed ostracised.

Athenian democracy is most closely associated with the name of Pericles (*c.* 495-429 BC), the statesman and general who led the Athenians during

Figure 1.6. The Parthenon (fifth century BC) on the Acropolis in Athens.

the first two years of the Peloponnesian war against Sparta, promoted the arts and letters, challenged the power of the aristocratic Areopagus, the ruling council of Athens, and initiated the construction of most of the buildings on the hill of the Acropolis, including the Parthenon (Figure 1.6), a temple to Athena, guardian goddess of Athens. Countless modern Western buildings are modelled on the Parthenon, from museums to town halls to university faculties.

The historian Thucydides (*c.* 460-*c.* 395 BC) records the following words from Pericles' funeral oration:

> Our polity does not copy the laws of neighbouring states; we are rather a pattern to others than imitators ourselves. It is called a democracy, because not the few but the many govern. If we look to the laws, they afford equal justice to all in their private differences; if to social standing, advancement in public life falls to reputation for capacity, class considerations not being allowed to interfere with merit; nor again does poverty bar the way; if a man is able to serve the state, he is not hindered by the obscurity of his condition.

The Assembly, the central institution of Athenian democracy, met around once every ten days. Decisions of war, peace and alliance were decided in this forum, in which all its members were allowed a voice. The executive branch of Athenian democracy was the Council of five hundred, on which all male citizens over the age of thirty were eligible to serve, together with seven hundred or so officials. Posts to the Council were usually chosen by lot. After the death of Pericles, Athenian democracy is thought by some to have descended into mob rule, but from its growth in the fourth century BC to its dissolution some one hundred and fifty years after Pericles' death, it brought relative stability to the Athenian city-state.

It has been hastily but nevertheless usefully said that, while Greek culture conquered Rome, Roman armies conquered Greece. Rome annexed the Greek provinces in the first and second centuries BC, but the Romans admired the achievements of Greek culture and fancied themselves as the natural successors of Greek civilisation, shaping their literature, philosophy and art to a large extent according to Greek conventions and carrying on the development and expansion of Greek ideas and artistic forms. Virgil (70-19 BC) modelled his Latin epic *Aeneid* on Homer's two epics, conspicuously tipping his poetic hat in the very first line of the *Aeneid* both to the weaponry of the *Iliad* and to the focus on Odysseus in the *Odyssey*: 'Arma virumque cano' ('I sing of arms and of a man'). Donatus, an early biographer of Virgil, tells that the poet was so dissatisfied with the unfinished work that, at his death, he demanded it be burned. Thankfully, the emperor Augustus intervened and ordered the work to be preserved, winning the eternal thanks of generations of scholars.

It was the principles of Roman private law that formed the basis of the European systems of 'civil law' today. The term civil law (Latin 'ius civile') describes those systems where law is codified in a major authoritative document; it is contrasted to systems of 'common law' or 'case law' where the law develops through appeals to precedent and the decisions of judges in individual cases. The strength in Roman civil law was that it contained a sense of objective rationality; judgments were no longer down to the whim and caprice of an absolute ruler but were passed down – in theory at least – according to public principles of justice. This gave a predictable reliability to contractual agreements and allowed rights of ownership to be normalised, crucial factors for the subsequent growth and development of Western society.

The greatest digest and systematisation of Roman law, and one of the most influential legal texts in Western history, was the legal code of the emperor Justinian (reigned 527-565 AD), comprising the *Digest* (a collection of writings from classical Roman jurists), the *Institutes* (a law textbook) and the *Code* (a systematised presentation of imperial legislation). His work provides modern-day scholars with their most important source of Roman law. The *Institutes* begins with the grand-sounding declaration that 'Justice is an unswerving and perpetual determination to acknowledge all men's rights [...] The commandments of the law are these: live honourably; harm nobody; give everyone his due.'

The government of Rome passed through three stages: monarchy, republic and empire. As legend has it, the early Roman monarchy was overthrown in 509 BC. For almost five centuries Rome was a republic, governed by a senate of three hundred adult landowning males who had held previous public office and whose appointment was approved by a vote of the senate itself. By the first century BC Rome had become the capital of a vast empire, and its laws allowed for provision, in time of war, for a 'dictatorship' in which one man could be given the power to veto the senate for a six-month period. In 44 BC Julius Caesar was made perpetual dictator, and later in the same year a group of senators disturbed by Caesar's increasing accumulation of power surrounded him in the senate and curtailed his authority in that most effective of ways: by stabbing him to death. After a season of civil war, the imperial period of Roman history was inaugurated with the rise to power of Caesar's grand-nephew Octavian (whose imperial title, Augustus Caesar, was taken by every subsequent emperor). Augustus is considered the first 'Roman emperor', a convenient shorthand title that indicates the accumulation of an increasing number of offices of state in one person.

An extended period of relative peace, both within and on the borders of the empire, began with the reforms of Augustus (63 BC-14 AD), 'reforms' which consisted for the most part of Augustus arrogating ever-greater power to himself. This has become known as the *pax Romana* (Roman peace). Crucially, Augustus' reforms were not merely political. He promoted a view of Rome as a world capital charged with securing a global peace, whose destiny would shape the fate of all of humankind. This notion of a special role in world history is one important difference between Greek and Roman ambition, and one reason why the thesis that Rome adopted Greek culture can be only partially true.

A good case can be made that it is first with the expansion of the Roman empire that we can talk about 'the West' as a cultural as well as geographical entity. After the conquests of the emperor Trajan (*c.* 53-117 AD) the Roman empire stretched from Egypt in the south to Hadrian's wall on the border between England and Scotland in the north, and from modern-day Portugal in the west to Syria in the east, dwarfing even Alexander's conquests. According to the historian Cassius Dio (*c.* 163-*c.* 235 AD), when Constantine the Great (*c.* 274-337 AD) made Christianity a state religion in 324, the Roman empire had already dwindled 'from a kingdom of gold to one of iron and rust', and the once mighty western Roman empire fell when the Visigoths sacked Rome in 410 AD. Romulus (reigned 475-476 AD), the last Roman emperor in the West, was deposed in 476. At its height the empire paved the way for the rapid spread of Christianity, a story that we shall take up in our second chapter.

2

The Roots of Western Culture: Christianity

Introduction

In a temperate outpost of the Roman empire, nearly 1,500 miles east of the imperial capital of Tiberius I, stepson of the great Augustus Caesar, a man hangs in agony, blood dripping from his punctured forehead. A small group of family and friends watch from a distance while attendant Roman soldiers pass the morning quietly, waiting for the convicts to die. Around thirty-three years earlier this criminal was born in a shed to a young teenage mother from a backwater northern town under foreign occupation. He had been given the name Yeshua, Aramaic for 'the Lord is salvation', and as a young man he had earned his keep swinging a hammer in his father's carpentry business. Around the age of thirty he embarked on three short years travelling in the Middle East, never moving more than two hundred miles from his place of birth and avoiding the nation's capital city. He never commanded an army and had no more than a handful of close followers during his lifetime.

In the final three years of his life, Yeshua is homeless and poor, relying on the hospitality of friends and sympathisers. After a series of increasingly hostile encounters with the political leaders of his own people, he is put to death by a method of execution forbidden to Roman citizens, a method intended to humiliate and prolong the agony of the naked criminal who eventually suffocates to death, unable to support his own body-weight. And yet this man, who never set foot in the modern-day West, has shaped its story perhaps more than any other. No one knows what he looked like, yet he is the most painted man in Western history. He never wrote a word, yet his teachings have stamped their shape deep into the Western sensibility. He died in shame and humiliation, yet the claim that this man is divine has been the single most important religious influence on Western thought and culture for the past two millennia. Yeshua's title of 'the anointed' (*mashiah* in Hebrew, *christos* in Greek) captures not just a religious claim but a fundamental way of thinking and living in the world, a set of responses to the great philosophical questions and a set of values that helps define Western attitudes to everything from the ethics of leadership to the meaning of the good life. This carpenter's son is an anomaly perhaps, but an anomaly which defines new norm. In this chapter we explore the story that makes sense of Jesus Christ the executed carpenter's son, for it is also a story through which the West comes to make sense of itself.

The Bible: unity and diversity

What we know of Jesus we know from the Bible, from the New Testament written after his death and, Christians would argue, from the prophesies about him in the Old Testament, written centuries before his birth. Both as a literary source (providing subjects and themes to write about) and a literary influence (predisposing us to write in certain ways), the Bible is without equal in the West. In his *Anatomy of Criticism* (1957), one of the most influential works of literary criticism published in the twentieth century, Canadian literary theorist Northrop Frye argues that the Bible is 'the major informing influence on literary symbolism', and that 'once our view of the Bible comes into proper focus, a great mass of literary symbols [...] take on meaning'. The influence of the Bible and Christian thought is also felt more broadly in our Western culture, to the point where the West's understanding of humanity and the world grows out of Christian soil. In this section we shall see how the Christian Bible as a whole has been understood to tell one coherent story through a wide variety of literary genres, and how this combination of unity and diversity has profoundly shaped the Western mind and ethos.

Before we dig into the Bible, it is worth being clear on how we shall navigate its pages. The chapter numbers by which modern readers divide the books of the Bible are not original to the biblical documents. They were added by Stephen Langton, who served as Archbishop of Canterbury between 1207 and 1228. Though the oldest manuscripts of the Hebrew Bible do include verse divisions, the Arabic numbered divisions familiar to modern readers were standardised and added to Langton's chapter numbers by Isaac Nathan ben Kalonymus around the 1440s in the case of the Old Testament, and for the Christian New Testament by Robert Estienne (1503-1559) in 1555.

The Bible as a unified mosaic

In John's gospel it is Jesus' own idea that the whole of the Bible, Old and New Testaments, bears witness to himself. In John 5:39 he says to a group of religious teachers 'You search the Scriptures because you think that in them you have eternal life; and it is they that bear witness about me'. This idea of the whole Bible bearing witness to Jesus is taken up in the second century by the church father Irenaeus of Lyons (died *c*. 200 AD). We know very little about Irenaeus, other than that he became bishop of Lyons (in Gaul, modern-day France) after faithful service to the church during the persecution under the Roman emperor Marcus Aurelius (121-180). In his lively and combative *Against Heresies* (*c*. 180) Irenaeus argues that the whole Christian Bible has a single 'hypothesis' an argument (Greek: *thesis*) beneath (Greek: *hypo*) its surface. Irenaeus likens the hypothesis of the Bible to so many jewels and mosaic pieces which, when rightly assembled, reveal the portrait of a great king. The heretics, he wryly adds, are like those who take the pieces of this mosaic and rearrange them to make a dog or a fox. It is a hypothesis that can be understood in three broad moments, with the third moment taking up the vast majority of the biblical material. Those three moments are creation, fall and redemption or, expressed as three questions: 'What is there?', 'What has gone wrong with it?', and 'How can it be put right?'

Creation: what is there?

The Bible's account of creation in Genesis 1 bears some marked differences to other ancient creation stories. Greek creation myth as recorded in Hesiod's (eighth/seventh century BC) *Theogony* reads like a particularly gruesome family soap opera. The story begins with chaos, out of which come forth the female Gaia (the earth) and male Uranus (the sky). Uranus imprisons Gaia's children in Tartarus (Gaia's bowels), for which Gaia seeks revenge by asking her sons to castrate Uranus with a flint sickle. Cronus, the youngest son, lies in wait for his father, and when Uranus – let us use a euphemism – approaches his wife's bowels, Cronus leaps out and severs his father's testicles, casting them into the sea. This pattern is paralleled in the creation myth of the Hittites (from modern-day Turkey), preserved in the *Song of Kumarbi* (c. fourteenth/thirteenth century BC), in which the god Anu is defeated by his son Alau, who is in turn deposed by his son Kumarbi. In a struggle with Alau, Kumarbi bites off his father's testicles and, swallowing them, impregnates himself, spitting out three further gods. A story of conflict also shapes the creation myth of the Babylonians (from modern-day Iraq), preserved in the *Enuma Elish* (earliest possible date: eighteenth century BC; latest date: eleventh century BC), in which a war between many gods is won by the young Marduk. The victor then kills Tiamat, goddess of the ocean, and divides her body in two, making the sky out of one part and the earth out of the other.

The first thing we notice when turning from these stories to the biblical account in Genesis chapter 1 is that there is no sense of conflict. No family rivalries, no blood, no testicles, no theogony (birth of the gods), just one God, *Elohim*, who creates not by war or by mutilation but by speaking: 'And God said, "Let there be light," and there was light' (Genesis 1:3). *Elohim* does not emerge from the chaos like Gaia and Uranus but forms the chaos into a cosmos. He has no birth and, unlike the Greek account, his origin is not explained. Genesis 1:1 simply begins: 'In the beginning, God ...'. Furthermore, *Elohim* has no rivals, and no peers; the sun, moon and stars are elements of his creation, not additional deities, and in this way Genesis 1 presents a comparatively demythologised creation story. Furthermore, and in contrast to Plato's insistence that ultimate reality can only be reached by abandoning the material and exercising the intellect, the material creation in Genesis is not considered as something to be risen above: 'And God saw everything that he had made, and behold, it was very good' (Genesis 1:31).

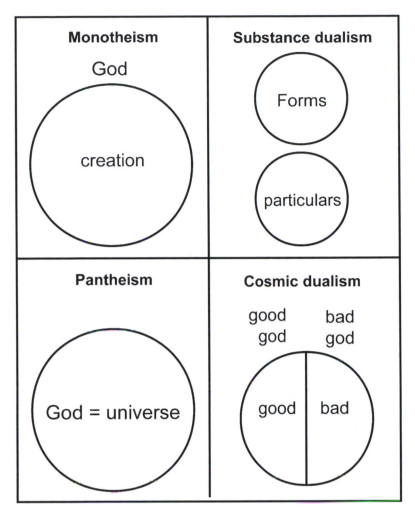

Figure 2.1.

Biblical monotheism presents a God who is unique and separate from the world he has created (Figure 2.1). This is different from Plato's 'substance dualism', according to which everything that exists, exists in two different worlds. It differs also from pantheism, in which the universe is identical with God, and from 'cosmic dualism', in which an equally powerful good god and bad god battle for control of the earth. The real uniqueness of the Genesis account of creation for the history of the West comes into focus when we consider that it marries monotheism with personhood: there is only one God, but that God speaks, sees and judges. The Roman Stoics held that there was one deity, but the Stoic God is a divine fire or an impersonal force, part of the material world. The God of the Christian Bible is a person. This combination of monotheism and personhood has two important implications for the Western view of the world. First, if the universe is created by one God alone, it is a place of order, predictability and structure, not chaos, conflict and inexplicable change. This conviction played its part in motivating the birth of Western science, based as it is on the belief that the workings of an ordered universe can be penetrated by human reason. Secondly, God's personhood is irreducible to more fundamental constituent parts, and so is the personhood of Adam and Eve, the human beings whom he creates in Genesis 1. Like God, they are persons; like God, they speak; like God, they bring order to the world. In the language of Genesis 1, human beings are created in the 'image of God' (1:26-7).

Such an insistence on the God-likeness of humanity has led to a high value being placed on all human life by the Judeo-Christian tradition and has laid the foundation for modern notions of human dignity and inalienable human rights. For example, the early Christians distinguished themselves in the Roman empire by their resistance to abortion and the exposure of infants, the practice of abandoning unwanted new-borns to the elements to die. The practice was finally outlawed in 374 by the Christian emperor Valentinian I (321-375). The Christian respect for life also extended to the ill and diseased. In *A History of Christianity* (1976), Paul Johnson quotes a letter from the Roman emperor Julian (reigned 361-363) in which he refers to the Christians by Jesus' home town of Galilee. Julian complains that 'I think that when the poor happened to be neglected and overlooked by the [Roman] priests, the impious Galileans observed this and devoted themselves to benevolence. [...] The impious Galileans support not only their own poor, but ours as well, everyone can see that our people lack aid from us.' Johnson concludes that the early Christians were operating 'a miniature welfare state in an empire which for the most part lacked social services'. Roman society had hospitals only for soldiers or gladiators; the West's first hospices for a broader public were established under the direction of the Christian council of Nicaea in 325 AD, with the first hospital built by Saint Basil in 369 in the city of Caesarea.

Fall: what has gone wrong?

The second great moment in the Bible's storyline comes in Genesis 3, shortly after the creation narrative, and tells how Adam and Eve disobey God. In Genesis 2 God invites Adam to eat fruit from all the trees of the garden of Eden save one, the tree of the knowledge of good and evil, with the warning 'in the day that you eat of it you shall surely die'. Goaded on by the serpent who is 'more crafty than any other beast of the field that the Lord God had made' (3:1), Adam and Eve disobey God and eat the fruit. This fruit is often represented in Western art and mythology by an apple, but there is no warrant for this in the biblical account. The confusion probably arises from the Latin translation of Genesis 3, where the word *malum* can mean both 'evil' and 'apple'.

For their disobedience, God curses the man, the woman and the serpent, and the 'very good' creation becomes a place of pain and conflict, in what Christian theology calls the Fall. Adam and Eve are banished from the garden of Eden, and the world after Genesis 3 is no longer the world of Genesis 1-2. Human sin exerts an effect on the whole of the created order; there is now a profound and ineradicable dysfunction in the natural world, in human relationships and in the relationship between God and human beings. The belief in Christian theology that this rebellion against God is a universal human condition – 'all have sinned and fallen short of the glory of God' (Romans 3:23) – has left its mark on Western notions of equality and hierarchy. If human beings are equal in bearing the image of God then they are also equal in sin, equal in a 'democracy of sin' in which everyone, regardless of their place in society, stands in need of God's mercy to forgive them. Medieval church murals of the final judgment frequently depict kings, bishops and even popes being ushered into hell alongside taverners and workers. All strata of society are on the same footing. It is not a position that the Christian church has always respected.

Redemption: how can it be put right?

In a Christian understanding, the rest of the biblical mosaic pieces tell the story of God's plan to redeem people from sin through Jesus Christ, the Old Testament providing a number of models of this coming redemption and the New Testament presenting its fulfilment.

Abraham and God's blessing

One of the first models of God's redemption of humanity in the Old Testament is the story of Abram (later called Abraham) in Genesis 12. Abraham is important in the story of redemption because he is told by God that blessing will come to all people through his bloodline:

> Go from your country and your kindred and your father's house to the land that I will show you. And I will make of you a great nation, and I will bless you and make your name great, so that you will be a blessing. I will bless those who bless you, and him who dishonours you I will curse, and in you all the families of the earth shall be blessed (Genesis 12:1-3).

Abraham's family does indeed grow, and at the beginning of Exodus, the second book of the Bible, we find them a 'great nation' living as slaves in Egypt at a time dated to around the end of the late Stone Age and the beginning of the Bronze Age (turn of the second and third millennia BC).

Moses, the Passover and the Ten Commandments

Fearing that the Hebrew nation will become too powerful, the Egyptian Pharaoh commands that all male Hebrew babies be killed. The parents of a Hebrew baby called Moses abandon him in a basket among the reeds of the river Nile, only for Moses to be found by Pharaoh's own daughter and brought up as an Egyptian. God addresses Moses from a burning bush (Exodus 3), sending him to Pharaoh with a demand to let the Hebrew nation leave Egypt for the land promised to Abraham. After God sends on Egypt nine plagues of increasing severity which serve only to harden the Pharaoh's heart, he tells Moses that he will send a tenth plague: 'I will pass through the land of Egypt that night, and I will strike all the firstborn in the land of Egypt, both man and beast; and on all the gods of Egypt I will execute judgments: I am the Lord' (12:12). In order to escape the same fate, the Hebrew households are commanded to kill a lamb and smear its blood around the doors of their houses. The lamb will die in the place of the Hebrew firstborn, and seeing the lamb's blood God will 'pass over' the Hebrew households. On the night when God slays the Egyptian firstborn, Moses leads the Israelites in an 'exodus' (Greek: *exodus*, 'exit' or 'departing') out of slavery towards the promised land. Centuries later, in the New Testament, the lamb is taken up as a foreshadowing or type of Christ, 'our Passover lamb' who 'takes away the sin of the world', and Jesus is recorded as having been crucified on the day before the annual Passover celebration. The Bible presents Jesus, like the lamb, as the one who dies in the place of those under God's judgment, setting them free.

Moses and the Hebrews finally leave Egypt on the night of the Passover, and enter a period of wandering in the desert (the original 'wilderness years'), during which time God makes two important revelations to Moses. First, God gives Moses instructions for building a tabernacle, or tent, where the Israelite priests are to offer sacrifices for the people's ongoing sins. Secondly, God reveals to Moses the 'law' or 'teaching' (*torah*) which is to govern the redeemed nation. In Exodus 19 Moses ascends Mount Sinai (in modern-day Egypt) to receive the law from God, descending in chapter 32 with two stone tablets containing the ten commandments. In the film *The Ten Commandments* (1956), the biggest grossing movie of the 1950s, Charlton Heston played the character of Moses. Heston insisted that, in the scene recreating his descent from the mountain, he should carry two tablets of real stone. Two large tablets were made but proved impossible for Heston to wield. The two 'stone' tablets we see in the film are in fact made of wood.

Once again, Moses leading the people out of slavery to the promised land is taken up in the New Testament as a model of redemption through Jesus Christ. The imagery of the tabernacle is used in the New Testament as a model of Christ who, according to John 1 'dwelt [literally: tabernacled] among us'. Christ is pictured as a priest who, like the priests serving in the tabernacle, offers the sacrifice that redeems people from sin. In the New Testament letter to the Hebrews, the wilderness tabernacle is described as a 'copy and shadow' of Christ's priestly service 'in the true tent that the Lord set up, not man'.

The ten commandments and revelation

The direct gift of the tablets to Moses by Yahweh (God's personal name, considered too holy to be pronounced in traditional Judaism) highlights a particular biblical emphasis about the way to know ultimate truth. Rather than Plato's intellectual contemplation of the Forms, or Aristotle's emphasis on the accumulation of knowledge through sense experience, in the Bible knowledge of ultimate truth is gained primarily through

God's self-revelation: God speaks and tells people what they otherwise could not find out for themselves. Whereas both investigation of the natural world and intellect are, so to speak, 'bottom-up' epistemologies – human beings striving by one means or another to attain knowledge of ultimate reality – revelation is (on Mount Sinai quite literally) 'top-down', accomplished not by the human search for truth but a divine initiative of self-disclosure. With the addition of revelation, we are now acquainted with three of the four ways of acquiring knowledge that weave themselves through Western intellectual history. The fourth is tradition, a reliance on what has been thought or said in the past. Each important movement or era in the West will strike its own relative emphases among these four paradigms of intellect, experience, revelation and tradition. The notion of revelation also marks an important difference between the Bible and the Homeric epic poems. Though the *Odyssey* and the *Iliad* are imbued with a religiosity and each epic begins with an appeal to a muse for inspiration, the Bible and Homer stand as two distinct trajectories for the Western religious sensibility: despite the reverence in which Homer's writing was held and its centrality to the education of Greek boys, it does not carry the same revelatory authority in the Greek mind as the Bible does for Christians.

Monarchy and exile

The history books of the Bible from Leviticus to 2 Chronicles tell the story of the Hebrew nation's slow conquering of the promised land, and the establishment of the Israelite nation as a monarchy with its capital in Jerusalem. The nation prospers under the kingship of David (eleventh century BC), a shepherd boy chosen by God to rule after Israel's first king, Saul, disobeyed Yahweh over a matter of sacrifice. David is succeeded by his son Solomon, under whose rule Israel enjoys its greatest period of *shalom* (peace and flourishing). Both David and Solomon are taken up in the New Testament as 'types', or models, of Jesus' own kingship. Nevertheless, Solomon's disobedience to God leads to a power struggle among his sons that results in the splintering of the Israelite nation into two separate kingdoms in 922 BC (mid Iron Age). Ten of the twelve Israelite tribes form the northern kingdom, retaining the name Israel, and the two remaining tribes form the southern kingdom of Judah, with Jerusalem as its capital.

The story of redemption is seemingly derailed in the eighth century BC by the dominant power in the Middle East, Assyria, the first empire to dominate both the Nile and Tigris-Euphrates river valleys. In 722 BC Assyria conquered the northern kingdom of Israel and resettled large numbers of its population in Assyrian lands, while Israel's own territory was in turn colonised by peoples loyal to the Assyrian empire. The mixed population that resulted became known as the Samaritans. A series of reliefs from the palace of the Assyrian king Sennacherib in Nineveh (now in the British Museum) depict the Assyrian siege of Lachish, 25 miles

Figure 2.2. Exiles being led from Lachish (Judah) to Assyria (*c*. 700-681 BC).
Alabaster panel. British Museum.

south-east of Jerusalem, in 701 BC. The detail of one of the reliefs (Figure 2.2) shows a line of Israelite refugees being led into exile.

In the south, the city of Jerusalem held out until 586 BC when Babylon, having now taken over from Assyria as the local bully boy, first besieged and then sacked the Judaean capital, taking the cream of Judaean society into exile and resettling them in Babylon. After the Fall, the exile is the great trauma of the Old Testament for Christian theology, and a cause of great distress for the Old Testament writers. Behind the military story of Assyria and Babylon, the exile is presented as God's judgment on his people for their disobedience to him and their persistence in unjust practices.

When Cyrus the Great of Persia (reigned *c*. 559-530 BC) conquered the Babylonian empire around 540, he decreed that the exiles be allowed to return and rebuild Jerusalem. The eventual return from exile, as recorded in the Old Testament books of Ezra and Nehemiah, is monumentally anticlimactic. Those who remember the old Jerusalem weep with sadness upon seeing it rebuilt on a much smaller scale, and the former glory is never recaptured. On this note of mourning mixed with expectant hope for a future saviour of the nation, the Old Testament draws to an end.

Jesus Christ: incarnation

From the closing of the Old Testament canon and the birth of Jesus four centuries pass, during which time Jerusalem becomes first part of the Seleucid empire, created from Alexander's conquests in the east, and then a province of the Roman empire, conquered by the General Pompey in 63

**The incarnation of
Jesus Christ**

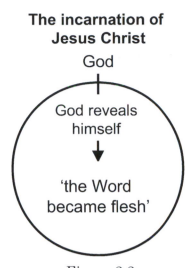

Figure 2.3.

BC. The New Testament begins in the first century AD with the account of the birth of Jesus to Mary, a young teenage woman betrothed but not yet married, in a squalid stable in Bethlehem, far from the nation's capital. In fact, modern scholarship now dates Jesus' birth to no later than 4 BC, on account of most scholars placing the death of Herod the Great in that year, in whose reign Christ is said to have been born. The Western dating convention of using the abbreviation AD (Latin: *anno domini*, 'in the year of the Lord') was devised in the sixth century by the monk and scholar Dionysius Exiguus ('Dennis the Small', *c*. 470-*c*. 554) during his attempts to draw up tables for the moveable date of Easter. Years had previously been reckoned on a regnal basis – for example 'the third year of the reign of Diocletian' – with days calculated according to a complicated system involving the 'Nones' 'Ides' and 'Calends' of each month. Exiguus' method of dating was not widely used until it was taken up by the Northumbrian monk the Venerable Bede (672/3-735) who used it in his *On the Reckoning of Time*, annotating dates before Christ as 'ante incarnationem Dominicam' (before the Incarnation of the Lord). The abbreviation BC became commonplace only in the seventeenth century.

The culmination of a Christian understanding of God's self-revelation is Christ's incarnation (see Figure 2.3). It is an idea developed most fully in the latest of the four gospels to be written: the gospel according to John (written perhaps around AD 90). John presents Jesus' incarnation in terms of the word (*logos*) becoming flesh (*sarx*). The passage bears quoting at length here because it provides an illuminating contrast with Plato's account of knowledge:

In the beginning was the Word, and the Word was with God, and the Word was God. He was in the beginning with God. All things were made through him, and without him was not any thing made that was made. In him was life, and the life was the light of men. The light shines in the darkness, and the darkness has not overcome it. [...] And the Word became flesh and dwelt among us, and we have seen his glory, glory as of the only Son from the Father, full of grace and truth. (John 1:1-5, 14)

For the Greek tradition, *logos* expresses the idea of the organising principle of order, the glue that makes sense of the world and holds it together. The first chapter of John's gospel presents a different *logos*, identifying this principle with Jesus himself: the *logos* is a person. In a further contrast between Greek and Christian thought, the prisoner who escapes from Plato's cave 'sees' the Forms and realises that all he has experienced hitherto has been unreal, whereas Jesus, in entering the physical world, affirms that world's reality. Finally, both Plato and John employ the image of light but whereas in Plato's cave the emancipated prisoner must travel upwards and out of the cave into the blinding light, for John the direction of travel is reversed, and 'the light shines in the darkness'.

Jesus Christ: death and resurrection

Many details are recorded in the gospel accounts about the itinerant public ministry of Jesus in the last three or so years of his life: he teaches in parables, heals the sick, drives out demons, calls twelve disciples to travel with him, and engages in increasingly hostile exchanges with the ruling Jewish authorities. Yet around half of the material in each gospel deals with the week before, and the days after, his death. The preponderance of material dedicated to Jesus' last days sets the stage for the central place that the crucifixion has played in Christian thought for the past twenty centuries.

This centrality has not been without controversy however. The notion of a suffering and dying God scandalised the ancient world as it does many today. Jesus' crucifixion was considered an ignoble death and a point of ridicule for early Christians, a point amply illustrated by the 'Alexamenos graffito' found scratched into a wall near the Palatine Hill in Rome and dating probably from the beginning of the third century (see Figure 2.4). The graffito shows a depiction of a man with a donkey's head hanging on a cross, with a second man standing in an attitude of worship above the inscription 'Alexamenos worships [his] God'. As for the biblical documents, Jesus' crucifixion itself is described with sparing detail, and in the letters of the New Testament the focus is not on his physical suffering but on the theological meaning of Jesus' death: 'For Christ also suffered once for sins, the righteous for the unrighteous, that he might bring us to God' (1 Peter 3:18). Christ's death is 'for' – or 'in the place of' – sinners, bearing the suffering for their sin and reconciling them to the God from whom they were alienated back in Genesis 3.

The pattern of Christ's lowly birth and suffering would give the West a new type of hero, a hero from humble beginnings who triumphs not in indomitable strength but through weakness. In fact, this pattern of weakness is typical of the types of Christ found in the Bible: Abraham the impotent senior citizen who fathers a great nation, Jacob the younger son who gains his father's inheritance, Joseph the brother abandoned and left for dead who saves his whole family, David the shepherd boy who becomes king, Gideon the coward who wins a great battle, and of course

Figure 2.4. Tracing of the Alexamenos graffito (first-third century AD). Plaster. Palatine Museum, Rome.

Jesus the carpenter's son from a backwater town who suffers for sin, 'that he might bring us to God'. This model of the humble hero also gave the West a new ethic of leadership, in the wake of the Jesus who stoops to wash his disciples' feet (a task that not even slaves were compelled to perform in first-century Jewish culture). Jesus embodies the subversive idea that leaders, be they religious or political, should be not our despots but our servants, our 'ministers' (*minister* is Latin for 'servant'), for Jesus commands 'If anyone would be first, he must be last of all and servant of all' (Mark 9:35). It is interesting to speculate on the extent to which this subversion of hierarchy, along with the 'democracy of sin' mentioned above, give Christianity and Western culture its bent of self-critical satire and a readiness to undermine overblown claims to power.

Finally, the very idea that God cares for human beings to the point of loving them self-sacrificially was a new idea in the West. For Aristotle the only fit object of the Prime Mover's thought is the Prime Mover itself;

such a god could feel no love for mortals. For the Epicureans the gods do not care about human beings. Much less would a god suffer and die for people, as the Christians claimed Christ had done on the cross. In *The Rise of Christianity*, sociologist Rodney Stark argues that 'what was new was the notion that more than self-interested exchange relations were possible between humans and the supernatural'. As an echo of God's self-giving love in dying for sinners, the early Christians developed a new ethic of *agapê*, love. The verb *agapao*, I love, predates the New Testament, but it seems that the early Christians invented the noun *agapê* to talk of God's love for people and the love Christians were expected to have among each other. In terms of social relations, Roman *liberalis* characterised a generosity with a view to a reciprocal return, whereas Christian *agapê* (Greek) or *caritas* (Latin) promoted giving to those unable to repay.

The gospel accounts record that after lying in the grave from Friday evening until Sunday morning, Jesus rose from the dead. The resurrection differs from a resuscitation in that Jesus is presented not as coming back to this life only to die once again at a later date, but as 'the first fruits of those who have fallen asleep' (1 Corinthians 15:20): the first of many to enter a new everlasting resurrection age. Finally, the New Testament teaches that Christ will return at an unspecified time in the future to 'judge the living and the dead' (2 Timothy 4:1), taking some to be with himself in the resurrection age and condemning others to hell, which he describes as a place 'where their worm does not die and the fire is not quenched' (Mark 9:48).

This final piece in the biblical mosaic also illustrates another important contribution of early Christianity to the Western ethos: the notion of eschatological time. Aristotle considered the cosmos to be eternal, arguing in the *Metaphysics* that is impossible 'that generation should take place from nothing', and the Stoics held that the cosmos cycles through eternal phases of expansion and contraction. By contrast, the biblical notion is of a 'last day' when the dead will be raised and Christ will judge the world. This linear notion of time as an irreversible and meaningful progress towards a final judgment shapes history as a trajectory leading to a predefined end. Its main contrast with Greek and Roman notions of time is not primarily the often asserted difference between 'linear' and 'cyclical' time. The Greco-Roman world was quite capable of seeing history in a linear way, for example in the destined rise and dominance of the Roman empire. The great difference is that the biblical conception of history is providential, directed by one God in supreme sovereign control, working all things out in accordance with his will, in contrast to Greco-Roman idea of fate or an impersonal force of destiny.

The Bible as a library of genres

In relation to Plato, we have already seen that we must take account of the genre in which philosophy is written. This is not only true of Plato, and it is not only true of philosophy. Indeed, it is nowhere more important than when we consider the way in which Western thought and Western sensibilities have been shaped by the Bible. The generically diverse literature of the Bible has left its mark on Western culture in three main ways. First, the imagery of the Bible has enriched Western languages by bringing into common circulation a large number of aphorisms and idioms. From the 1611 King James translation of Matthew's gospel alone we have in English turning the other cheek, going the extra mile, casting your pearls before swine, doing unto others as you would have them do unto you, an eye for an eye, a faith that can move mountains, the blind leading the blind, love thy neighbour, the salt of the earth, the spirit is willing but the flesh is weak, walking the straight and narrow, a wolf in sheep's clothing, and having a cross to bear.

Secondly, the Bible has given to the Western mind many of its 'archetypes': events, people or stories that – like the Greco-Roman gods and goddesses – transcend their own particularity to symbolise a common situation or truth of the human condition in a way that becomes part of the shared mental furniture of a culture. Archetypes play an important role in any culture. For the psychologist Carl Jung (1875-1961) they 'make up the groundwork of the human psyche'. A full survey of biblical archetypes would run far beyond the scope of this book (the *Dictionary of Biblical Imagery* published in 1998 weighs in at a hefty 1,058 pages), and I shall only mention very few here by way of illustrative example. The Babylonian exile stands in Western art and literature for the pain of forced banishment, and the promised land and new Jerusalem for many a homeland; the relationship between Jesus and Mary his mother is an archetype of all mother-child relationships, and Judas' betrayal of Jesus an archetype of treachery (just remember the famous 'Judas' heckle when Bob Dylan dared to abandon his folk music roots for an electric guitar in his Royal Albert Hall concert of 1966). The massacre of the innocents – when Herod 'killed all the male children in Bethlehem and in all that region who were two years old or under' (Matthew 2:16) – is an archetype of the horror of systematic slaughter, in the same way that the word 'Auschwitz' now stands as an archetype of evil in the Western mind.

Thirdly, biblical writing has provided generic forms and intellectual inspiration for sacred and secular authors alike throughout the subsequent history of Western literature, as well as for the Western mind more broadly. Rather than listing notable subsequent works influenced by the Bible – an inexhaustible task of limited interest – we shall explore the deeper influence that some of the major genres of the Bible have provided for the Western sensibility as a whole.

The writing of the Old Testament

As with the Homeric epics and the writings of Herodotus (*c.* 484-*c.* 425 BC) the father of Greek history, biblical history cannot be rightly understood apart from the context of divine plans and influence. The Babylonian exile is both the defeat of one weaker nation by a stronger empire and the judgment of God on his disobedient people. Babylon is both God's 'hammer' to break nations (Jeremiah 51:20) and also responsible for her atrocities against Israel (Jeremiah 51:24). This providential view of history, along with the language the Bible uses to articulate it, has often been taken up by Western nations to suggest that they, like the Israel of the Old Testament, have a special place in the plans of God. Towards the end of the fourth century AD the city of Constantinople proclaimed itself the 'New Jerusalem', the world centre of true worship and of God's dealings with the world. In the 800s AD Alcuin of York proclaimed the court of Charlemagne (*c.* 742-814) at Aachen to be a new Jerusalem, and Charlemagne called his subjects a new Israel. The Puritan colonisation of New England in the seventeenth century was dripping with references to the 'promised land' and with the idea that the colonisers were a 'chosen nation', a 'New Jerusalem', a 'city on a hill' with a God-given responsibility to be a light to the nations. The theme continues to be articulated by some today in relation to the place of the United States among the nations of the world.

Jewish scholars divide the Hebrew Bible (containing substantially the same books as Christian Old Testament) into three broad genres: the law (or *torah*), the prophets (or *nevi'im*) and the writings (or *kethuvim*). Taking the initial letters of these three Hebrew words, together they make the Tanach. The biblical genre of law – though in certain ways resembling other ancient law codes like the Babylonian code of Hammurabi (*c.* 1700 BC) – is notable in that it grounds universal ethical demands in the character of God. Kings and emperors are not absolute rulers but are themselves subject to God's law. This was vividly illustrated on one memorable occasion around the year 390 when Ambrose, bishop of Milan, refused to serve mass to the Roman emperor Theodosius the Great (reigned 379-395), on account of his slaughter of seven hundred inhabitants of Thessalonica that same year. Eight months after this stand-off, Theodosius repented and vowed henceforth to wait thirty days between passing a death sentence and carrying it out. The Greco-Roman gods, frequently in conflict with each other, laid no universal moral injunctions upon humanity, but the commandments of Yahweh are given as universal commands to the whole Israelite nation. The importance for the Western tradition of the notion of a law above the nation's sovereign – its modern avatar is the national constitution – is hard to overestimate, providing a stability and predictability in the areas of contract and property that allow for the building of modern society.

The biblical genre of prophecy is strikingly different from Greco-Roman oracles. The oracle was consulted by a supplicant who would ask a question to which he or she would receive an oracular, opaque answer that often required much interpretation. By contrast, the pattern of biblical prophecy is that the (often reluctant) prophet is given a verbal message directly from God to proclaim to the nation, more often than not in plain language and often falling on deaf ears. The prophets are not only foretellers but forth-tellers, messengers reminding the nation of God's covenant with them – his solemn and binding promise – and bringing God's words of judgment and comfort, often with vivid accompanying actions. The prophet Hosea is commanded by God to marry a prostitute to show Yahweh's own commitment to his people who have committed spiritual adultery. Ezekiel cooks his food on animal dung to show how conditions will be in the future siege of Jerusalem, and Isaiah walks naked through the streets of Jerusalem for three years, proclaiming 'so shall the king of Assyria lead away the Egyptian captives and the Cushite exiles, both the young and the old, naked and barefoot, with buttocks uncovered' (Isaiah 20:4).

The third broad genre after the law and the prophets is the 'writings', also referred to as 'wisdom literature'. The wisdom in question (Hebrew: *chokmah*) is a practical reason, a correct understanding that goes hand in hand with sound judgment and skill in the daily practical affairs of life. The wisdom books present two distinct outlooks on the world. The book of Proverbs presents a view according to which virtue is rewarded, vice is punished and people receive what they deserve. By stark contrast, the book of Ecclesiastes presents a chaotic world in which the wicked frequently prosper and the righteous are thwarted and suffer. The 150 Psalms of the Bible sit in the middle of this duality, on occasion praising God for the manifest justice in the world, at times bewailing its absence.

Whereas Greek and Latin poetry are constructed according to metre, the Psalms and other examples of Hebrew poetry in the Bible (three quarters of the Old Testament is written in poetic form) privilege the device of parallelism, the restatement of an idea in order to amplify or qualify it. A synonymous parallelism restates an idea in different terms:

> Your word is
> > a lamp to my feet
> > and a light to my path. (Psalm 119:105)

Antithetical parallelism strengthens a point by stressing its negation:

> A wise son makes a glad father,
> > but a foolish son is a sorrow to his mother. (Proverbs 10:1)

And synthetic parallelism progressively develops a thought over a number of repetitions:

> The voice of the Lord is powerful;
> > the voice of the Lord is full of majesty.
> The voice of the Lord breaks the cedars;
> > the Lord breaks the cedars of Lebanon. (Psalm 29:4-5)

This parallelism builds meaning through progressively adding blocks of sense, each line providing one unit of sense. This has led some scholars to speak of a 'Hebrew logic' as distinct from 'Greek logic' exerting its influence in the Western tradition. The theory goes like this. Greek (read: Aristotelian) thought is abstract and concerned with universals, encountering the world through the mind and deploying a linear logic that constructs syllogistic arguments. The Hebrew mind by contrast is concrete and particular, encountering the world through the senses and reasoning with a 'block logic' that, as in the case of poetic parallelism, builds units of sense out of smaller blocks of meaning. As with most such theories, this schema is good servant but a bad master, helpful in clarifying some of the different emphases of Greek and Hebrew thought but unpardonably reductive when used as the only grid through which to appreciate these two traditions.

An example of concrete thinking can be found in the Hebrew of Exodus 34:6, where Yahweh reveals his name to Moses. Modern translations render the name as a series of abstract nouns: 'The Lord, the Lord, a God merciful and gracious, slow to anger, and abounding in steadfast love and faithfulness'. The word translated 'anger', however, is the Hebrew *apaim* (nostrils, noses). Hebrew expresses anger through its concrete embodiment, the flaring of the nostrils, whereas modern English and ancient Greek both use an abstract noun. Similarly, 'gracious' is from *chanan*, meaning bending or stooping, and 'merciful' is from *racham*, to fondle, from which Hebrew also derives the word for the womb or uterus. Though it is by no means unknown in other languages to take concrete ideas to stand for abstract concepts, it is the relative frequency of such examples of concrete thinking in Hebrew that leads some to argue for Hebrew and Greek thought as the concrete and abstract poles between which the future development of Western thinking was to swing.

The writing of the New Testament

The New Testament is not written in the elegant Greek of Aeschylus or Plato but in koinê Greek (literally 'common Greek'), a spoken dialect with a simplified grammar and shorter sentences. The first complete New Testament we possess (called the Codex Sinaiticus) dates from around 350, and papyrus fragments of individual books date back to the second century AD. Figure 2.5 shows the recto of a papyrus of John's gospel (from chapter 18) dated somewhere in the first half of the second century and held in the John Rylands library in Manchester.

In *Mimesis* (1946), a seminal and highly influential study of the Western literary tradition, Erich Auerbach argues that the New Testament documents and in particular the gospel accounts also introduce a new type of character into Western literature. Characters from the lower classes appear in Greco-Roman literature either for comic effect or as illustrations of vice and ignorance, but the group of Jesus' closest disciples – including fishermen, a freedom fighter (Simon the Zealot) and a tax collector (Matthew) among others – are presented as 'the image of man in the highest and deepest and most tragic sense'. Auerbach traces this mode back to the simultaneous humility and nobility of the incarnate Christ, suggesting that this marriage of the divine and the everyday

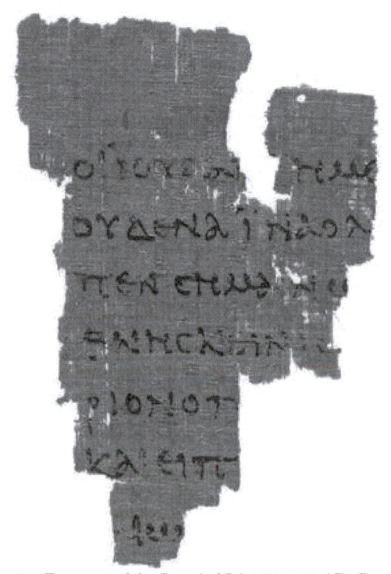

Figure 2.5. Fragment of the Gospel of John (125-150 AD). Papyrus.
John Rylands Library, Manchester.

forges the new 'mixed style' of the gospels: neither tragic nor comic. The new style exerts 'a most decisive bearing upon man's conception of the tragic and the sublime', the awakening of 'a new heart and a new spirit'. The gospels not only bring a new shape to religious belief, with the worship of a suffering, dying and rising God, but they also introduce a new literary sensibility to the West, a literature of the fully human common person.

The history of Christianity until the fifth century

The story of the rise of early Christianity is one of rapid growth, from just over 1% of the Roman empire around 100 AD to 50% by 350. In its first three centuries Christianity was primarily an urban religion. In fact, the word 'pagan' comes from the Latin *paganus*, meaning 'country dweller'. Rejecting as they did the entire pantheon of Roman deities, the Christians often found themselves accused of atheism.

The early Christians were certainly a persecuted minority, though the extent of the persecution is a matter of disagreement among scholars. The main waves of persecution came under the Roman emperors Nero (reigned 54-68) and Diocletian (reigned 284-305). The historian Tacitus (56-117) writes of the Christians that 'in their very deaths they were made the subjects of sport: for they were covered with the hides of wild beasts, and worried to death by dogs, or nailed to crosses, or set fire to, and when the day waned, burned to serve for the evening lights'.

Martyrdom stories in early Christianity are gruesome and varied (and often embellished). Lawrence, the patron saint of cooks, was slowly roasted in Rome for his refusal to hand over the names of Christians to the emperor Valerian, and is said to have encouraged his executioners to turn his body on the grill when one side was 'done'. Agatha, among other tortures, had her breasts cut off; Bartholomew, patron saint of tanners, was skinned alive and then crucified upside down. Sebastian, frequently represented in Renaissance art, was 'martyred twice'. He was a Roman officer under the emperor Diocletian who converted to Christianity and convinced other soldiers to become Christians. Diocletian ordered that he be shot by archers, but he survived and returned to preach to the emperor, who then had him beaten to death.

Whatever the reasons were for the growth of early Christianity, the number of Christians had risen sufficiently by 313 AD that the emperor Constantine I gave them official recognition in the Edict of Milan, decreeing that 'no man should be denied leave of attaching himself to the rites of the Christians, or to whatever other religion his mind directed him', after having himself professed Christian belief a year earlier. Constantine also granted tax exemptions to the Christian church and relieved its priests of military service. In the year 380, Christianity was declared the official religion of the Roman empire, with pagan worship outlawed in 391 and the imperial cult of emperor worship partly dying out, partly subsumed under the category of Christian sainthood. In Constantine's new imperial state church, the boundary between secular and ecclesiastical rule became increasingly blurred, as it had been before the adoption of Christianity as the official religion. Finance increasingly flowed into the building of churches, and wealthy artistic patrons demanded Christian works. In the centuries to come, the synthesis of sacred and secular power would be concentrated by the emergence of the Roman papacy. It was Damasus, Bishop of Rome (368-384) who first referred to the church in Rome as the 'apostolic see' (in other words, the jurisdiction that claims direct descent from Jesus' apostles in general and Peter in particular). Leo I (440-461) is commonly recognised as the first Pope; he argued for Peter's primacy among the apostles and claimed that Peter himself spoke through the Pope. The rise in power of the Pope coincided with the increasing weakness of the western Roman empire.

The church fathers

The first eight or so centuries of Christianity are known as the patristic era, and the thinkers who developed and defended the Christian faith in this period are known as the church fathers. The flowering of Christian thought and writing at this time is vigorous and broad, and one of the main questions to preoccupy the church fathers is the relation between Christian doctrine and pagan philosophy. The attitude of the church fathers to Greco-Roman learning varies greatly. Foremost among those opposing the appropriation of pagan learning was Tertullian (*c.* 160-*c.* 240), African father of the church born in Carthage (near modern-day Tunis). In his *Heretics*, Tertullian argues that:

> philosophy is the material of the world's wisdom, the rash interpreter of the nature and dispensation of God. Indeed heresies are themselves instigated by philosophy [...] What indeed has Athens to do with Jerusalem? What has the Academy to do with the Church? What have heretics to do with Christians? Our instruction comes from the porch of Solomon, who had himself taught that the Lord should be sought in simplicity of heart. Away with all attempts to produce a Stoic, Platonic, and dialectic Christianity!

Elsewhere in his writing Tertullian refers to Plato, Zeno and Epicurus as authorities, and it is unclear whether in the quotation above he is rejecting philosophy as a whole or merely the Christian heresies he thinks it leads to. Nevertheless, his rhetorical question 'What indeed has Athens to do with Jerusalem?' has been taken as emblematic of one possible Christian attitude to pagan philosophy.

Augustine of Hippo (354-430), the greatest of all the church fathers, takes the opposite view. Augustine converted to Christianity in 386 under the teaching of bishop Ambrose of Milan, after delaying the decision with the prayer he records in his *Confessions* 'Grant me chastity and self-control, but please not yet'. He served first as a monk and then became bishop of Hippo in 396, dying there when the city was besieged by the Vandals in 430. In his *On Christian Doctrine* (published between 397 and 426 AD) Augustine writes:

> we ought not to refuse to learn letters because they say that Mercury discovered them. Nor (because they have dedicated temples to Justice and Virtue, and prefer to worship in the form of stones things that ought to have their place in the heart) ought we on that account to forsake justice and virtue. Nay, but let every good and true Christian understand that wherever truth may be found, it belongs to his Master; and while he recognises and acknowledges the truth, even in their religious literature, let him reject the figments of superstition.

Augustine's greatest contribution to the Christian appropriation of pagan philosophy was in bringing together Plato's Forms and the *logos* of John 1. Plato is the privileged philosophical interlocutor for Augustine, leading him to the conclusion that the Forms (referred to here as Ideas) exist in the mind of God:

> Ideas are certain principal, stable and immutable forms or reasons of things. They are not themselves formed, and hence they are eternal and always stand in the same relations, and they are contained in the divine understanding.

Augustine differs however from Plato's position that knowledge of ultimate reality is gained through the intellect. For Augustine faith is necessary for all true knowledge, for 'if you do not believe, you will not understand'.

Augustine is one of the last great writers of antiquity and one of the first of the Christian era, giving the West two of its most important volumes, the *Confessions* (397-400) and the *City of God* (413-426). The *Confessions*, written as a prayer addressing God directly, is the beginning of the Western tradition of autobiographical writing. In its pages Augustine searches his heart and motivations, drawing wider conclusions about the human condition and about God. He tells of the love and prayers of his Christian mother Monica, of his dissolute youth when he considered Christianity as nothing more than a religion for old women, and of his eventual conversion to Christianity after being confronted with his own wickedness when he stole a 'huge load of pears' from a pear tree, not out of hunger but out of a love for doing wrong:

> I became evil for no reason. I had no motive for my wickedness except wickedness itself. It was foul, and I loved it. I loved the self-destruction, I loved my fall, not the object for which I had fallen but my fall itself.

Augustine's story is one of dissatisfaction and disgust at his own behaviour and his own heart, leading to the realisation that 'You have made us for yourself, O Lord, and our hearts are restless until they rest in you.' The *Confessions* is also an important step in the development of the Western notion of interiority, the exploration of an 'inner space' or 'inner world' of the mind or soul.

The writing of *The City of God Against the Pagans* was precipitated by the sacking of Rome in 410 by the Visigoths, an act which was widely interpreted as punishment for Rome abandoning its traditional gods and turning to Christianity. In *The City of God* Augustine seeks to refute this interpretation by showing that Rome suffered calamities during the period of its pagan worship, that the longevity of the Roman empire must in fact be ascribed to Yahweh, the God of the Bible, and that pagan gods provide no benefits either in this life or the next. Augustine divides civilisation into two distinct categories, the *civitas dei* (city of God) and the *civitas mundi* (city of the world), two opposing orders that exist intermingled in the present time but will be divided on the final day of God's judgment. This 'two kingdoms' theology exerted a powerful influence on subsequent Christian thought, including on the reformer Martin Luther (1483-1546).

Books 11 to 22 of the *City of God* elaborate a Christian philosophy of history, tracing the two cities from their origin, through the whole sweep of biblical and human history, to their final separation in the future. This second half of the *City of God* was instrumental in developing the notion of linear progress and eschatological time at the heart of the Western ethos, as well as strengthening the view that 'secular' history cannot be adequately understood apart from sacred history. With good reason, the theologian B.B. Warfield argues that Augustine's writing does not merely bring into being 'an epoch in the history of the Church, but has determined the course of its history in the West up to the present day'.

Christian art until the thirteenth century

Having briefly discussed the influence of the biblical genres and Augustine's writing on the course of Western literature, we turn now to early Christian art, taking in a span from the origins of Christianity in first-century Rome to the high Middle Ages around 1200. The development of Western sacred art in this period is a story of increasing abstraction. The earliest Christian paintings are to be found on the walls of the catacombs under the city of Rome, where early Christians buried their dead. The volcanic tufo rock on which Rome is built has the peculiarity of being relatively soft when first exposed to air but then hardening with time, making it ideal for the excavation of catacombs. The Christian paintings of this period portray a very human and humble Christ, typically a beardless shepherd watching over his sheep (Figure 2.6).

After Constantine's adoption of Christianity as the official religion of the Roman empire, state sanctioned and financed Christian art moves away from the depiction of a simple agrarian Christ to the resurrected Christ in glory. The apse mosaic (526-547) of the Basilica of San Vitale in Ravenna (Figure 2.7) already shows a much more majestic Christ, seated upon a heavenly orb and offering a martyr's crown to San Vitale on a shimmering golden background with a cross-shaped halo and surrounded by angels. Nevertheless, the face of this Christ still retains a look of common humanity, unshaven like the good shepherd of the catacombs. Apart from Christ's grandeur, there is one noticeable development in the San Vitale mosaics: the large staring eyes so typical of Byzantine art, intended as windows onto the pure souls of the characters depicted.

As we skip down the centuries from San Vitale to the Cathedral of Monreale (in modern-day Sicily) in the late twelfth century, we can see the full flourishing of the Byzantine aesthetic. In the Monreale mosaics Christ has become more abstract, more distant, more majestic, depicted now not as a humble shepherd but as an eternal and universal king: *Christus pantokrator*, 'Christ ruler of all' (Figure 2.8). The depiction is more Platonic, a symbolic representation of Truth that lifts the contemplative soul up to the divine. This allegorical depiction of deity in symbolic terms is a particular legacy of Byzantine art to the Western

Figure 2.6. The Good Shepherd (third century AD). Fresco. Catacomb of Priscilla, Rome.

Figure 2.7. Detail from the apse mosaic (526-547), Basilica of San Vitale, Ravenna.

Figure 2.8. Christus Pantrokator mosaic (twelfth-thirteenth century),
Cathedral of Monreale, Sicily.

Figure 2.9. Pantokrator image from the deesis mosaic
(thirteenth century), Hagia Sophia, Istanbul.

tradition, a new way of imagining invisible divinity through visible depictions that takes its lead from the incarnate 'word become flesh' and that uses gold and glass to paint with a heavenly light. Byzantine art is not mimetic, seeking faithfully to represent a particular earthly reality, but iconic, evoking a universal heavenly truth through symbol and abstraction from the everyday and bringing a symbolic richness into the Western tradition not seen in the art of Greece and Rome.

The basilica of Hagia Sophia, originally built by Constantine II (reigned 337-340) was at the centre of Christian and Muslim rivalries in the early Middle Ages, being captured and ransacked on more than one occasion. The Pantocrator image from the thirteenth century deesis mosaic in the basilica (Figure 2.9) still displays the pronounced eyes and abstract golden grandeur of the Byzantine style, but Christ's expression now has a new tenderness. The powerfully abstract aesthetic is softening to reveal something of the humanity of the pre-sixth-century depictions. Within two hundred years of the Hagia Sophia deesis mosaic, the Italian painters Cimabue and Giotto would be setting off in search of a new naturalism that would surpass anything the Western world had seen before. But before we can tell that story we must explore the thought, architecture and literature of the Middle Ages that accompanied this trajectory of Byzantine art.

3

From Catacombs to Cathedrals:
The Middle Ages

As unexpected events go, it must rank among the most far-reaching in Western history. Charles, King of the Franks, has been on a visit to Rome, ostensibly to investigate a set of accusations circulating against the Pope. A faithful servant of the Catholic church, Charles has already expanded the Frankish Christian empire by conquering the Saxons (modern-day north Germany), Lombards (northern Italy) and Avars (Hungary), overseeing their forced conversion to the Catholic religion. In Rome he is received cordially enough, and the people of the city even sing hymns in his honour as he walks through the streets. Then, on Christmas day in the year 800, as Charles is kneeling at the high altar of St Peter's Basilica, to his surprise and anger (if we are to believe his rather romanticised biography) Pope Innocent III produces a crown and hails the kneeling monarch as *Imperator Romanorum* (emperor of the Romans), giving him the name taken by every Roman emperor: Augustus. The attendant congregation obligingly strike up in chorus a well-rehearsed 'To Charles, most pious Augustus, crowned by God, great and peace-loving emperor, life and victory', and the West has its first emperor since 476 AD. With an empire covering most of modern-day Belgium, Germany, northern Italy, northern Spain and north-eastern France, there is some justification in claiming that Charles is the Father of Europe, for his coronation marks the birth of the West as an entity distinct from the eastern Byzantine empire.

The coronation of Charlemagne (*Carolus Magnus*, Charles the Great, see Figure 3.1) as Holy Roman Emperor marks a watershed in Western history, a marriage of spiritual and political power that would remain, in one form or another, until 1806 when the last Holy Roman Emperor, Francis II (1768-1835), abdicated after defeat by Napoleon at the battle of Austerlitz, his empire only a fraction of the size of Charles's. Charlemagne's reign and the writing that surrounds it is an exercise in historical symbolism, with many of the different threads we have followed through the Greco-Roman and Judaeo-Christian roots of Western culture taken up and re-woven to serve new ends. In Virgil's *Aeneid* it is the Trojan hero Aeneas who founds the city of Rome, and Charlemagne is now the new Aeneas, founding a *Roma secunda*, a 'second Rome' at his imperial court in Aachen (modern Aix-la-Chapelle, on the border between France and Germany). Lest this symbolism be lost, Charlemagne ordered that stone for the construction of his palace at Aachen be brought from

Figure 3.1. Golden reliquary bust of Charlemagne (possibly thirteenth century), Aachen Cathedral, Germany.

Rome itself. His people, the Franks, became the object of myths of their own, their lineage rather fancifully being traced back to the city of Troy immortalised in Homer's *Iliad*. Turning to a Hebrew frame, Charlemagne is hailed as the new king David, ruling over a united kingdom from the 'New Jerusalem' of Aachen. His ethnically mixed dominion of Saxons, Bavarians and Franks is cast in the mould of Augustine's 'city of God', and would come to be known as 'Christ's kingdom', or 'Christendom'. In this chapter we first examine the period between the fall of the western Roman empire to Charlemagne's reign in the early Middle Ages, and then we turn our attention the great flowering of culture that followed in the high Middle Ages. The term 'Middle Ages' itself (Latin: *medium aevum*) was not used until much later, first appearing in the seventeenth century.

The early Middle Ages (600-1000)

The two centuries following the sack of Rome on 24 August 410 AD were a period of instability for a fading Roman empire harassed by barbarian tribes. The overthrow of Rome's dominance in the West saw the splintering of power into rival barbarian kingdoms, among which the Franks made gains in much of modern-day Germany and France and established themselves as the dominant power in central Europe under Clovis I (*c.* 466-511), a convert to Catholicism.

By the dawn of the seventh century, the two main influences that would sculpt the Western ethos and Western culture were in place. The Greco-Roman and the Judaeo-Christian legacies would be re-interpreted during the centuries that followed and invested with ever-changing meanings. During the same period there was a decline in the great cities of antiquity. It is estimated that one million people lived in Rome during the time of Augustus Caesar (reigned 27 BC-14 AD), but that number had dwindled to around thirty thousand by the year 800, and even at this modest number it was still the most populous city in Europe. The period from the fifth to the beginning of the ninth century was also a period of imperial decline. From the seventh century onwards, Christianity had to reckon with the rise of Islam in the east. The eastern Roman empire, also known as Byzantium, lost most of its territory to Islam in the seventh century, but still maintained Christianity in Constantinople, its capital city, until its fall in 1453. With the advance of Islam, Europe emerged as the new centre of Christendom.

Charlemagne (742-814)

Charlemagne dominates the early Middle Ages like a colossus, both in terms of his achievements and his stature. When a tomb said to belong to the emperor was opened in 1861, it contained a skeleton over 6 feet tall (1.82 metres), when average male height in the 800s was not more than 5.5 feet (1.67 metres). As with Alexander the Great it was Charlemagne's father, Pepin the Short, who began to unite the empire that his son would rule and further expand. Like Alexander, Charlemagne's empire stretched over most of western Europe, but the eastern extent of his rule stopped at the Elbe in the modern-day Czech Republic, far short of Alexander's eastern conquests. At his court in Aachen Charlemagne built a magnificent octagonal chapel named after the Palatine, the centremost of Rome's seven hills. The exterior diameter of the chapel's cupola (dome) was 144 Carolingian feet (equal to 157.5 standard feet, or 48 metres), reflecting the 144 cubit thickness of the wall of the New Jerusalem in Revelation 21:17. Charlemagne brought to his court the finest scholars in his empire: Franks, Lombards, Visigoths and Saxons. None was greater than Alcuin of York (*c.* 740-804) whom he placed in charge of the palace school and scriptorium at Aachen. Charlemagne and Alcuin introduced unprecedented educational reforms to the empire, requiring every cathedral and monastery to establish a school and teaching a curriculum that dates back at least as far as Augustine and that consists of grammar, rhetoric and logic, together known as the trivium. These reforms have come to be known as the 'Carolingian Renaissance' and, along with

Alfred the Great's (849-99) promotion of learning in the British Isles, Charlemagne's fostering of scholarship and the arts was in large part to thank for preparing the way for Europe's transition out of the Dark Ages. By the twelfth century, a further four subjects (the quadrivium) had been added: arithmetic, music, geometry and astronomy, and together the trivium and the quadrivium comprise the seven liberal arts that formed the backbone of medieval education. We can see the seven liberal arts represented in the foreground of Raphael's *School of Athens* (see. p. 91).

Charlemagne made Latin the official legal and business language in his empire, and had monastic scribes embark on the task of copying and disseminating the Bible and the writings of the Latin church fathers. A new script was developed called Carolingian minuscule, which was clearer and quicker to write than the large, rounded characters of the former uncial script. This increased the speed at which documents could be copied, as well as forming the basis of many modern typefaces. Important as Charlemagne's educational reforms were, they reached only a small minority of the population, 90% of whom remained illiterate. Although Charles himself could read Latin, Frankish and a little Greek, even he never learned to write because writing was considered a professional manual labour separate from general literacy.

As well as educational reforms, Charlemagne also brought sweeping changes to church and government, requiring all holders of ecclesiastical or governmental high office to swear a personal oath of allegiance to him. Charlemagne's papal coronation and the consequent blurring of the distinction between the power of church and state was to lead to bitter struggles throughout the Middle Ages. The conquests of Charles's Holy Roman Empire were often brutal, its borders more often than not volatile, and the emperor's wives frequently plural, to the disapproval of the ecclesiastical hierarchy. The eighteenth-century French *philosophe* Voltaire (1694-1778) was not altogether frivolous in suggesting that Charlemagne's rule was 'neither Holy, nor Roman, nor an Empire'.

Literature and art in the early Middle Ages

Perhaps the most famous work of literature dating from the early Middle Ages comes not from Charlemagne's empire but from the Anglo-Saxons, inhabitants of Angeln (modern-day north Germany), Saxony (east Germany) and the Jutland peninsula (modern-day Denmark) who came in the fifth century to settle in Ængla land, or England. The anonymous 3,182-line Old English epic poem *Beowulf*, composed some time between the eighth and eleventh centuries, tells of the eponymous hero's search for *þrym* (power, glory; the letter þ, 'thorn', is pronounced 'th') and *ellen* (valour) in his battles with the monster Grendel, Grendel's mother and an unnamed dragon. *þrym* and *ellen* present a rougher, less refined ethic than the Greek 'excellence' (*aretê*), and certainly more pugnacious than Christian *agapê*.

It was for a long time a commonplace of commentaries on *Beowulf* to suggest that the monsters and dragons were an embarrassment to its main themes, but in an influential paper of 1936, *Lord of the Rings* author J.R.R. Tolkien argued that the three monsters, symbolising evil and death, are central to the epic's concerns. His comments serve as a justification of the more fanciful aspects of the epic genre more broadly:

> It is just because the main foes in *Beowulf* are inhuman that the story is larger and more significant than this imaginary poem of a great king's fall. It glimpses the cosmic and moves with the thought of all men concerning the fate of human life and efforts; it stands amid but above the petty wars of princes, and surpasses the dates and limits of historical periods, however important. At the beginning, and during its process, and most of all at the end, we look down as if from a visionary height upon the house of man in the valley of the world.

One striking feature of *Beowulf*, shared by other Old English and Norse poetry, is its 'kenning'. It will be remembered that Homer's epics are peppered with epithets ('swift-footed Achilles', 'the wine-dark sea'); the technique of kenning replaces the noun with its paraphrase, rather than qualifying it with an adjective. So in *Beowulf* blood becomes 'battle sweat', death is the 'sleep of the sword', the king is the 'giver of rings' and, perhaps most poetically of all, the sea is the 'whale road', the 'sail road' or the 'swan road'. Kenning shares with Homeric epithets the feature of helping create the world of the text, giving the reader an indication not only of what is happening but also of an ethos, how people and events are to be viewed and valued.

Although the Carolingian empire did produce a notable body of both epic and lyric poetry of its own, its greatest contribution to Western literature is the careful preservation and propagation of learning under Alcuin and his successors. Along with the preservation of ancient texts, the Carolingian monasteries also developed the art of decorative calligraphy. Figure 3.2 shows an illumination of Christ's ascension from the Drogo Sacramentary (*c.* 850). The floral motif on the letter 'C' shows influences of the decorative geometric patterns of earlier Celtic art.

Philosophy in late Antiquity and the early Middle Ages: Neoplatonism and Christianity

The dominant philosophy of the Carolingian era was Neoplatonist. Neoplatonism is a term used to identify a tendency in philosophy beginning with Plotinus (204/5-270 AD), though many of the Neoplatonists themselves would reject the charge that they are departing from Plato at all. In book 6 of his *Republic*, Plato evokes the Good as the highest of the Forms, describing the Good in relation to being (to what exists) as 'not being, but superior to it in rank and power'. It is from references such as this that Plotinus speaks in his *Enneads* of an invisible and transcendent One which is simple, infinite, beyond being and beyond goodness, yet which makes possible both good and evil, both unity and multiplicity,

61

Figure 3.2. Detail from the *Drogo Sacramentary* (*c*. 850).
Bibliothèque Nationale de France, Paris.

both justice and injustice. As such, it is beyond any positive description. Everything in the world, including the world itself, has its origin in the One and will flow back to the One.

The Roman aristocrat and statesman Boethius (*c*. 475-*c*. 526 AD) sought to marry aspects of Neoplatonist doctrine with Christian belief, and his work stands alongside Plato and Aristotle as a pre-eminent influence on the thought of the Middle Ages. A noted translator and commentator of Aristotle, Boethius' most influential work is the *Consolation of Philosophy* (*c*. 524), written under house arrest while he was awaiting execution at the hand of the Ostrogothic king Theodoric the Great, whom he had displeased through his championing of Roman traditions and institutions. The work takes the form of a dialogue between Boethius and a female personification of philosophy, written with a beauty of style that has earned Boethius the title 'the last Roman'. The *Consolation*, looking beyond immediate injustice to a Platonic-Christian providence governing the affairs of the world, became a medieval bestseller and was translated by no lesser figures than King Alfred (into Old English), Jean de Meun (into Occitan), and Geoffrey Chaucer (into Middle English). It popularised in Western culture the idea of the wheel of fortune (Latin:

rota fortunae), a large wheel turned by the goddess Fortuna with people tied to its rim. The literal rising and falling of individuals as the wheel rotates symbolises the rise and fall of their fortunes over time.

Perhaps the greatest thinker of the early Middle Ages is the Irishman John Scottus Eriugena (*c.* 810-*c.* 877). Unusually for the time, Eriugena had a sound command of Greek as well as the more usual Latin, giving him access both to the Christian and Greek traditions of thought. His philosophy seeks to unite these two traditions in a Christian Neoplatonism in which, as with Plotinus, all things issue from and return to a self-identical One. The Plotinian One becomes for Eriugena the God who is in 'darkness' beyond the distinction between being and non-being. His illustrious career took him to the Frankish court around 845, where he succeeded Alcuin at the Palace School in Aachen. The story is told that, when seated for a meal opposite the Frankish king, Eriugena was noted with disapproval to transgress the court rules of etiquette. The king pointedly asked the philosopher what separates a drunkard (*sottum*) from an Irishman (*scottum*), to which Eriugena is said to have replied: 'only a table'. Despite the great influence of his synthesis of Christianity and Neoplatonism on later thinking, his views on predestination received a less fulsome welcome; they were dismissed by the Council of Valence in 855 as 'Irish porridge' and the Council of Sens (1225) described his Neoplatonism as 'swarming with worms of heretical perversity'.

The high (1000-1300) and late (1300-1400) Middle Ages

The period from around 1000 to 1300 saw a flourishing of what was increasingly recognisable as 'Western culture'. In *The Making of Europe*, historian Christopher Dawson justly claims that 'there is no doubt that the eleventh century marks a decisive turning point in European history [...] with the eleventh century a movement of progress begins which was to continue almost without intermission down to modern times'. The period witnessed dramatic improvement in agricultural efficiency. The introduction of the wheeled plough with an iron ploughshare allowed the heavy soils of northern Europe to be cultivated more effectively, and the new three-field system of crop rotation allowed for a more sustainable exploitation of the soil. At the beginning of this period, a good harvest would yield four seeds for every one seed sown, but by 1300 the ratio was ten to one. The population of Europe also rocketed in this period. By best estimates, it grew from thirty million in 1000 to fifty-five or perhaps sixty million in 1200, helped by the 'medieval warm period', a rise in sea temperature of around one degree from 950 to 1250 that resulted in a warmer and drier climate in the North Atlantic. The period also saw dramatic cultural developments. During the course of the twelfth and thirteenth centuries almost the entirety of Aristotle's surviving works began to circulate in Latin translation, and the period saw the development of the new philosophy of scholasticism and the new Gothic style in architecture.

Philosophy in the high Middle Ages: the problem of universals

Plato and Aristotle differed on the question of universals, or qualities that can apply to any number of particular objects ('green', 'beautiful', 'dog', 'good'). For Plato, universals have real existence as Forms outside of space and time, whereas for Aristotle, though universals do indeed exist they only exist in things (there is no 'sphere' apart from things that are spherical). Augustine, adopting a broadly Platonic position, maintained that universals exist in the mind of God, and Eriugena took a moderated Platonic stance in holding that universal categories are more real than the particular things that instantiate them. The controversy around universals continued to rage throughout the Middle Ages, reaching a climax in the twelfth century. The problem is not merely of esoteric interest, for taking one position or another on the status of universals leads to a particular view of the cosmos and whether it will yield its secrets to human reason: do the things that exist fall into necessary categories, or not? The thinking of the high Middle Ages on this question is summed up in the conflict between the scholastic realists and nominalists.

Scholastic realism: Thomas Aquinas (1225-1274)

Scholasticism is not as much a philosophy as a method. The scholastic method is a way of seeking to understand and engage with an argument – usually in Aristotle or the Bible – by closely reading the primary text and extracting the basic units of its arguments. *Quaestiones* (questions) are then asked in relation to the argument, usually eliciting a yes/no answer. After this, a range of commentaries on the text are consulted, and their arguments arrayed in a list of *sententiae* or short propositions on both sides of the yes/no question. The scholastic philosopher first gives the case with which he disagrees from the secondary sources, then the case with which he agrees, before setting out his own arguments and returning to the opposing arguments in order either to refute them or show them to be irrelevant.

Under the influence of Peter Abelard (1079-1142), both scholastic realism and nominalism gave a new prominence to human reason. Rejecting Augustine's dictum *credo ut intelligam* ('I believe in order to understand'), Abelard asserts with pride in his *History of My Misfortunes* that his own pupils 'asked for the human and philosophical reasons and insisted that it was not enough for something just to be said – it had to be understood'. Abelard was one of the first writers to call himself a theologian, and it is with this new privileging of reason that we see the birth of 'theology' in its modern sense, as distinct from biblical exegesis. In the wake of Abelard, later scholastic philosophy seeks to give reasons (*rationes*) for Christian faith, attempting to reconcile the teaching of Aristotle with biblical doctrine by showing that Christian theology is rational and that a correct use of reason must lead to Christian faith. Unlike Abelard however, later scholastics retain the notion that faith precedes, and leads to, understanding.

The greatest high medieval scholastic philosopher is Thomas Aquinas (1225-1274), born into the Italian nobility and marked out from his early years for monastic service. Thomas (he is often referred to by his first name only, and with the adjective 'Thomistic') failed his first *disputatio* at the University of Paris, an oral debate between a master and student that served as an examination. Even in failure he still impressed the chair in theology Albert the Great (*c.* 1200-1280), who commented 'We call him the dumb ox, but in his teaching he will one day produce such a bellowing that it will be heard throughout the world'. Albert's prophecy proved correct, and Thomas the 'Angelic Doctor' is held by many to be the Christian Aristotle, bending the ear of popes and academics alike. Thomas has such esteem for Aristotle himself that he simply calls him 'the Philosopher'. Thomas's position on universals is heavily indebted to Aristotelian moderate realism (also called Thomistic realism). Thomas gave to Aristotelian realism a new religious significance. It is said that Aquinas 'baptised' Aristotle, but it is equally true that Aquinas re-made medieval Christianity in Aristotle's image.

In his magnum opus the *Summa Theologica* (*Summary of Theology*, written between 1265 and 1274), Thomas distinguishes two types of truth: natural truths accessible to anyone (for example: God exists), and truths of grace, given only by revelation (for example: the nature of the Christian Trinity).

The realms of nature and grace are not divorced from each other, Thomas insists in the *Summa*, for 'there is no reason why those things which are dealt with in the philosophical sciences, so far as they can be known by the light of natural reason, may not also be taught us by another science, so far as they fall within revelation'. Two principal efforts are made to link the realms of grace and nature (see Figure 3.3): first, philosophical proofs of God's existence guide the thinker towards divine grace; secondly, the idea that nature itself reveals something of God to us brings the experience of God within the grasp of human reason. In this respect, Thomas took his lead from the first chapter of the Apostle

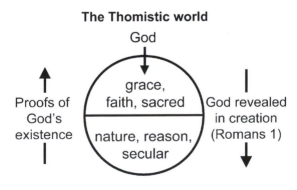

Figure 3.3.

Paul's letter to the Romans: 'the invisible things of God are clearly seen [...] by the things that are made'. Notwithstanding recent arguments to the contrary (notably by Henri de Lubac, 1896-1991), nature and grace for Aquinas are not continuous. At the opening of the *Summa* Thomas affirms that 'those things which are beyond man's knowledge may not be sought for by man through his reason, nevertheless, once they are revealed by God they must be accepted by faith'. Despite the revelation of God in creation, then, there is a discontinuity between faith and reason, a discontinuity that opens in the Western ethos a secular space where law, politics, and natural investigation can be conducted without explicit recourse to the Bible or God. This possibility of investigating the natural world unaided by revelation can be seen as one important step towards the birth of Western modernity.

Scholastic nominalism: William of Ockham (1285-1349)

Scholastics like Abelard, Thomas and Anselm of Canterbury (*c.* 1033-1109) sought to reconcile apparent contradictions in the scriptures and Patristic writings. By contrast, Hildegard of Bingen (1098-1179) and Bernard of Clairvaux (1090-1153) exemplified a contrary trend in high medieval thought that scorned the attempted synthesis of faith and reason. For Bernard, scholasticism in general and Abelard in particular were 'attempting to bring the Christian faith to naught because he supposes that human reason can comprehend all that is God'. For Bernard, Abelard's theology was nothing more than a 'stupidology' (*stultilogia*). For his own part, Bernard held that 'it is desire that drives me, not reason', a desire most eloquently communicated in his series of eighty-six sermons on that passionate biblical book, the Song of Songs. In subsequent chapters we shall see how this growing dispute between the primacy of the intellect and the primacy of feeling or desire becomes increasingly acute until, from the eighteenth century onwards, it dramatically fractures the Western sensibility in two.

If the rationalism of Dominican monks like Abelard, Thomas and Anselm was opposed by Bernard and his Cistercian order, then the moderate realism of the Dominicans was opposed by William of Ockham, the redoubtable fourteenth-century English Franciscan. So far we have seen two broad positions on the question of universals. Plato and the Neoplatonists held an 'extreme realism' in which universals exist independently outside the mind, while Aristotle and the Thomistic realists argued for a 'moderate realism' in which universals really exist, but only in particulars. Ockham, by contrast with both positions, moved to reject the real existence of universals altogether.

Roscellinus (1050-1125) had argued two centuries previously that universals are merely *flatus vocis* (airy or arrogant words), nothing more than names (*nomina*) and not things (*res*). By the turn of the fourteenth century, however, the late medieval West was facing a number of crises. The period of high medieval prosperity was brought to a cruel end with the great famine in Europe from 1315-1322, when a drop in temperatures was accompanied by unusually heavy rain. Then in 1348-9 the Black Death or 'the great mortality' wiped out fully 25-35% of Europe's entire population, returning with devastating effect in 1363. In addition, the Catholic church had fallen into schism, with up to three rival popes claiming authority at one time. In these late Middle Ages, a new philosophy asserted itself, building both on Roscellinus' nominalism and on Aquinas' realism, with Ockham as its greatest proponent.

For Ockham, the idea that universals could ever be the object of human knowledge was 'the worst error of philosophy'. He held that only concrete experience can lead to knowledge, that nothing exists apart from individual beings, and that general categories – like 'table', 'man', 'green' or 'beauty' – exist only within language (see Figure 3.4). The principle from which he argued was that 'plurality must never be posited without necessity', or in other words: the simplest and most economical explanation should always be sought. This principle of economical thought has become known as 'Ockham's razor', slicing away all but necessary assumptions.

Nominalism and universals

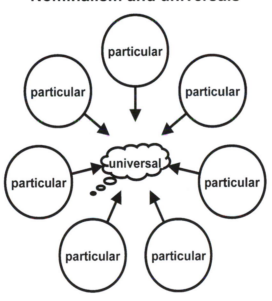

Figure 3.4.

Ockham did, however, still hold that revelation was a source of true knowledge, but in an extreme version of Thomas's discontinuity between faith and reason he argued for an absolute break between knowledge gained empirically or through reason and knowledge gained by revelation. Ockham's is a 'double truth' universe: there is truth as given by immediate mystical experience of the divine, which is both certain and also impenetrable to rational investigation, and there is truth as experienced through the senses and by reason. However, there is no bridge between revelation and reason, or between faith and experience

The nominalist divide

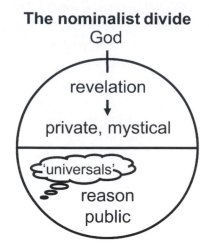

Figure 3.5.

(see Figure 3.5). This dichotomy slowly began to change the nature of belief in the West. The idea of philosophical proofs of God's existence was, in this context at least, on the wane, and in its place came the necessity of what would later be called a 'leap of faith'.

The move away from a Dominican Thomistic realism to a Franciscan nominalism is an important moment in the West's move to the post-medieval period of modernity. The importance of nominalism for future Western thought can be appreciated when we consider the place of universals in organising a society. Universals do not merely name abstract concepts like 'beauty' or 'goodness'; they also provide for the real existence of groups within a social network: the family, the nation, the social class. If universals are lost, then so is the basis of the medieval social order.

Eckhart and the new mysticism

Flourishing at the same time as Ockham, a new mysticism was growing in the church, exemplified in the writings of the Dominican Meister Eckhart (*c.* 1260-c 1327). Eckhart was certainly a mystic, but not a recluse. He travelled round Europe propounding his ideas, though always on foot, according to the rule of the Dominican order. On the question of universals Eckhart was a realist, but he sought to marry the Thomistic system with the burning desire of a Bernard of Clairvaux. In a way that reminds us of early Neoplatonist thought about the origin and destiny of the universe in the One, Eckhart holds that human origin and human destiny are a perfect union with God. He also holds that such a union can be tasted during mortal life through mystical experience. In his *Confessions* Augustine states that God is 'closer to me than I am to myself', and Eckhart uses this passage in order to evoke a burning intimacy between the soul and its creator. However, even this intimacy was not enough for Eckhart; he sought a passion in which the difference between Lover and Beloved, between the soul and its God, is completely dissolved. His prayer 'I pray God to rid me of God' is a plea to be rid of any fixed idea of God that gets in the way of his communion with the real but unknowable God. For Plato, it is the intellect that allows us access to an ultimate reality outside the world of sense experience; for the late medieval mystics such fundamental truth is not grasped with the rational mind but experienced in a communion that exceeds and on occasions contradicts the intellect.

The three great high medieval institutions: monastery, cathedral and university

When we turn our attention from philosophy to high medieval society, we can see scholastic and mystical influences in the three great medieval institutions that shaped not only the architecture of Western medieval cities but also their culture of learning and the arts. These three institutions are the monastery, the cathedral and the university.

Monasteries

After Constantine's creation of the imperial state church there grew within Christendom a desire for a life separated from the common civic space and apart, at least in principle, from the increasingly complicated relationships between secular and ecclesiastical power. Over the course of the Middle Ages coenobitic monastic orders proliferated in Europe, each with its own rule and peculiarities (see Figure 3.6), providing just this separation from the machinery of the state.

Scholarly Dominicans such as Abelard, Thomas and Anselm contrasted starkly with the Franciscans, who were pledged to a vow of poverty, as well as with the austere Cistercians with their emphasis on manual labour. The monasteries almost single-handedly saved Western civilisation during the early Middle Ages, playing a crucial role in preserving documents and fostering scholarship during the unstable centuries following the decline in power of the western Roman empire. Situated outside cities, monasteries were often spared the ravages of war; they were also a stabilising influence during volatile political times.

Cathedrals

The high Middle Ages is the age of grand cathedral building in Europe. Cathedrals could take over a hundred years to erect to the original design, but were commonly modified and expanded across subsequent centuries. The cathedral in Cologne stands at 152 metres high (the height of thirty-three double-decker buses) and was finally finished in 1880, 632 years after it was begun. When finished, medieval cathedrals were often large enough to contain the entire populations of the cities in which they were built. Over a hundred cathedrals were erected in the brief span of one hundred and fifty years from 1150 to 1300. The word itself comes

Order	Founder/inspiration	Prominent members	Characteristics
Augustinian	Augustine of Hippo (354-430)	Martin Luther (1483-1546) Gregor Mendel (1822-1884)	contemplative: 'mendicant' vow of poverty
Benedictine (Black Monks)	Benedict of Nursia (480–547)	Anselm (1033-1109) Peter Abelard (1079-1142)	contemplative: 'prayer and work'
Cistercian (White Monks)	Robert of Molesme (1028-1111)	Bernard of Clairvaux (1090-1153)	contemplative: manual labour, self-sufficiency. Split from the Benedictines.
Carthusian (Silent Monks)	Bruno (*c.* 1030-1101)		contemplative: solitude, 'community of hermits'
Dominican	Dominic (1170-1221)	Thomas Aquinas (1225-1274) Catherine of Sienna (1347-1380) Meister Eckhart (*c.* 1260-*c.* 1327)	active: preaching and teaching
Franciscan	Francis of Assisi (1181/1182-1226)	John Duns Scotus (*c.* 1265-1308) William of Ockham (1288-*c.* 1348)	active: vow of poverty, simplicity, penance, love for the poor
Carmelite	no named founder; founded early thirteenth century	Teresa of Ávila (1515-1582) Thérèse of Lisieux (1873-1897)	contemplative: prayer

Figure 3.6. Monastic orders.

from *cathedra* ('seat' or 'chair' in Latin), referring to the bishop's or archbishop's throne, a feature of every cathedral building. Cathedrals built in the early Middle Ages were mostly in the Romanesque style, with its characteristic rounded arches and sturdy right-angled simplicity, and Figure 3.7 shows the Romanesque elevation of the Basilica of St Sernin in Toulouse, built between *c.* 1080 and 1120.

By the twelfth century Romanesque architecture was overtaken by the flamboyant, soaring new Gothic style with its characteristic ogival (pointed) arches, ornate and expressive stonework, lavish decoration, ribbed vaults and flying buttresses. All these features are present in the east side of the Cathedral of Notre Dame de Paris (Figure 3.8), completed in 1345.

The medieval cathedrals were much more than places of Christian

Figure 3.7. Romanesque elevation of the east face of the Saint Sernin Basilica (1080-1120), Toulouse.

Figure 3.8. East face of Notre Dame Cathedral (twelfth century), Paris.

worship, acting as repositories of local records, disseminating education through the cathedral schools, and providing relief to the poor. The city would wake, worship and sleep to the rhythm of the cathedral bell. Unencumbered by pews (which were only widely introduced into churches from the Protestant Reformation of the fifteenth century to reflect the new importance given to the sermon), medieval cathedrals also served as market halls, each trade gathering in a different area of the building.

The intricate construction of the Gothic cathedral echoes the medieval rediscovery of the mathematical writings of Euclid (flourished 300 BC) and the elegant, intricate reasoning characteristic of the scholastic method. Just as, for Thomas, God shines his light in the whole of nature, so the medieval cathedral with its high ceilings and large windows created a space rising to heaven infused with a colourful, celestial light. 'Gothic' began as a term of abuse in the sixteenth century for a style so monstrous, it was thought, that only the heathen and uncivilised Goths, the wreckers of Roman civilisation, could have dreamt of it, but the Gothic cathedrals stand as testimony to the soaring ambition and grandeur of the style.

Universities

Out of the medieval monasteries and cathedrals, both of which served as centres of education, there emerged an institution new to the West and central to its subsequent development: the university. The birth of the university coincided with a reaffirmation of the value of studying the natural world. Hugh of Saint-Victor (c. 1078-1141), canon of the Abbey of Saint-Victor in Paris, maintained that, far from being incompatible with the religious life, a secular study of the world provided the necessary foundation for higher religious contemplation. His new Paris school followed the curriculum of Alcuin's seven liberal arts, and it was at the school of Saint-Victor that the University of Paris was founded in 1170. Paris was to be one of the great medieval universities, though it was not the first. Bologna was founded, it is generally thought, in 1088, and teaching began in Oxford in 1096, thriving as never before when Henry II (reigned 1154-1189) forbade English students from attending the University of Paris in 1167 over a disagreement with the 'turbulent priest' Thomas Becket, who had fled to Normandy. Cambridge University, in turn, was founded when a group of scholars left Oxford in 1209, probably fleeing the volatility that existed between townsfolk and the university. Students entering a medieval university would first take a bachelor's degree from the faculty of arts, covering the seven liberal arts, and then could choose to continue to a master's degree in any of the other three faculties: theology, law or medicine. The university played an important role in the life of medieval culture, providing training for the professions, furnishing a context for the dispassionate pursuit of truth and discovery, and facilitating a Europe-wide community of Latin-speaking scholars.

Literature of the high Middle Ages

In addition to the monasteries, cathedrals and universities, the princely or ducal court was a centre of high medieval culture. The period saw the birth of the chanson de geste, a new genre re-working aspects of the ancient epic, and court poets called troubadours composed a new form of love lyric. In the late twelfth century there also emerges the genre of romance, marking an important transition away from the epic genre epitomised by Homer's *Odyssey* and *Iliad*.

Chanson de geste: a new form of epic

The first high medieval generic innovation is the chanson de geste, literally a 'song of deeds'. These vernacular verse compositions were usually in lines of ten syllables and typically had as their subject matter the life and reign of Charlemagne. Over one hundred chansons de geste survive in over three hundred manuscripts, of which the earliest and the most influential is the *Chanson de Roland* (c. 1100), a 4,002-line tale of a battle in 778 between Charlemagne's army and a Muslim force, and of the valiant warrior Roland, nephew of Charlemagne. In the *Chanson* Roland and his force of twenty thousand men are overwhelmed by a Saracen ambush numbering (rather fancifully) four hundred thousand, and in the final throes of a heroic but fatal last stand, Roland summons up strength to blow his olifant horn ('olifant' is the Old French word for elephant), calling to his aid Charlemagne and the bulk of the Frankish force. Roland blows with such force, and he is so wounded from the battle, that his temples burst and he expires before Charlemagne, hearing the horn, returns and routs the Saracens.

Unlike Homeric epics, the events upon which the chanson de geste is based were usually (at least in their origin) historical and widely known at the time, though in the case of the *Chanson de Roland*, written some 300 years after the events it describes, the action is transformed – with not a little poetic licence – from a Basque attack on a baggage train at the Battle of Roncevaux Pass on 15 August 778 to a crusade-like war against the Saracen army. Stylistically, the chanson de geste is characterised by assonance, rhyming vowel sounds echoing across the two halves of each ten-syllable line, as we can see in the opening four lines of the *Chanson de Roland*:

> Carles li reis, nostre empere magnes
> Set anz tuz pleins ad estet en Espaigne:
> Tresqu'en la mer cunquist la tere altaigne.
> N'i ad castel ki devant lui remaigne;

> Charles the King, our Lord and Sovereign,
> Full seven years hath sojourned in Spain,
> Conquered the land, and won the western main,
> Now no fortress against him doth remain,

The *chansons* also introduce elements largely foreign to ancient and early medieval epic: passages of greater length dealing with sentiment and emotion, magical or extraordinary objects described in sumptuous detail, and narrator's asides. If the *chanson* recovers elements of previous epic poetry, then it does so only by transforming it.

Troubadour poetry: courtly love

Another vernacular innovation in the eleventh to thirteenth centuries was the rise of troubadour poetry. The troubadours, writing in the southern French Occitan language, and the trouvières, writing in 'Old French', the language of northern France, forged a new type of poetry as they travelled from court to court. Troubadour poetry was written to be sung and performed, often by the troubadour himself or herself (a female troubadour is called a trobairitz) and sometimes by a *jongleur* (performer) or *cantaire* (singer). From the end of the twelfth century onwards, poetry on the theme of love was called a *canso*, but this was a form of love never before seen in the Western sensibility. Courtly love, or *fin'amor*, is notoriously difficult to define. It can be seen as one of the expressions of high medieval chivalry, a somewhat fluid notion that from the twelfth century onwards prescribes a code of duty and honour for the knight (in service to his lord), for the Christian (in service to his God), and the lover (in service to his lady).

Courtly love both seeks and dreads satisfaction as it luxuriates in a mixture of pleasure and suffering, courting the affections of a woman usually of more elevated status than her pursuer, to whom her would-be lover pledges absolute allegiance as to a feudal lord. A mixture of inner tumult and outward elegant seemliness, this love is expressed through radical, often extreme service of the beloved, though it rarely ends in marriage (the pursued woman is usually another man's wife). The male lover is tormented and enraptured in equal measure as he waits at an excruciating – but poetically convenient – distance for a recompense or recognition from the unattainable object of his suit. The tradition shows influences of Neoplatonism in its treatment of love in this world as a weak imitation of a perfect, heavenly love. Very different from the *aretê* of Achilles, from the Christian ethic of *agapê* or from the *þrym* and *ellen* of Beowulf, though taking elements of each, courtly love also draws on the love poetry of Ovid (43 BC-18 AD) and the lyric poetry of Muslim Spain. In *The Allegory of Love*, twentieth-century medievalist C.S. Lewis argues that the rise of courtly love marks a 'real change in human sentiment', and that 'the troubadours effected a change which has left no corner of our ethics, our imagination, or our daily life untouched, and they erected impossible barriers between us and the classical past or the Oriental present'.

Romance and medieval allegory

In the middle of the twelfth century another new genre is introduced to Western literature, one that will eclipse the epic. The new genre is romance, a term that derives from the French expression *mettre en roman*, meaning 'to translate into the vernacular'. Over time it also came to have a more specific meaning, blending tales of chivalric exploits with a much greater and richer allegorical tapestry of love than was usual in troubadour poetry or in the chanson de geste. For its material, medieval romance commonly draws on classical themes (often Troy or Alexander) or the English court of King Arthur (*c.* fifth/sixth century), but as for its generic inspiration it looks to lyric poetry, placing love firmly at the centre of its thematic concerns. Shot through with magic and quests, romance often presents an individual's pursuit of self-discovery through any number of amorous encounters and knightly exploits, frequently recounted by an ironic, clerical narrator. The world of romance reflects the concerns and preoccupations of the medieval court, and its horizons (love and chivalry) are those of courtly ambition. The romance also gives the West a new sense of adventure, and an important departure from the Greco-Roman notion of fate that blows Odysseus off course as he struggles to return home. The point is made by Michael Nerith in *The Ideology of Adventure*:

> *Aventure*, which in its literary occurrences before the courtly romance means fate, chance, has become, in the knightly-courtly system of relations, an event that the knight must seek out and endure, although this event does continue to be unpredictable, a surprise of fate. The decisive factor, however, is that the surprising event, the *aventure*, is *sought*, and within the framework of this intentionality it is planned for and hence predicted. A change has taken place from *aventure* as fate to *aventure* as 'adventure'.

This new sense of questing complements the emphasis on questioning in the scholastic method, and it is nowhere more beautifully and compellingly present than in the greatest of all medieval romances, the *Roman de la rose* (*Romance of the Rose*), by Guillaume de Lorris (dates unknown) and Jean De Meun (*c.* 1250-*c.* 1305). The *Roman de la rose* is narrated by Lover, who tells of a dream in which he sets out on a quest for love 'in which the entire art of love is contained'. The romance is layered with at times impenetrably intricate and interwoven meanings, reminiscent of the mystical absorption of troubadour poetry and of Patristic interpretations of the Bible, particularly of the Song of Songs. The text is full of personified abstractions reminiscent of Roman gods and goddesses. We meet Idleness, Pleasure, Evil Tongue, Rebuff, Reason, and Rose, as well as characters taken directly from Greco-Roman mythology such as Cupid, Narcissus and Venus. The *Roman de la rose* concludes with the lover plucking his Rose (read: consummating his relationship with his beloved) in a manner that by no means resolves the mysteries of the text. The plot is rounded off in obedience to Aristotle's pattern of the well-wrought story, but not at the expense of unravelling the romance's rich layers of mystery.

The invention of courtly love is part of a broader move towards a new aesthetic in the high Middle Ages. As Kenneth Clark notes in his *Civilisation*, women in early medieval painting and sculpture can often be presented as stern, austere and ugly, but around the 1300s there begins to emerge the depiction of what we would today more readily recognise as beauty. Statues of the Madonna from the thirteenth century take on a new delicacy and aesthetic tenderness that was to be brought to poetic rapture in the work of Dante Alighieri.

The 'Pre-Renaissance': Dante Alighieri (1265-1321)

As Jean de Meun was crafting the allegorical beauty of the *Roman de la rose*, Dante Alighieri was a young Florentine boy. If the *Roman* beautifully typified a moment in the evolution of the medieval sensibility, then Dante's *Divina Commedia* (*Divine Comedy*, written between 1308 and 1321) both encapsulated the high medieval moment, with its intricately linked social hierarchies, deep religiosity, heroism and sentimentality, and at the same time helped forge a new Western ethos. Though the dates of the *Divina Commedia* would classify it as a medieval text, it opens a door for us to the world of the Renaissance.

Dante was born into a noble Florentine family and became involved in Florentine political struggles on the side of the white Guelfs (in favour of Florence becoming a commune independent of papal rule) against the black Guelfs (supporters of the Papacy). When the black Guelfs took control of Florence in 1301 Dante was sent into exile, settling in Ravenna. Realising the embarrassing error of having exiled its greatest writer, the city of Florence later passionately sued for the return of Dante's remains, even building a tomb for him in the basilica of Santa Croce in 1829. As recently as 2008 Florence City Council voted by a majority of one to rescind Dante's exile, but his nearest living descendent, winemaker Count Pieralvise Serego Alighieri, refused to accept the city's honour of the Golden Florin.

In his *Vita Nuova* (*New Life*, c. 1290-4), Dante describes his love for Beatrice Portinari in a way that intertwined worldly and divine love even more perfectly than the romance tradition. Far from Dante's passionate desire for Beatrice being a distraction from devotion to God, the poet is drawn upward to heaven by his love for her. With the *Vita Nuova*, the Western (male) mind discovers a new kind of love, and no longer has to choose between love for God and love for a woman; Dante learns to see Christ by seeing him reflected in Beatrice's eyes as she herself looks at Christ.

The *Divina Commedia* is written not in Latin but in vernacular Tuscan, in *la dolce stil nuovo* (the 'sweet new style', or 'sweet new genre'). The *dolce stil nuovo* has roots in troubadour lyric and also draws on the symbols and metaphors of medieval romance. Its dominant theme of love is expressed in divine terms, often treated with a deal of introspection on the part of the poet. The three books of the *Divina Commedia* (*Inferno*, or Hell, *Purgatorio*, or Purgatory, and *Paradiso*, or Paradise) enact a monumental fusion of the Aristotelian cosmos with the Christian sensibility in a way that accomplishes on the level of the imagination the 'baptism' of Aristotle that Thomas wrought in his philosophy. By doubling the cosmos of concentric spheres in Aristotle's cosmos with the concentric circles of hell and the expanding spheres of heaven, Dante is forging a combined mythology that transcends the classical-Christian divide and exerts a profound (though complicated) influence on the subsequent development of Christian thought. Strikingly, the *Commedia* breaks with the third person narrative tradition of Homer and Virgil to introduce into the epic a protagonist and narrator who speaks in the first person 'I'.

As well as providing the superlative synthesis of the medieval ethos, Dante is part of a new interest in Greco-Roman writers and artists that was to set the stage for an explosion in art and learning the intensity of which has rarely if ever been equalled in the history of the West. That explosion is called the Renaissance.

Man the Measure of All Things:
The Renaissance

'In the normal course of events many men and women are born with remarkable talents; but occasionally, in a way that transcends nature, a single person is marvellously endowed by Heaven with beauty, grace and talent in such abundance that he leaves other men far behind; all his actions seem inspired and indeed everything he does clearly comes from God rather than from human skill.' With these words the painter and historian Giorgio Vasari (1511-1574) opens the chapter of his *Lives of the Artists* dedicated to the life of Leonardo da Vinci (1452-1519). Leonardo's gifts may have come from God, but the fame belonged to the man himself in an age when the individual artist enjoyed unprecedented prestige, almost veneration. Such was Leonardo's fame, Vasari reports, that as he lay dying King Francis I of France lent over his body, cradling Leonardo's head in his hands in order to receive his final breath.

Leonardo witnessed and contributed to an audacious – some would say arrogant – age of expression, exploration and innovation, leaving thirteen thousand pages of sketches and notes, many of which he sought to protect from rivals by writing the text backwards so that it could only be read with a mirror. His notebook musings encompass an alphabet of human inquiry, ranging through aerodynamics, anatomy, architecture, astronomy, botany, cartography, geology, geometry, hydraulics, literature, mechanics, meteorology, optics, religion, weaponry and zoology, and including designs for a spring-powered car, flying and gliding machines, a parachute and a machine gun, as well as drawings and caricatures of men and women of all ages. With his *Mona Lisa* (1503-6) and *Last Supper* (1495-1498) Leonardo left the West with two of its most recognisable and reproduced works of art. Such an extraordinary breadth of interest and learning is indicative of the new age that followed the high medieval Gothic, an age that saw Luther challenge the Catholic church, Magellan circumnavigate the globe, Raphael, Michelangelo and Leonardo himself redefine painting, and Copernicus pioneer the Scientific Revolution. It was an age that aspired to the dictum of the ancient Greek Protagoras: 'man is the measure of all things'.

Renaissance humanism

Renaissance means 'rebirth', and what was reborn in the European Renaissance of the fifteenth century was an interest in the culture of the ancient Greco-Roman world. We could be forgiven for thinking that, thanks to Boethius, Aquinas and Ockham, and with the many references to Virgil and Troy dotted throughout medieval literature, the influence of classical culture had never gone away, and we would be correct. It was the uses to which classical culture was put in the Renaissance that opened a new horizon in the Western sensibility, as the art, rhetoric and aesthetics of ancient Greece and Rome were used to shape a self-understanding of humanity that was bolder, freer and more self-possessed than we see in the medieval period. The poet, scholar and father of the Renaissance Francesco Petrarca (1304-1374, known in English as Petrarch) lamented that, while the scholastic method stops at determining the truth, the moral philosophy of antiquity sows into our hearts love of the best. Petrarch was at the forefront of developing a new relation to classical culture and mythology, filling his Italian and Latin works with references and allusions to classical sources. While always a devout Christian, Petrarch evoked the authority of the ancient classics with a new belief in their pertinence and immediacy, paving the way for the flourishing of Renaissance humanism.

The manifesto of this new exaltation of humanity was Giovanni Pico della Mirandola's (1463-1494) *Oration on the Dignity of Man* (1486). First, the *Oration* dramatically presents a description of how God the Father has set humankind in the midst of nature with a unique destiny to rule over it. This celebration of the human is woven together with a powerful vindication of the liberal arts, a praise of the 'heavenly' and 'angelic' practice of philosophical reasoning, and a hymn to humanity that, alone among the animals, can forge its own destiny through the exercise of its will and its divine rationality: 'You will have the power to sink to the lower forms of life, which are brutish. You will have the power, through your own judgment, to be reborn into the higher forms, which are divine.'

The Renaissance humanism of the fourteenth and fifteenth centuries continues the medieval trend, initiated by Peter Abelard and the Dominican tradition, of privileging human reason as the final arbiter in all matters of faith and knowledge. But this was not the desiccated reason of the lengthy scholastic handbooks. Humanist education abandoned the scholastic emphasis on logic – barren, turgid and lifeless as it now appeared – for a new cultivation of rhetoric and style, expanding the trivium to include history, poetry, Greek and moral philosophy and hailing the Roman orator Cicero (106-43 BC) as its great hero. This new curriculum was renamed *studia humanitatis* (approximating to the modern-day 'humanities'), and appealed to ancient Greece and Rome in order to assert the humanist present in the face of the medieval past. The appeals to authority that characterised the scholastic method were replaced by the rallying cry of *ad fontes* ('back to the sources!'). The primary texts of the Bible and ancient writers were to be studied directly, not through the lens of medieval commentators. This rallying cry was followed by the Renaissance humanist Erasmus of Rotterdam (*c.* 1467-1536) in his *On the Method of Study and Reading and Interpreting*

Authors (1511) to plead for a direct engagement with Greek and Latin sources unmediated by endless medieval authorities. Erasmus's own critical edition of the Greek New Testament (1516) corrected a number of apparent errors in the Latin Vulgate version, which had been accepted as the standard text by the medieval church since its translation by Jerome in the fourth century.

The new humanistic sensibility

Along with the new humanist philosophy and education came a further change to the Western ethos, an change that would supplant the medieval chivalric code of *fin'amor* for an age where the life of the knight errant was no longer an ideal. In fashionable courts like Urbino (modern-day north-east Italy), refinement and elegance were increasingly prised over valour in battle. Nowhere was this new ethos more perfectly captured than in Baldassare Castiglione's (1478-1529) transformation of the medieval knight into the Renaissance gentleman. Castiglione came from an aristocratic family and, in the service of the Duke of Urbino, undertook diplomatic missions, later serving as envoy to Pope Clement VIII. His *Il Libro del Cortegiano* (*The Book of the Courtier*, 1528) takes the form of four fictional discourses set in the ducal palace of Urbino, in which Castiglione distils through a variety of characters the wisdom he has accumulated through spending time in Italian courts. The courtier should carry himself with *sprezzatura*: a controlled yet seemingly unstudied naturalness and self-preserving ability to hide one's desires and feelings behind a studied mask of external calm.

If Castiglione's *sprezzatura* was the presentable side of Renaissance manners, then its brutal but effective underbelly is exposed in Niccolò Machiavelli's (1469-1527) notion of *virtù*. Virtù (from the Latin *vir*, man) was used by early humanists almost exclusively to connote traditional Christian virtues of generosity, love and prudence, but Machiavelli gives it a new meaning in *Il Principe* (*The Prince*, written in 1513 and published in 1532), recovering and reinterpreting its ancient sense of 'manliness', 'inner strength' and 'leadership'. *Il Principe* is written in the guise of offering advice to Lorenzo de' Medici (1449-1492), the ruler of the Florentine republic from 1469 to 1492 in a time when the city was threatened and partially overrun by French, Spanish and German armies, and when the self-government of Florence had deteriorated through Milanese and Venetian incursions.

Machiavelli was a fervent humanist, and *The Prince* echoes some elements of the new humanist outlook. Lorenzo is counselled that, in order to gain, keep and exploit power he must abandon the morals of Christian society and exert rule by force, not merely by law, and that although he may hope to be loved he must above all ensure that he is feared, for 'love endures by a bond which men, being scoundrels, may break whenever it serves their advantage to do so; but fear is supported by the dread of pain, which is ever present'. In departing from recognised Christian notions of agapic virtue and reducing religion to one tool among many for social control, Machiavelli is taking up a position in the secular political space opened by the Thomistic discontinuity between reason and faith and further cemented by the nominalist dichotomy between revelation and natural knowledge. It was an approach that led to Machiavelli's name becoming a synonym for the Devil himself ('Old Nick'), and to the pejorative adjective 'Machiavellian'.

Florence: the early Renaissance (mid-fourteenth to fifteenth centuries)

In 1115 the city of Florence threw off the rule of the Holy Roman Empire and became a republic, maintaining its republicanism through many bitter intrigues until 1532, when hereditary rule was restored by Alessandro de' Medici, appointed 'Duke of the Florentine Republic' by Pope Clement VII (1478-1534), who quite conveniently also happened to be from the powerful Medici family. By the early decades of the fourteenth century, the Republic of Florence was at the heart of the cultural world. Its population had increased more than six-fold from around fifteen thousand in 1200 to ninety-six thousand only a century later. The dominant system of social organisation in medieval Europe had been feudalism. In the feudal system, there are (schematically) four strata of society: the monarch, the lords or barons, the vassals (or knights) and the peasants. The monarch leases a plot of land to a lord, in return for the lord's military and governmental services. The lord then grants fiefdoms, or parcels of land, to his vassals, in exchange for which the vassals would provide the lord with military service. The people who worked this land on behalf of the vassals were the peasants, or serfs. Serfs did not own the land they worked, and they had to give a proportion of their crops in tax, along with additional taxes and rent. Serfdom was a form of wage slavery.

However, the thirteenth century saw the establishment of the most extensive Europe-wide trading network since the mercantilism (or merchant capitalism) of the western Roman empire. The new network was based on the shipping of goods from one location to another in order to realise a profit on their sale, and fourteenth-century Italy (sometimes called the *quattrocento*) was to see the rise in importance of the city as a trading hub. Those in the best position to prosper from this new increase in trade were the merchants, and over the course of the *quattrocento* their influence grew. The establishment of an international banking system, along with the invention of the balance sheet and early foreign exchange markets as well as an international currency (the Florentine florin) all contributed to the growing power of the merchant class. Increasingly independent of both the Pope and the Holy Roman Empire, the power in Italian city states was concentrated in the hands of merchants. The medieval system of guilds, the bodies of master tradesmen that regulated standards of production, prices and the right to practice a profession, gradually diminished in importance, and new terms like 'bank' and 'bankrupt' entered the language. Florentine moneychangers would operate from a table or counter (Italian: *banca*), which would be broken if they became bankrupt (the Italian *banca rotta* means 'broken counter').

This economic transformation was accompanied by a change in attitudes towards the nature of human identity. The feudal system, not to mention a Neoplatonic view of universals, predisposed the medieval mind to think of identity in terms of one's place within the greater whole, both the whole of the feudal system and the whole of the mother church. But with the rise of the cities and their mercantile economies, standing began to depend on disposable capital rather than on one's place within the feudal hierarchy.

Art and architecture of the early Renaissance

If the soaring vaults of Gothic cathedral architecture reflect the huge systematic complexity of the scholastic method, then in the early Renaissance both philosophy and architecture take on more human proportions. In his *De re aedificatoria* (*Ten Books of Architecture*, 1452), the 'universal man' Leon Battista Alberti (1404-1472) looks back to Greco-Roman ideas of proportion in asserting that the design of buildings should be based on 'main lines in strict proportion and regularity, lest the pleasing harmony of the whole should be lost in the attraction of individual parts'. No edifice is more illustrative of Alberti's principles

Figure 4.1. Filippo Brunelleschi, Pazzi Chapel (1440s-1460s), Basilica of Santa Croce, Florence.

than Filippo Brunelleschi's (1377-1446) Pazzi Chapel (Figure 4.1) in Florence, with its modest dome and regular, well-proportioned cloister.

Increasing naturalism in painting: from Cimabue to Dürer

What Dante and Petrarch achieved in opening the way for Renaissance literature, Giotto di Bondone (1267-1337) accomplished in the medium of painting. The young Giotto was apprenticed to the great Florentine artist Cimabue (1240-1302), the last major exponent of the Byzantine style in Italy. Although Cimabue explored an increasing naturalism within the limits of the Byzantine style, his painting still communicates the powerful, symbolic, contemplative aesthetic of Neoplatonic Christian art. In his *Maestà* (*Madonna in Majesty*, 1280-1285, Figure 4.2) the Madonna's throne has a three-dimensional reality novel in the Byzantine tradition, and her features are more natural than would be usual in

Figure 4.2. Cimabue, *Maestà* (1280-1285). Tempera on panel.
Uffizi Gallery, Florence.

Figure 4.3. Giotto, *The Deposition of Christ* (1304-06). Fresco.
Capella degli Scrovegni, Padua.

iconography of the time. Giotto however went far beyond his teacher
in pioneering the two-dimensional rendering of realistic architectural
space, as well as in conveying a naturalistic emotional intensity rarely if
ever equalled since antiquity. His *Deposition* is reproduced here (Figure
4.3), with all its movement and energy. According to Vasari, the young
Giotto was discovered by Cimabue when, as a twelve-year-old shepherd
boy he was seen sketching on a rock with a piece of flint. Later, the
apprentice mischievously painted a fly on the nose of one of Cimabue's
figures, causing his master to attempt several times to brush it away
before realising Giotto's prank.

By the last decades of the fifteenth century, the naturalism of Florentine
painting had developed far beyond even Giotto's pioneering works, with
artists like Domenico Ghirlandaio (1449-1494) producing 'warts and all'
likenesses of living patrons. Florence was by no means the only city in Europe
to be embracing a new artistic naturalism however. At the same time or
in some cases even before the Italian masters, the 'northern Renaissance'
produced artists capable of a dazzling naturalism, like Jan van Eyck (*c.*
1395-1441) in the modern-day Netherlands and Albrecht Dürer (1471-

Figure 4.4. Jan van Eyck, *Portrait of Cardinal Albergati* (1431-2).
Oil on wood. Kunsthistorisches Museum, Vienna.

1528) in modern-day Germany. Van Eyck's tender but unflatteringly realistic portrait of Cardinal Niccolò Albergati is reproduced here (Figure 4.4). Van Eyck's technique of minute observation is consonant with, if not directly influenced by, the particularism and attention to individuality of the nominalists, and of course also with Renaissance humanism.

Albrecht Dürer, another giant of the northern Renaissance, produced what is undoubtedly the most enigmatic of all Renaissance portraits. In his *Self-Portrait* of 1500 (Figure 4.5), Dürer fixes the viewer in a direct gaze, with his flowing Christ-like golden hair and his hand poised to offer a blessing. The hair and pose evoke a whole tradition of Christian icon painting, including the Pantocrator image at Monreale (see p. 55). Dürer's *Self-Portrait* and the Monreale Christ are similar, down to the lock of hair curling on the artist's forehead. The shapes of Dürer's characteristic 'AD' monogram, on his eye-line to the left of his face, gently echo the Greek letters alpha and omega (A and Ω) in Jesus Christ's declaration that 'I am the Alpha and the Omega, the first and the last,

Figure 4.5. Albrecht Dürer, *Self-Portrait at 28* (1500).
Oil on panel. Alte Pinakothek, Munich.

the beginning and the end' (Revelation 22:13). There is a twist in the tale, however: the 'I' here is none other than the artist himself: the individual human being has taken his place at the very centre of Renaissance iconography, and this Christ wears the fur coat characteristic of the humanists. Nothing could more powerfully convey the new place of the artist in Renaissance society. During the period of high medieval Gothic, artists were predominantly seen as craftsmen, manual labourers making something according to the rules of their guild and working as largely anonymous parts of a greater whole. Whereas we cannot be sure of the names of the master architects behind most medieval cathedrals, with the Renaissance the individual artist rises to a glorious new prominence, and fine art becomes ever more distinct from the crafts. The creation of art is now not a manual, but an intellectual labour and authorship, along with it ownership, becomes central to the ethos of an increasingly capitalist society. Finally, early Renaissance Florence also saw the development of theories of perspective. It was Filippo Brunelleschi again who, in 1415, brought geometrical perspective to the attention of Florentine artists through his use of mirrors to demonstrate the possibilities of painting three-dimensional objects on a two-dimensional plane. In the decades that followed, the number of paintings with chequered marble floors in

Figure 4.6. Paolo Uccello, *Battle of San Romano*, left panel (*c.* 1454-57).
Tempera on wood. National Gallery, London.

the most inappropriate places – notably in the stable of Christ's birth in one case! – testify to artists' excitement at the discovery. One of the most striking exponents of perspective in Renaissance art is Paolo Uccello (*c.* 1397-1475). In his *Niccolò Mauruzi da Tolentino at the Battle of San Romano* (Figure 4.6), we see that the broken lances lying on the ground rather conspicuously point towards the painting's single vanishing point in the distance. Vasari writes that, although Uccello liked to challenge himself artistically, the strain of his efforts is too evident in his work, and this judgment has dogged his reputation ever since.

Rome: the high Renaissance (mid-fifteenth to mid-sixteenth centuries)

Around 1500, a change takes place in the direction of the Italian Renaissance. The scene changes from Florence to Rome as Pope Julius II (reigned 1503-1513) asserts himself as a great patron of the arts. With this geographical shift also comes an aesthetic transformation, for what we see in the Roman Renaissance is an idea of man in heroic proportions: more audacious, more monumental and limitless. It is a new aesthetic embodied in the work and the reputations of the three great Roman masters: Leonardo da Vinci, Michelangelo and Raphael.

Leonardo da Vinci (1452-1519)

No one exemplifies the Renaissance spirit of fertile curiosity better than Leonardo di ser Piero da Vinci. Leonardo's scientific disposition shaped his approach to painting. He rendered horizons not as sharp lines but with *sfumato* (from *sfumare*: to vanish or shade), a technique of graduated shading that lightens darker tones and darkens lighter ones. As he explains in his notebooks, 'I know that the greater or less quantity of air that lies between the eye and the object makes the outlines of that object more or less distinct'. His portrait of Lisa del Giocondo, famous as the *Mona Lisa* (*Mona* is a contraction of *madonna*, from the Italian *ma donna*, 'my lady'), is a study in the guarded expression and controlled posture characteristic of Castiglione's *sprezzatura*. The painting has become the most famous single canvas the Western tradition, not least for the intrigue that has surrounded it. In 1911 the *Mona Lisa* was stolen from its home in the Louvre in Paris by Italian carpenter Vincenzo Peruggia, who had designed the painting's protective display box. Peruggia kept the masterpiece for over a year and it was only discovered when he rather unadvisedly sought to sell it to the Uffizi Gallery in Florence. In a stirring show of patriotic justice the Italian court where he was tried eventually passed a lenient sentence on Peruggia, and what is more, during the painting's absence visitor numbers to the Louvre actually rose, as people flocked to see the empty place where the stolen masterpiece had previously hung.

Michelangelo (1475-1564)

In 1488 Michelangelo di Lodovico Buonarroti Simoni became apprenticed to the great Ghirlandaio in Florence, but in 1496, at the age of twenty-one, he moved to Rome. The story is told that Michelangelo had sculpted a statue of St John the Baptist for Lorenzo de' Medici, who had asked him to create the impression that the work was an ancient original in order that Lorenzo might pocket a greater sum when selling it. When the eventual buyer, a certain Cardinal Raffaele Riario, discovered the ruse, he was so taken by the quality of the forgery that he invited Michelangelo to Rome himself.

It was in Rome that Michelangelo set to work on 'The Giant', an unwieldy block of marble over five metres high from Carrara in northern Tuscany. Michelangelo turned the Giant, the size of which had deterred other sculptors from working on it, into the most iconic sculpture of the high Roman Renaissance, and perhaps the most recognised sculpture in Western history. *David* (1501-4, Figure 4.7) stands over four metres high, completely nude, and bears a look of intense energetic defiance, a statement of confidence in the limitless potential of Renaissance humanity. It was perhaps Michelangelo's Neoplatonist convictions that enabled him to take the commission where others, including Leonardo, had refused. He believed that the form of beauty was contained within the stone, and that to sculpt was merely to liberate the form in a process that he likened to religious salvation.

In 1508 Michelangelo reluctantly accepted a commission from Pope Julius II to fresco the more than 1,000 square metres of the Sistine Chapel in the Vatican's Apostolic Palace, a task that was to take him

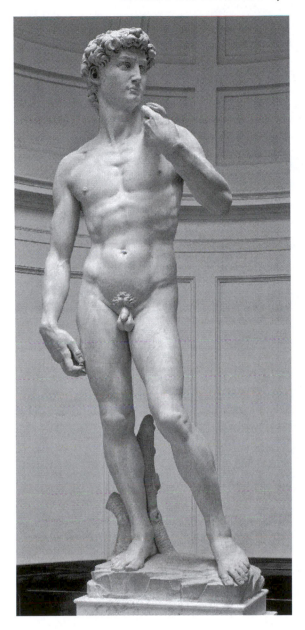

Figure 4.7.
Michelangelo, *David*
(1501-1504). Marble.
Galleria dell'Accademia,
Florence.

until 1512. It is characteristic of the high Renaissance, and especially of the work of Michelangelo, that the characters he depicted in the Chapel are presented in almost superhumanly muscular proportions. This is true not only of gods and heroes, whom one might expect to cut a heroic dash, but also of fishermen and labourers. It should not surprise us however, for the Neoplatonist Michelangelo considered bodily perfection to be a sign spiritual beauty. None of his characters, however, is depicted in more colossal proportions than the Jesus who forms the focal point of the Last Judgment on the altar wall of the chapel (Figure 4.8). David and Jesus provide a powerful contrast with Michelangelo's own *Pietà* (*Pity*, 1499), depicting a seated Mary with her dead son Jesus lying limply in her arms, and sculpted when the artist was only twenty-four years old. In contrast to the invincibility of David and Jesus, the *Pietà* remains one of the most tender evocations of the fragility of human life in the history

Figure 4.8. Michelangelo, detail of Jesus from *The Last Judgment* (1534-1541). Fresco. Sistine Chapel, Vatican.

of Western art. In 1546 Michelangelo was commissioned as architect of the new St Peter's Basilica in Rome. The cupola, a huge 42.3 metres in diameter, remains to this day the world's tallest dome.

Raphael (1483-1520)

Raffaello Sanzio da Urbino came to Rome in 1508 at the invitation of Pope Julius II, after around four years in Florence where he came under the influence of Leonardo's careful studies of human anatomy. This son of a painter was commissioned by Julius II to fresco the Pope's own private library in the Vatican's Apostolic palace, and he began work in the *Stanza della Segnatura*, the room in which, from the thirteenth century

Figure 4.9. Raphael, *School of Athens* (1509). Fresco.
Stanza della Segnatura, Vatican, Rome.

on, Popes would sign the judgments of cases that came before them. Raphael delivered a vision of this room as a harmony of worldly and divine wisdom. On the east wall he depicted the *School of Athens* (Figure 4.9), a gathering of the great philosophers of ancient Greece and Rome in the setting of a geometrically patterned series of receding arches. Though we are sure about the identity of Plato (modelled on Leonardo da Vinci) and Aristotle in the centre of the *School*, attempts to identify some of the other characters are more speculative. The numbers used here are more or less approximate: (1) Plato, (2) Aristotle, (3) Zeno, (4) Epicurus, (5) Averroes, (6) Pythagoras, (7) Alexander the Great, (8) Hypatia, (9) Socrates, (10) Heraclitus, (11) Diogenes, (12) Archimedes or Euclid, (13) Zoroaster, (14) Ptolemy, (15) Raphael himself. Visitors to the Stanza della Segnatura who stand side on to the fresco will notice that the figure sitting on the stairs in the middle (10) protrudes forward slightly. The story is told that after completing the *School of Athens* Raphael stole into the Sistine Chapel while Michelangelo was absent and, impressed by the muscular density of Michelangelo's figures, added Heraclitus to the *School*, a figure of noticeably more muscular build than the other philosophers and reputedly a portrait of Michelangelo himself.

Facing the *School of Athens*, Raphael filled the west wall with *The Disputation of the Holy Sacrament*, a depiction of the church as the meeting of heaven (with its perfect circular shapes) and earth (with its rectangular forms) in which figures from Old and New Testaments stand alongside Popes, Dante Alighieri and the architect Bramante. They are shown discussing the Eucharist, the bread and wine that become Christ's body and blood in the Catholic mass.

The legacy of high Renaissance art to the Western tradition is complex. In many ways it looks back to the past, to Greco-Roman and Judeo-Christian ideas and forms, but it presents them in a style of vivid naturalism, heroic Neoplatonic realism and tender humanity that are truly new in the Western artistic vocabulary. The breadth and depth of emotion and truth that is expressed by the 'Roman Trinity' of Leonardo, Raphael and Michelangelo may have been outdone for intensity by the tortured and ecstatic emotional spectrum of later Baroque art, but it was never surpassed.

Literature of the Renaissance

As in the case of Renaissance humanism, it was Petrarch who forged the way for the Renaissance literary recovery of the ancient world. It was Petrarch who first used the term 'Dark Ages' to describe the period from the fall of the western Roman empire to the beginning of the Renaissance, a term intended very transparently to make an artistic and cultural point, and it was Petrarch who proposed that new light would shine only with the recovery of the genius of Roman letters. When discussing literature it is customary among scholars to refer to the 'early modern' period, rather than to the Renaissance.

Montaigne and the essay

Fully two centuries after Petrarch's impassioned plea for a recovery of ancient rhetoric and style, Michel Eyquem de Montaigne (1533-1592), elected mayor of Bordeaux from 1581 to 1586, penned a three-volume work that was to introduce a new and important genre to the early modern West, along with a new way of exploring the human being. Like Ockham at the end of the medieval period, Montaigne was living in an age in which former certainties were beginning to unravel, an age when a resurgent interest in the thought of the ancient sceptic Sextus Empiricus (flourished *c.* 200 AD) and the discovery of non-European civilisations were combining to relativise Western assumptions about humanity and society. Echoing the Roman playwright Terence, Montaigne proclaims in his *Essais* (*Essays*, published 1580) that 'I am a man, and think that nothing human is foreign to me'. Montaigne's *Essais* are works of patient self-examination, not with the Augustinian aim of unearthing and confessing hidden sin, but in the spirit of a Socratic 'know thyself'. It is hard to improve on Montaigne's own characterisation of his work in 'On books' (*Essais II*): 'These are my fancies, by which I try to give knowledge not of things, but of myself [...] As my fancies present themselves, I pile them up.' Montaigne's *Essais* are an important milestone in what has been called the 'birth of private life' or the 'birth of the individual' in the West, when identity became increasingly understood not in terms of social class or function but in terms of inner thoughts and feelings.

The *Essais* signalled generic innovation on a number of fronts. They were, unusually for the time, written in the vernacular. They were, comparatively for the time, disordered and haphazard, and their focus, unheard of for the time, was on the non-heroic daily attitudes and behaviours of one man. Though Montaigne seems to have been inspired by Plutarch's *Parallel Lives*, a collection of short biographies of famous Greek and Roman men written in the latter part of the first century AD, his writing brought something to the Western canon that, we can say with confidence, had not been seen before. The exploratory, sometimes tentative nature of Montaigne's writing is indicated by the genre of *essai*, meaning an experiment, test or attempt. Montaigne's experiment was in self-understanding, and whatever the subject of an essay (war, culture, education, cannibals, drunkenness or thumbs), Montaigne is, in the end, talking about himself. The essay was a genre for an age of discovery and for an age of uncertainty. The unbounded range of the essay, discoursing on everything from sleep to kidney stones and from the rise and fall of nations to pedantry, reflects the curiosity of an age pushing back geographical, scientific and theological boundaries. By contrast, the hesitant, probing form speaks of a world in which many old certainties are being challenged by a new scepticism, summed up in Montaigne's own famous interrogative 'Que sais-je?' ('What do I know?', *Essais* II.12). The nationalistic certainties of the epic genre seemed rash in this new sceptical age that viewed cultural differences largely or wholly as the effect of quirks of geography. The complex, fanciful traditions of romance would seem wholly undesirable in this world where a passage on the delights of love can sit happily alongside complaints about persistent flatulence or gout. This willingness to mix the humorous with the monumental, the everyday with the epochal, along with the same uncertain relation to the truths of the past, are also marks of the greatest of all early modern dramatists: William Shakespeare (1564-1616).

Shakespeare's tragedies and sonnets

Shakespeare's tragedies reflect and develop the new willingness to confront the human condition in all its facets and with all of its inherent frailties and doubts. Shakespeare's heroes are no longer hounded by merciless Furies or vengeful gods; the deities are now elusive and sometimes absent, and it is this elusiveness that brings to Shakespeare's world a new shadow of pessimism, instability and uncertainty. As Hamlet laments:

> ... this goodly frame, the earth, seems to me a sterile promontory. This most excellent canopy, the air, look you ... this majestical roof fretted with golden fire – why, it appears no other thing to me than a foul and pestilent congregation of vapours.

Some have ascribed this sense of instability and the latent atmosphere of impending catastrophe to the onset of capitalist society and the decline of feudalism with its hierarchical certainties. Whatever the truth of this conjecture, the direct and personal influence of the gods that was characteristic of much Greek tragedy has vanished, and if there is a notion of fate which draws the Shakespearean tragic hero or heroine on to their death then it is an elusive fate, born of the lethal mix of human circumstances, including the hero's own flaw, and chance. There is scant help from above either. On her inexorable way to death, Juliet cries:

> Is there no pity sitting in the clouds
> That sees into the bottom of my grief?

This by no means implies a rationalistic universe devoid of any mystery, however. There is, as Hamlet reminds us, more in heaven and earth than is dreamed of in Horatio's philosophy, and the witches of Macbeth or the ghost of Hamlet's father preclude any quick conclusion that Shakespeare's universe is closed and transparent to reason. Nevertheless, the new willingness to write a tragedy in which the gods are vanishing and uncertain at most is both an indication towards, and a gentle questioning of, the Renaissance focus on humankind as the measure of its own destiny.

In terms of genre it is too easy to argue that Shakespeare's tragedies are so different from each other that nothing can be said about them as a whole, for while it is surely hasty to pass off generalisations as the last word on a given subject it is equally churlish to deny generalisation its proper place. The history of genres, as we shall continue to see in the chapters that follow, is often a story of repeated transformations, and Shakespeare transforms the tragic genre he inherits in a number of important ways. First of all, Shakespeare's tragedies deal with secular themes. Throughout the Middle Ages, theatre dealt overwhelmingly with sacred subjects: adaptations of biblical narrative or morality plays. Profane or secular drama was either unheard of or only performed in burlesque.

In taking a pattern for his own tragedies, Shakespeare reaches back not so much to the tragedy of the three Greek playwrights Sophocles, Euripides and Aeschylus, but to the plays of the Roman Stoic philosopher and orator Seneca (3 BC-65 AD), full as they are of rhetorical flourish and sensational events. Shakespearean tragedy tells of the downfall of mostly noble, often rich and always exceptional characters – exceptional in some human quality, whether it be love (Juliet and Romeo), jealousy (Othello), or ambition (Macbeth), an exceptional quality that draws them into their exceptional suffering and their exceptional fate which, in Shakespearean tragedy, is always death. The manner of death and/or the recognition of folly that precedes it restores somewhat the nobility of the tragic hero, and events which would have been implied rather than presented in classical tragedy – notably violent passion and gruesome death – are played out on Shakespeare's Elizabethan stage with relentless and eloquent scrutiny.

4. Man the Measure of All Things

The fourteen line poetic sonnet form (from *sonetto*, Italian for 'little song') dates back to thirteenth-century Italy. The Petrarchan sonnet breaks its fourteen lines into an eight-line stanza (octet), usually rhyming *abbaaba*, and a six-line stanza (sestet), combining three rhymes in any number of ways. In contrast to this inheritance, the Shakespearean sonnet signals a new, modern love poetry. Shakespeare wrote a hundred and fifty-four sonnets, and in sonnet 130 he mocks the excesses and conventions of the Petrarchan formula and of the fanciful symbols of medieval romance. I cannot resist quoting this wicked lampoon in full:

> My mistress' eyes are nothing like the sun;
> Coral is far more red than her lips' red;
> If snow be white, why then her breasts are dun;
> If hairs be wires, black wires grow on her head.
>
> I have seen roses damask'd, red and white,
> But no such roses see I in her cheeks;
> And in some perfumes is there more delight
> Than in the breath that from my mistress reeks.
>
> I love to hear her speak, yet well I know
> That music hath a far more pleasing sound;
> I grant I never saw a goddess go;
> My mistress, when she walks, treads on the ground:
>
> And yet, by heaven, I think my love as rare
> As any she belied with false compare.

The measure of love here is the 'I think' of line 13, an 'I think' that echoes Hamlet's judgment that there is 'nothing either good or bad, but thinking makes it so'. These judgments of beauty and goodness rest on human shoulders, rather than on those of an absent God, and man is once more the measure of all things.

Cervantes and the modern age

Shakespeare is writing during an early modern age increasingly without myths (other than the myth that there are no myths) and without the paraphernalia of cosmic deities to breathe warm meaning into a cold world. Active at the same time as Shakespeare, the Spanish novelist Miguel de Cervantes Saavedra (1547-1616) was the self-educated son of an unsuccessful surgeon, whose life was not without incident. The Ottoman empire was a powerful collection of provinces under Muslim control that, in the sixteenth century, stretched over much of Eastern Europe and almost as far west as Vienna, and in 1571 Cervantes fought with the Spanish coalition against the Ottoman empire in the battle of Lepanto, defeating the main Ottoman fleet off the west coast of Greece. After the battle Cervantes was captured by pirates and imprisoned in Algiers for five years, but his own dramatic life story stands in sharp contrast to that of his most famous fictional creation, Alonso Quijano, a retired country gentleman who vainly attempts to inhabit the world of gallantry and heroism about which he reads in books of medieval chivalry. However, as everyone apart from Alonso himself can quite plainly see, such a magical world of storybook heroism does not exist, nor ever did. Alonso re-names himself Don Quixote, taking the persona of a 'knight-errant' and setting out with his squire Sancho Panza (one of Alonso's slow-witted neighbours) on aimless quests to duel with ferocious giants (windmills to you and me) and lodge in castles (country inns). But Don Quixote (published in two volumes, in 1605 and 1615) is more than a biting satire on medieval romance (and, through romance, on ancient epic) from the standpoint of an age rapidly losing its illusions. It is also the invention, out of the prose romances of the Middle Ages, of the most important literary genre of the modern period: the novel.

Don Quixote is often credited as being the first modern novel, though extended prose fiction is not itself a modern invention. Petronius' (died 66 AD) *Satyricon* and Apuleius' (born *c.* 123 AD) *Metamorphoses* (commonly known as *The Golden Ass*) both develop individual and vivid characters involved in romantic escapades, and there is no shortage of prose romances in the fourteenth and fifteenth centuries. Nevertheless, there is an air of disenchantment about *Don Quixote* that marks it out as a genre for the new modern age. The opening line of the first chapter contrasts rudely with the almost incantatory evocations of the poetic muse that begin Homer's epics: 'In a village of La Mancha, the name of which I have no desire to call to mind, there lived not long since one of those gentlemen that keep a lance in the lance-rack, an old buckler, a lean hack, and a greyhound for coursing.' As well as thumbing its nose at Homer, this opening sentence gently parodies the scene-setting of medieval romance, and in Cervantes' disenchanted narrative point of view the West is given a template for literary realism that will mark novelistic production to the present day. Furthermore, in *Don Quixote*'s literary inventiveness, wordplay, interweaving of prose styles and foregrounding of the theme of literature and its relation to the society in which it is produced and read, the way is paved for modern introspective novels that foreground the play of language and that blur the boundary between reality and fiction. Cervantes presents in acute and pathological form what will become a commonplace assumption of the modern novel: 'reality' is the construct of the individual mind. In 'Don Quixote and the Invention of the Novel' critic Anthony J. Cascardi writes:

> no matter which way the picture is turned the *Quixote* remains a watershed work in the history of literature. Before it, things seem relatively remote; after it, we are in a far more familiar universe. During the four centuries since the publication of *Don Quixote* there has been no doubt that to write a major work of fiction was to write a novel.

Cascardi no doubt exaggerates a little (people still do, after all, write major plays and poems), though we do indeed no longer see epics or romances in the fiction bestseller lists. However, like the ancient epic the modern novel is an omnibus genre that defies any definition more specific than 'extended prose fiction'.

Thus far we have told only half the story of the Renaissance period, and in the next chapter our centre of gravity moves to northern Europe to consider two movements which, along with the Renaissance, helped to shape the modern world: the protestant Reformation and the Scientific Revolution.

5

Into the Modern Age:
Religious Reformation and
Scientific Revolution

In Arundel House in Highgate, near London, a man lies at death's door. According to his biographer, it is a case of death by experiment. The dying man is Sir Francis Bacon (1561-1626), the great politician, scientist and philosopher, and Bacon's biographer John Arundel tells how, as he was travelling to Highgate through the snow in the winter of 1626, Bacon had insisted on performing an experiment on the preservation of meat. After buying a hen from one of the Highgate residents, Bacon had the animal disembowelled and stuffed it with snow in order to see whether the cold would slow its decomposition. It was Bacon himself who suffered a chill, however, and he fell so ill from his exposure to the cold that he had to seek shelter at the Earl of Arundel's house, where a damp bed compounded his fever and he died two or three days later. Although this may well be an appropriate way to go for one of the founders of modern scientific practice, the true story is sadly not as Arundel tells it. To begin with, records show that it did not snow that year in London. Nevertheless, it does seem that Bacon's scientific experiments were partially to blame for his death. In a letter to the absent Lord Arundel written from his Highgate deathbed, Bacon mentions wanting to conduct 'an experiment or two touching the conservation and induration of bodies', and likens his own possible demise to that of the Roman Pliny the Elder (23-79 AD) who died from inhaling noxious fumes when he strayed too close to the erupting Mount Vesuvius.

Bacon authored over thirty books and collections of essays including the *Novum Organum* (*New Method*, 1620), a volume that was to spearhead a transformation in the course of scientific enquiry in the West. As well as being a pioneer of the new experimental method in science, Bacon was also a Protestant believer, publishing *A Translation of Certain Psalms* (1625) and a volume on the state of the Church of England. Like Thomas Aquinas before him Bacon held the importance of studying both God's word and God's world, and in *The Advancement of Learning* (1605) he writes: 'There are two books laid before us to study, to prevent our falling into error; first, the volume of the Scriptures, which reveal the will of God;

then the volume of the Creatures, which express His power'. Moreover, in the *Novum Organum* Bacon argues that scientific and theological inquiry serve the same end:

> if the matter be truly considered, natural philosophy is, after the word of God, at once the surest medicine against superstition and the most approved nourishment for faith, and therefore she is rightly given to religion as her most faithful handmaid, since the one displays the will of God, the other his power.

In this chapter we examine in turn Bacon's two books, exploring how a new understanding of the Bible and a new approach to the natural world both grew in the soil of Renaissance humanism, and both shaped the West in the period running from the early sixteenth to the late seventeenth century. The Protestant Reformation and the Scientific Revolution are two mileposts that mark our arrival into the modern Western world.

The Protestant Reformation (early sixteenth to mid-seventeenth centuries)

Reformation, culture and philosophy

The Protestant Reformation is sufficiently complex that any attempt to list its causes is doomed to failure. Nevertheless it is possible to discern a number of broad trends that, taken together, led much of the West into a period of religious upheaval. The event which more than any other remains emblematic of the beginning of the Reformation occurred on 31 October 1517, when the Augustinian monk Martin Luther (1483-1546; Figure 5.1) nailed to the wooden church door in Wittenberg a list of ninety-five 'theses' or statements. Luther's ninety-five theses take issue with a Roman Catholic church that, at this stage, he was seeking to reform from the inside. Much of Luther's disagreement was directed at particular practices within the Roman church, notably penance (according to which acts could be performed to secure the forgiveness of sin) and indulgences (a mechanism for paying money to the church in order to release souls from purgatory, a place where the dead who were not deserving of hell were thought to go in order to be purged of sin before entering heaven).

In addition, the ground was prepared for the Reformation by a number of social and technological advances in the fifteenth century. The invention of the printing press by Johannes Gutenberg in Mainz around 1439, with a capacity to produce up to two hundred and forty prints per hour, made affordable copies of the Bible and other texts available to a much wider public than those who could afford the painstakingly hand-copied manuscripts from the monastic scriptoria. Indeed, it was largely due to the rapid circulation of printed copies of Luther's ninety-five theses that the Reformation became such a powerful force so quickly. In addition, Renaissance humanism helped foster a new readiness

Figure 5.1. Lucas Cranach the Elder, *Portrait of Martin Luther, aged 46* (1529). Oil on wood. Uffizi Gallery, Florence.

to scrutinise accepted authority and, in addition to the importance of Erasmus's 1516 critical edition of the Greek New Testament, Lorenzo Valla's (1407-1457) *Annotations on the New Testament* (1444) inspired a generation of humanist scholars to subject not only the Latin Vulgate but other important ecclesiastical documents to a new level of scrutiny. The humanist principle of *ad fontes* ('back to the original sources') provoked a fresh willingness to criticise Catholic teaching where it seemed to differ from the Bible. To the extent that the Reformation was about the interpretation of texts, primarily the Bible and Augustine, it grew in the soil of Renaissance humanistic textual criticism.

The particular inflection given to *ad fontes* by the Reformation is captured in the Latin motto *sola scriptura* ('by scripture alone'). *Sola scriptura* labels the position according to which the only sure knowledge of God (and therefore of ultimate reality) is to be gained through God's self-revelation in the Bible (Figure 5.2). Tradition, experience and reason, when they are called upon, are required to respect and work under the supervision of scriptural revelation, not to be masters over it.

Luther and *sola scriptura*

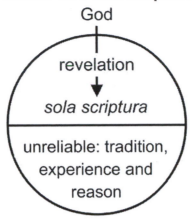

Figure 5.2.

Luther never developed a single theological system in the manner of the scholastics, preferring to draw his theology out of a close engagement with passages of the Bible rather than from a series of philosophical questions. It was through his own application of *ad fontes*, studying Paul's letter to the Romans in the New Testament, that Luther came to a theological understanding that was to define the terms of his quarrel with the Roman church. As Luther himself recounts it, the insight came from his meditation on the meaning of Romans 1:17, 'For in it [the gospel] the righteousness of God is revealed from faith for faith, as it is written, "The righteous shall live by faith".' Luther despairs that, if God's 'righteousness' is that justice by which he condemns the sinner, as Luther's own teachers propounded, then it cannot be 'gospel' (good news):

Night and day I pondered until [...] I grasped the truth that the righteousness of God is that righteousness whereby, through grace and sheer mercy, he justifies us by faith. Thereupon I felt myself to be reborn and to have gone through open doors into paradise. The whole of Scripture took on a new meaning, and whereas before the 'righteousness of God' had filled me with hate, now it became to me inexpressibly sweet in greater love. This passage of Paul became to me a gateway into heaven.

Along with *sola scriptura*, in this quotation we also see the Reformation emphases of *sola fide* (salvation is 'by faith alone', apart from performing good works), and *sola gratia* (salvation is 'by grace alone', a free gift from God rather than something to be achieved through human effort).

Another factor contributing to the Reformation was an increasingly educated laity. In other words, the Reformation was precipitated by the medieval church having done its job so well. The monastic and cathedral schools, along with the universities, had given the laity an ability and propensity to think for itself, a propensity which led to questioning the authority and practices of the church that had educated it. Finally, we see in Luther a violent rejection of the Aristotelian thought that had been embraced so warmly by the Roman church through the mediation of its

'Angelic doctor' Thomas Aquinas. Predating the ninety-five Wittenberg theses, Luther had published another series of theses in which he claimed that 'Almost the entire *Ethics* of Aristotle is bad and against grace', and 'the whole work of Aristotle relates to theology as darkness to light'. Whereas Aquinas had used philosophical vocabulary to elucidate the sense of the Bible, Luther argued that it did nothing but obscure the meaning of the text.

After Luther refused to recant at the command of Pope Leo X in 1520, the Holy Roman Emperor Charles V called Luther to appear before the imperial Diet (parliament) in the city of Worms, once again demanding that Luther renounce his views. Luther is said to have replied 'unless I am convicted by the testimony of Scripture and by clear reason – for I do not trust either in the Pope or in councils alone, since it is well-known that they have often contradicted themselves – I cannot and will not recant anything, for it is neither safe nor right to go against conscience'. At the conclusion of the Diet, Luther was denounced as a 'notorious heretic', and hid from the authorities in Wartburg castle, where he embarked on translating the Bible into German.

The second generation of reformers was spearheaded by Jean Calvin (1509-1564). Calvin had been trained as a lawyer in the humanist mould, and having fled to Geneva from his native France he sought to refashion the city as a 'Christian commonwealth'. It was a more modest ambition than Charlemagne's 'New Israel' but a similar attempt to bring politics under the rule of theology (and thereby a strong rejection of the nominalist-inspired dichotomy of revelation and reason). According to the belief that it was the church's duty 'to cherish and protect the outward worship of God, to defend sound doctrine of piety and the position of the church [...] and to promote general peace and tranquillity', public officials in Calvin's Geneva were designated 'vicars of God'. Calvin's two-volume systematic presentation of biblical teaching, *Institutes of the Christian Religion* (first published in Latin in 1536, then in French in 1541), echoes Augustine's emphases on 'total depravity' (that every human faculty has been tainted by the Fall) and the sovereignty of God in the predestination of Christian believers to heaven. Unlike a scholastic exercise of rational questions and answers, the *Institutes* presents itself as an aid to studying the Bible in the now familiar *ad fontes* manner.

Legacies of the Reformation

The Reformation changed the course of European religious expression irreversibly, but its consequences stretch far beyond issues of theology and religious life. Among other political and dynastic factors, the division between Catholic and Protestant beliefs led to civil wars in England and France, and to the Thirty Years' War (1618-1648) in the Holy Roman Empire, a brutal period of hostilities that brought casualty figures of up to 30% in some German states. The Thirty Years' War finally ended with the peace of Westphalia in 1648 (referred to as the 'Peace of Exhaustion' by contemporaries), under which the prince of each province was given the right to determine the religion of his own state (Catholic, Lutheran or Calvinist) under the principle of *cuius regio, eius religio* (Latin: 'whose realm, his religion'), and where minority religious groups in a province were granted some limited rights. The Westphalian treaties are an important milestone in establishing the foundations of modern international legal order, based on the sovereignty of each state over its own territory and laws.

These trends were mirrored on the far side of the English channel in the growing popularity of Puritanism, a movement that considered the Protestant church of England to be only 'halfly reformed' and pressed for a more complete adoption of Calvinist principles. There is a streak of Puritan writing that militates for liberty of conscience, and in his *Areopagitica* speech (1664) Puritain John Milton (1608-1674) launches an impassioned critique of censorship and defence of freedom of speech:

> though all the winds of doctrine were let loose to play on the earth, so Truth be in the field, we do injuriously, by licensing and prohibiting, to misdoubt her strength. Let her and Falsehood grapple; who ever knew Truth put to the worse, in a free and open encounter?

Similarly, the Scottish Presbyterian minister Samuel Rutherford (*c.* 1600-1661) argued in his *Lex Rex* (1660) against absolute power (rex lex: 'the king is the law') in favour of the rule of law (lex rex: 'the law is king'). After the collapse of the Puritan commonwealth created by 'Lord Protector' Oliver Cromwell, and following the restoration of the English monarchy in 1660, *Lex Rex* was included in the last official book burning in England, at Oxford on 21 July 1683.

It has been argued that the Reformation played a pivotal role in the rise of capitalism. In his *The Protestant Ethic and the Spirit of Capitalism* (1904-5) Max Weber (1864-1920) argues that the Protestant understanding of vocation as working for God, not ultimately for the state or an employer, brought about a situation in which 'the earning of money within the modern economic order is, so long as it is done legally, the result and the expression of virtue and proficiency in a calling'. It is this 'spirit' of capitalism for Weber that is subsequently inscribed and codified in laws that rationalise the production of goods and that see the making of money as a virtue.

Another consequence of the Reformation was the Catholic Counter-Reformation of the sixteenth and seventeenth centuries. These Catholic reforms did not simply seek to respond to the new Protestantism but sought to equip the Catholic church with new institutions to meet the challenge of the early modern world. The Council of Trent (summoned in 1537 and meeting in sixteen sessions until 1551 and then again in 1561) brought about reforms in the understanding of indulgences, mandated seminaries in every diocese, and declared 'anathema' (Greek:

'a thing accursed or devoted to evil') many of the teachings of the new Protestantism. In the face of humanist biblical scholarship, Trent also reaffirmed Jerome's Latin Vulgate translation as the church's authorised text. As a result of the Counter-Reformation, modern-day Poland and southern Germany were brought back into the Catholic fold.

The Reformation, learning and literature

Luther's translation of the Bible from Hebrew and Greek helped to establish Modern High German as the standard literary language among the many German dialects. Luther sought to produce an earthy translation of the Bible intended to be read by all, and so he substituted the German coin Groschen for the Roman denarius and rendered the Greek *barbaros* (barbarian) as *undeutsch* (un-German). In the first forty years of its publication, more than a hundred thousand copies of Luther's Bible were printed.

Whereas the *Lutherbibel* helped to standardise the German language, the English Bibles of John Wycliffe (1328-1384), William Tyndale (1494-1536) and the Authorised (King James) Version (1611) enriched the English tongue. The Authorised Version exerted a powerful influence on English style, though in a deliberate move intended to lend its subject matter gravity and elevation it sounded somewhat archaic even at the date of publication. Along with Shakespeare, the Authorised Version (standing on the shoulders of Wycliffe and Tyndale) is the greatest influence on idiomatic English, coining phrases like 'clear as crystal', 'a law unto themselves', 'the fat of the land', 'a word in season' and 'a thief in the night'.

The vernacular translations of the Bible in the Reformation era did much to shape the languages of modern Europe, but their influence was felt more widely than in the area of linguistic reform. Translating the Bible into the mother tongue of ordinary people was itself a daring (and heretical) political gesture that challenged the control of the ecclesiastical authorities and their political allies. Tyndale, indeed, was strangled to death and then burned at the stake, and Wycliffe's bones were exhumed and burned posthumously in 1428.

The relationship between the Reformation and cultural production more broadly is complex. During Luther's imprisonment in Wartburg castle, the reform movement in Wittenberg was taken over by Andreas Karlstadt (1486-1541) who took a sterner line than Luther himself, condemning church music with the judgment that 'Gregorian chant lures the mind still further from God – to say nothing of the mumbling, the shrieking like geese of the choristers and lascivious sound of musical instruments, the wailing of organs'. Iconoclasm (the destruction of religious images) was to be a sporadic feature of the Reformation, the effects of which can still be seen in many northern European churches and cathedrals. If the likes of Karlstadt can be likened to latter-day Tertullians, with their own version of 'What indeed has Athens to do with Jerusalem?', then the attitude of Luther and Calvin themselves is closer to that of Augustine and his desire to reclaim the 'Egyptian gold', to use in the service of God everything good in the philosophy and culture around them. In 1524 Luther wrote in the preface to the church chorale book he published at Wittenberg that 'when natural music is sharpened and polished by art, then one begins to see with amazement the great and perfect wisdom of God in his wonderful work of music.' There are further hints of Augustine's Egyptian gold when Luther declares that 'nor am I at all of the opinion that all the arts are to be overthrown and cast aside by the Gospel, as some super-spiritual people protest; but I would gladly see all the arts, especially music, in the service of Him who has given and created them'. As for Calvin, in Book 2 of the *Institutes* he counsels that:

> in reading profane authors, the admirable light of truth displayed in them should remind us that the human mind, however perverted from its original integrity, is still adorned and invested with admirable gifts from its creator. If we reflect that the Spirit of God is the only fountain of truth, we will be careful, as we would avoid offering insults to him, not to reject or condemn truth wherever it appears. In despising the gifts we insult the giver.

As for its contribution to literature, Reformation culture is notable for John Milton's epic *Paradise Lost* (1667), a text of great generic richness and complexity. Like the myth surrounding a supposedly blind Homer, Milton is said to have composed *Paradise Lost* after turning completely blind, and like Virgil's *Aeneid, Paradise Lost* comprises twelve books (in its second edition), and opens with a very long sentence evoking the artist's muse. In the case of Milton, however, the muse is none other than God the Holy Spirit. Milton's Eden can be seen as a romance garden of love, and the structure of his epic resembles a tragedy in which the protagonists Adam and Eve fall by an excess of pride and undergo an Aristotelian *anagnorisis* (discovery) when they wake in Book 9 to realise their loss. Shakespeare no doubt would have approved of Satan being Milton's master of the Petrarchan sonnet. Yet Milton introduces a twist to the familiar tragic framework, transposing classical heroism into a Christian frame. God's grace in clothing Adam and Eve marks a departure from the undoing and death of both Greek and Shakespearean tragedy, and Milton confounds the expectations and conventions of 'pagan' genres with an injection of Christian hope.

John Bunyan's allegory *The Pilgrim's Progress* (1678) is no less influential than Milton's *Paradise Lost*. Bunyan himself was a tinker by trade, a Puritan who fought in Oliver Cromwell's parliamentary army during the English Civil War, and he began work on *The Pilgrim's Progress* while imprisoned for participating in religious services held outside the auspices of the Church of England. The work sold a hundred thousand copies in Bunyan's lifetime, and by some accounts it is the second best selling book of all time, after the Bible. The full title as printed on the cover of the first edition is *The Pilgrim's Progress from this world to that which is to come: delivered under the similitude of a dream*. In his verse introduction to the book, Bunyan defends his generic choice of 'similitude' or allegory:

> Solidity, indeed, becomes the pen
> Of him that writeth things divine to men;
> But must I needs want solidness, because
> By metaphors I speak? Were not God's laws,
> His gospel laws, in olden times held forth
> By types, shadows, and metaphors?

What Bunyan calls metaphor in his introduction is a sustained and rich allegory. Christian's journey from the City of Destruction to the Celestial City is undertaken after advice from Evangelist, delayed by Mr Worldly Wiseman, an inhabitant of Carnal Policy, and punctuated by – among a host of allegorical characters – a period of incarceration at the hands of Giant Despair in Doubting Castle and a meeting with the ferryman Vain Hope. We see here once again the influence of early Christian biblical interpretation on the Western sensibility. Both the incarnate Christ as 'word become flesh' and the approach to the Old Testament that sees it as a series of foreshadowings or types of Christ leave their mark here in Bunyan just as clearly as in the abstracted symbolic representations of Christ in Byzantine art. The West's understanding of signs and symbols more generally owes a great deal to this tradition of biblical interpretation.

Baroque art and music in Catholic and Protestant Europe

A divided Europe produced distinctively Protestant and Catholic trends in the Baroque art and music that flourished in the late sixteenth to the early eighteenth century. The word 'baroque' comes from the Portuguese *barocco*, describing pearls of irregular shape, and was originally used in a derogatory sense to describe a style often full of dramatic movement and emotion that disrupted the classical order of the Renaissance.

Catholic Europe: Rubens and Monteverdi

With the possible exception of Diego Velázquez (1599-1660), the greatest painter of the Catholic Baroque is Peter Paul Rubens (1577-1640). Rubens' canvases bring dramatic and powerful movement and a vivid use of colour together with a sensuousness and a religious intensity that marries spirit and flesh in images that appeal directly to the emotions. In his *Descent From the Cross* (1611-14, Figure 5.3), completed in Antwerp where Rubens was court painter to Archduke Albert, the dramatically extended body of the dead Christ slumps down the canvas and, though lifeless, is endowed with movement by the eight characters assisting in the deposition. A sense of intensity is added by the strong light and the bright white cloth framing Christ's body, and the characters are shown with a muscularity reminiscent of Michelangelo's Sistine Chapel.

Figure 5.3. Peter Paul Rubens, *The Descent from the Cross*
(1611-1614). Oil on panel. Antwerp Cathedral.

The dramatic intensity throbbing through Baroque art also found a
new form of musical and theatrical expression in the genre of opera.
Opera was conceived as a way to capture what was thought to have been
the emotional power of the ancient Greek theatre of Sophocles, Euripides
and Aeschylus, with its religious or ritual setting and its sung chorus.
Like Baroque painting, opera was intended to make a direct emotional
appeal to its audience. The great pioneer and early Venetian master of
opera was Claudio Monteverdi (1567-1643), court musician the Duke of
Mantua, whose *L'Orfeo* (*Orpheus*, 1607) was described by its composer as
a 'fable in music' in which he successfully banished the layered polyphony
of Renaissance singing (where two or more notes or parts are sung

simultaneously, often making it difficult if not impossible to understand the words being sung) with a strong homophonic composition where the meaning of the libretto takes centre stage.

Protestant Europe: Rembrandt, Bach, Handel

If Rubens and the Catholic Baroque drew attention to the flesh in its spiritual intensity, then the Protestant Baroque, consonant with Calvin's refusal to divide sacred and secular authority, showed the divine accommodating itself to the quiet of the everyday. Medieval and Catholic culture was broadly characterised by a strong divide between the sacred and the secular, between clergy and laity, but depictions of the events of Christ's life in Protestant Baroque painting tend to be presented in the frame of everyday life, shorn of the evidently supernatural. In Rembrandt's (1606-1669) *Holy Family* (1640, Figure 5.4), the source of light is perfectly natural, no longer emanating from an intense and supernatural source outside the canvas as in Rubens' *Descent From the Cross*. The composition uses effects of *chiaroscuro* (contrasts between light and dark) but not to the point of losing the sense of natural light. Unlike Rubens and fellow Catholic Baroque painter Caravaggio (1571-1610), the light in which Rembrandt's mother and child are bathing does not create an otherworldly intensity. A sizable proportion of Rembrandt's composition is given over to the space above the holy family, but that space is not filled by choirs of angels or the finger of God, rather by the beams and supports of an ordinary Flemish house. Rembrandt's Mary no longer wears the usual blue (a particularly expensive pigment), but the natural browns of peasant clothing. In other canvases this everydayness is even more pronounced; one particularly delicious example is found in an etching of the parable of the good Samaritan (1633), where Rembrandt includes a dog defecating in the background.

Rembrandt's message is that the spiritual is not experienced by escaping this world, but in this world. Whereas Rubens looks back to the drama and heroism of the Renaissance, Rembrandt looks forward to a more sober, modern world. In Protestant countries there was a new willingness to paint everyday scenes not as symbols or allegories of a higher reality, but as proper subjects of artistic contemplation in their own right. It was also in the Netherlands of the seventeenth century that the genre of landscape (from Dutch *lantscap*, where *-scap* is the equivalent of the English suffix -ship) came to prominence, as the waning influence of patrons – and of their demand for portraits – allowed artists to experiment more freely.

The Baroque era in music can be dated from Monteverdi's first opera, *L'Orfeo*, in 1607, to the death of Johann Sebastian Bach in 1750. Born in 1685, Bach was the most talented member of a large and musically prolific Protestant family from the Duchy of Saxe-Eisenach, in the central region of modern-day Germany. Orphaned and raised by his brother Johann Christoph, during his lifetime Bach was better known as an organist than

Figure 5.4. Rembrandt, *Holy Family* (1640). Oil on wood.
Louvre, Paris.

as a composer. Although he was underappreciated in his lifetime, Bach's compositions are now acknowledged as a watershed in the development of Western music, and the authoritative *Grove Dictionary of Music* hails his work as 'of an encyclopaedic nature, drawing together and surmounting the techniques, the styles and the general achievements of his own and earlier generations and leading to a new perspective'. His *Well-Tempered Clavier* (1722) contains solo piano fugues in all twenty-four major and minor keys, providing a template for musical harmony through the Classical and Romantic eras and through to the early twentieth century.

Bach's music is shaped by an impulse to rational order, but his compositions also succeed in soaring with the emotional intensity characteristic of Baroque painting. For the composer Claude Debussy (1862-1918), Bach is 'a benevolent god, to whom musicians should offer a prayer before setting to work so that they may be preserved from mediocrity', and Beethoven (1770-1827), punning on the German word *Bach* (brook), proclaimed 'not brook but sea should be his name'. J.S. Bach is not to everyone's taste, however, and Sir Thomas Beecham (1879-1961), founder of the London Philharmonic Orchestra and artistic director of the Royal Opera House, grumbled that in Bach there is 'too much counterpoint – and what is worse, Protestant counterpoint!' Though Bach did not himself compose opera, the Baroque operatic form reached its climax with the works of Georg Friedrich Handel (1685-1759) who composed forty-two operas in addition to the famous oratorio *Messiah*, written in the space of just twenty-one days in London in 1741. In the complex layers of melody in Bach and the dramatic lyricism of Handel we can sense the first stirrings a new type of music, not music as craft but music as expression. It would take a further two centuries, however, for that new form to blossom.

The Scientific Revolution (sixteenth to late seventeenth centuries)

Like the Protestant Reformation, the Scientific Revolution owes a debt to the *ad fontes* rallying cry of Renaissance humanism, and like the Reformation it would not have been possible without the establishment of the medieval university as a centre of teaching and research. Technical inventions also played a pivotal role in forging the new scientific era. In *The Passion of the Western Mind* (1991), Richard Tarnas points to four in particular (all with Oriental precursors) that had come into widespread use in the West by the turn of the sixteenth century, each with immense cultural ramifications. First, the magnetic compass enabled the calculation of a ship's latitude (its north-south position) with a new level of exactitude and allowed explorers like Christopher Columbus to calculate their position at sea by reference to the stars and to determine a ship's direction even in overcast or foggy conditions. Secondly, the West's discovery of gunpowder meant that mounted cavalry and fortified castles were now vulnerable to infantrymen and canons, weakening the power of local feudal lords and increasing the dominance of larger nation-states. Thirdly, Christiaan Huygens' (1629-1695) invention of the mechanical clock in 1637 meant that time could be measured much more accurately than with previous pendulum models, allowing the modern world to organise itself in new ways that were impossible when the best indicators of time were the rising and setting of the sun. Finally, we have already seen how the printing press was a catalyst for the Protestant Reformation. Gutenberg's invention also made it possible for bourgeois households to consume educational and entertaining reading matter, and paved the way for mass communication through newspapers. The first English language newspaper was the *Oxford Gazette* of 1665.

The Scientific Revolution forges ahead with the Renaissance's desire to understand this sublunary world and the place of humanity in it. The notion of 'science' as we understand it today is a term of nineteenth-century coinage. The earliest reference to 'science' in the Oxford English Dictionary is from 1867, while the word 'scientist' is coined by philosopher, theologian and scientist William Whewell (1794-1866) in 1834. Before this date, 'science' simply meant knowledge, as when Geoffrey Chaucer (1343-1400) in the *Canterbury Tales* says that the soul has 'science of goode werkes'. At the time of the Scientific Revolution, the study of nature and the physical universe went under the name of 'natural philosophy', a discipline that included science, philosophy of science and (frequently) alchemy, in addition to certain branches of theology.

The Scientific Revolution was driven by a double impetus. First, it was propelled by a renewed conviction in the ancient Pythagorean idea that the order we perceive and can measure in the world obeys certain mathematical laws – in other words that the key of mathematics will open the door to nature's secrets. Secondly, it was fostered by the conviction that the Christian God is a God of order who has created a cosmos the regular workings of which are penetrable to human reason and investigation. We shall consider the importance of the Scientific Revolution for Western history in six steps, taking us from a new mathematical understanding of astronomy to a modern, mechanistic view of human society.

Nicolaus Copernicus (1473-1543): heliocentrism

The Scientific Revolution begins in the field of astronomy, with a renewed desire to explain the motions of heavenly bodies. Astronomy at this time was charged with a significance much wider than simply understanding the movements of the heavenly bodies, a significance that came as a legacy of Plato and Aristotle's sub/superlunary dichotomy and Aquinas and Dante's marriage of Western Christianity with an Aristotelian view of the world and the heavens. As Alfred North Whitehead (1861-1947) remarked, 'not the movement of the earth but the glory of the heavens was the point at issue'.

The Scientific Revolution began, quite literally, with a leap forward, when the West realised that its calendar was lagging over a week behind the sun. Since 45 BC the West had been using the Julian Calendar (named after Julius Caesar), relying on ancient measurements which did not accurately calculate the length of the solar year. As a result, by the sixteenth century the calendar had lost ten days, with the spring equinox falling on 11 rather than 21 March. In seeking to reform the Julian Calendar, Pope Paul III (reigned 1534-1549) called on the help of the Polish-born astronomer Nicolaus Copernicus. Copernicus realised that reforming the calendar would require updating astronomy, and in 1543 he published his *De revolutionibus orbium coelestium* (*On the Revolutions of the Heavenly Spheres*), with a dedication to Paul III. In 1582 the church issued the new Gregorian calendar, including Copernicus's ten-day correction. It is sometimes suggested that, when England adopted the new calendar in 1752 there were riots with incensed crowds demanding

111

'Give us back our eleven days!' (the necessary correction had increased by a day between 1582 and 1752). This story of the 'calendar riots' is now thought to be a myth, though the 'missing days' themselves were indeed lost, the dates in question being 3-13 September 1752.

The adoption of the Gregorian calendar also accounts for the United Kingdom financial year beginning on the peculiar date of 6 April. Previously, rents and other payments were made at the beginning of each quarter, on 25 March (Lady Day), 24 June (Midsummer Day), 29 September (Michaelmas Day) and 25 December (Christmas Day). Before 1751 the new year was calculated from Lady Day, but in that year it was moved by an act of Parliament to 1 January. Lady Day itself was moved forward eleven days, now falling on 6 April, which remains the beginning of the financial year.

The dominant cosmological paradigm before Copernicus was that of Ptolemy (*c*. 87-*c*. 170 AD), a Greek astronomer and geographer depicted in Raphael's *School of Athens* on the bottom right, holding a celestial globe (see p. 91). In his *Almagest* (150), Ptolemy developed the theory of 'epicycles' which sought to rationalise the movement of the planets. What came to be known the 'Copernican Revolution' was a re-modelling of the solar system with the sun, not the earth, at the centre, and with the planets, including the earth, now orbiting in perfect circles around the sun. This Copernican insight was later refined by the German astronomer Johannes Kepler (1571-1630), who first hypothesised and then proved that the planets do not move in perfect circles at all, but in elliptical conic sections. In so doing he solved the ancient problem of the 'wandering' planets, vindicating Plato's prediction that their orbits, despite appearances to the contrary, are in fact regular and mathematically ordered. It was Kepler, then, who finally responded to Plato's plea and 'saved the phenomena'. It is commonly thought that the Copernican Revolution is to be seen as a dethroning of man from his exalted place in the centre of the universe, but this is not accurate. Being at the centre of the solar system was not a place of privilege in Aristotle's model of the cosmos, rather the unmoving earth was a place of change and decay in contrast to the perfect motions of the heavenly spheres.

Galileo Galilei (1564-1642): the telescope and laws of motion

In 1609, while Kepler was refining and publishing his new theory of planetary motion, Galileo Galilei began to make observations through his newly invented telescope, constructed out of a leather casing and two glass lenses. The telescope allowed him to perceive hitherto invisible bodies in the sky, such as the four largest satellites of Jupiter known today as the Galilean moons. Significantly, he also observed 'imperfections' in the solar system – sunspots and lunar craters – that further threw into doubt the Platonic and Aristotelian hypothesis of a perfect superlunary reality.

Legend has it that it was through comparing the regular swaying of a chandelier in Pisa Cathedral with his own pulse that Galileo came to understand the regular motion of a pendulum. His many experiments (including the wonderful, if apocryphal, story of dropping objects of different weights from the top of the leaning tower of Pisa) were driven on by the conviction that the universe is 'written in the language of mathematics', and they led him to formulate the law of the uniform acceleration of falling bodies and the parabolic path of projectiles. Galileo was confined to house arrest after being tried by the Roman Catholic inquisition for his 'heretical' view that the earth moves around the sun. Upon receiving his condemnation for holding that the earth is not stationary, he is said to have muttered the words 'eppur si muove' ('and yet it moves').

Francis Bacon (1561-1626): the scientific method

While Galileo was conducting his experiments in Padua and Pisa, over in Elizabethan England Francis Bacon was arguing for a new approach to scientific enquiry. Like Luther but for different reasons, Bacon set himself up as the implacable opponent of Aristotle. He objected to Aristotle's doctrine that the form of a substance dictates not only what it is but what it is 'good for', its purpose or 'final cause'. Bacon rejected Aristotle's final causes as 'barren virgins', thereby stripping the natural world of any speculatively imposed purpose or teleology and creating, for the first time in the West, a world of 'facts' separated from any values or purposes. He also rejected Aristotle's propensity to proceed from axioms to conclusions by chains of reason with little need to gather new data from the natural world. 'The present system of logic is useless for the discovery of the sciences,' Bacon complained, for it 'rather exists in confirming and rendering inveterate the errors founded on former notions than in searching after the truth, and is therefore more hurtful than useful.' We do not simply need to improve the logic we use to deduce conclusions, Bacon argued, rather we need to jettison our whole method in favour of a *novum organum*, a 'new method' of scientific enquiry. Bacon's new approach was called the inductive or empirical method (sometimes also referred to as the 'scientific method' or the 'Baconian method') which 'constructs its axioms from the senses and particulars, ascending continually and gradually, until it finally arrives at the most general axioms'.

Bacon does not throw out reason in favour of experiment, but seeks to give both their due. In a passage from the *Novum organum* he likens three different scientific methods to three different animals:

> Those who have handled sciences have been either men of experiment or men of dogmas. The men of experiment are like the ant, they only collect and use; the reasoners resemble spiders, who make cobwebs out of their own substance. But the bee takes a middle course; it gathers its material from the flowers of the garden and of the field, but transforms and digests it by a power of its own.

The Baconian bee provides the fundamental orientation of scientific enquiry to this day, though Bacon's emphasis on the goal of scientific investigation being 'man's empire over nature' is now more controversial.

René Descartes (1596-1650): mathematisation of space and the cogito

If Bacon stands in the Scientific Revolution for that position which most privileges empirical enquiry, then in René Descartes we find the revolution's most ardent champion of reason. Descartes' first great contribution to the Scientific Revolution is in his mathematisation of space. He was not the first to understand space mathematically, indeed Greek astronomy and Euclid's theorems had been doing that for millennia. Rather, he was among the first to put forward that the entirety of space, even movements and changes that may seem erratic, chaotic or *alogon*, can be exhaustively mathematised. Descartes' notion of space as infinitely extendable in every direction (from which we get our 'Cartesian co-ordinates') replaced the notion of place in Aristotle's *Physics*, according to which every element is 'carried to its own place, provided that nothing interferes', i.e. stones belong to earth and will return downwards if thrown into the air. This replacement of a hierarchical model with one universal set of co-ordinates parallels the more fluid and de-structured society of early modernity's urbanisation and growing capitalism that displaced the strict ranks of the feudal order.

Descartes' mathematised universe had a number of crucial consequences. The medieval cosmos required the constant and personal intervention of its creator to guarantee its correct functioning, whereas Descartes' universe needed no such interference, and therefore it paved the way for the deism of the eighteenth century. Furthermore, if the mathematised universe was governed by natural laws and not by a personal deity, it could – in principle at least – be understood by physicists and mathematicians without the help of theologians.

As well as developing a new conception of space, Descartes was commissioned by Cardinal Pierre de Bérulle (1575-1629) to confute the growing Pyrrhonian scepticism that, in the wake of Montaigne and his Pyrrhonist-influenced *Essais*, was gaining ground in the French universities and troubling the Roman Catholic church. The result was to be a seismic philosophical shift with its roots in Abelard's promotion of reason in theology and the implications of which stretch deep into the thought of our own day.

In his *Discourse on the Method of Rightly Conducting One's Reason and of Seeking Truth in the Sciences* (1637), Descartes sketches his new approach. This relatively short text is written in the first person and relates how Descartes shut himself away in a small heated room (sometimes translated as an oven!) in order to give himself over to an exercise of hyperbolic scepticism, seeking to doubt everything he possibly could and going so far as to posit a powerful evil genius whose mission it is simply to deceive Descartes' senses. From within this radical scepticism he set out to find one piece of irrefutable knowledge it would be impossible for him to doubt. Then, by a series of careful deductions, he could build out from this one irrefutable truth to establish knowledge on a basis that even the hypothetical evil genius could not shake. The one truth that Descartes thinks he cannot doubt, he tells the reader, is that he is thinking. Even if he is mistaken, he still *thinks* he is mistaken. This was the foundation on which he would build his epistemology: *cogito ergo sum*, 'I am thinking, therefore I exist' (or, as it is often but unhelpfully translated, 'I think therefore I am'). Descartes' *cogito* echoes Augustine's earlier refutation of scepticism with the proposition *si fallor sum* ('If I err, I exist'), but it could not be more different from Augustine's approach to knowledge summarised in his 'credo ut intelligam' ('I believe in order to understand'). For Descartes – at least as he has been taken up by subsequent thinkers – belief no longer has a central place in our knowledge; human beings can themselves attain certain knowledge through the proper exercise of reason. In Descartes' modern autonomous self, God is no longer needed to provide or guarantee knowledge.

Note also that the *cogito* is focused on the individual: *I* am thinking therefore *I* exist. The medieval feudal ideal in which personal identity is understood only as part of a greater collective is fast fading, to be replaced by the modern individual with its roots in late medieval nominalism. In the modern age, divine revelation is no longer the final court of appeal in matters of knowledge; now it is the human *cogito* that takes centre stage. It is, furthermore, ironic, that at the time when the Scientific Revolution is busy evicting the earth from its central place in the cosmos, the thinking individual comes to occupy the foundational position in this new account of knowledge.

Descartes' new foundation for knowledge, it should be noted, is based in the mind ('I am thinking ...') and not in the natural world. Descartes had been chastened when, despite careful observations that seemed to corroborate it, the Aristotelian model of the cosmos had collapsed so definitively, and this led him to reject sense data as an unreliable basis on which to build certain knowledge, a position that reinforced his opposition to Bacon's scientific method (see Figure 5.5). By contrast with Bacon's inductive reasoning (moving from observation to general rule in a way that adds new knowledge), Descartes favoured deductive reasoning (starting with unmovable first principles and deducing what those principles necessarily entail, rather than adding new knowledge to them), a method which was not weakened by an appeal to fallible sensory experience. Descartes spent relatively little time in his French homeland. For what were to be the final years of his life he moved to Sweden at the invitation of Queen Christina (reigned 1632 to 1654), where the cold climate and the Queen's insistence on early-morning tutorials with her in-house philosopher conspired to hasten his early death.

Deductive and inductive reasoning in the scientific revolution

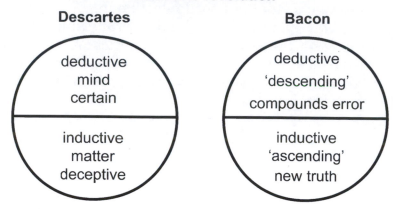

Figure 5.5.

Sir Isaac Newton (1643-1727): the law of gravity

Along with Descartes, Isaac Newton did more than anyone else to mathematise the physical sciences, pioneering the idea of the mathematical model to predict and verify empirical observations. Among his many contributions, certainly the most famous and perhaps the most significant is his theory of gravity, that the force holding the moon to its orbit around the earth decreases as the inverse square of the distance separating the two bodies, an equation which also explains the effects of gravity on objects on the earth's surface (including the famous if unverifiable incident of the falling apple). The significance of this one law of gravity explaining both the behaviour of planets orbiting the sun and the behaviour of apples falling to the ground is huge. It shows once more that the heavens obey the same laws as the earth, putting another nail in the coffin of the Platonic and Aristotelian sub/superlunary dichotomy.

Although he wrote as many words on alchemy as he did on science (though there was no absolute distinction between the two areas of investigation in Newton's day), his *Philosophiae Naturalis Principia Mathematica* (1687, *Mathematical Principles of Natural Philosophy*, often shortened to *The Principia Mathematica*) epitomises more than any other volume the power and influence of the new scientific method, as Newton grounds his understanding of the physical world, his laws of motion and laws of gravitation in a rigorous mathematical method that was far in advance of any other scientific work of the time and was to set the standard in the Western world for scientific and mathematical rigour.

Thomas Hobbes (1588-1679): a mechanistic view of society

The mechanistic understanding of material reality that came from Bacon, Newton and Descartes had proved itself to have great predictive power, and soon it was being imported into disciplines previously considered non-scientific, with the aim of investigating the whole of material and human reality with the tools crafted for the West by the Scientific Revolution. Politics and ethics sought to emulate the success of the scientific method by establishing universal truths of human conduct through careful observation. For Descartes, physical objects, animals and human beings are machines, but they are animated by minds which themselves are not material. This 'Cartesian dualism' of mind and matter was collapsed by Thomas Hobbes, who saw no need to posit an immaterial mind: man for Hobbes is a machine. Hobbes employed this modified Cartesian mechanistic view to the realm of politics and society in his *Leviathan* (1651), setting out an understanding of the human body that reflects the mechanistic spirit of the dawning modern age: 'For what is the Heart, but a Spring; and the Nerves, but so many Strings; and the Joynts, but so many Wheeles, giving motion to the whole Body, such as was intended by the Artificer?' Hobbes presents a picture of society in terms of the interaction of human atoms, and just as atoms are governed by physical forces so also human bodies are moved by appetites and desires. Hobbes understood the state as a machine that controlled the disorder caused by the interaction of these appetites. The desire to view all of reality in this way risked becoming a scientism, a belief that the tools of scientific enquiry can be applied to human society as a whole and can provide answers to human problems in all spheres of inquiry. The mechanistic view reached its most radical expression with Julien Offray de La Mettrie (1709-1751): 'let us conclude boldly then, that man is a machine and that there is only one substance, differently modified, in the whole world'. La Mettrie's conclusion harkens back to ancient atomism and to the search of the pre-Socratic philosophers for an *archê*, the one element out of which everything is made.

The discovery of the New World

Finally, an important chapter in both the history of the Scientific Revolution and the Protestant Reformation is the discovery of the New World. Using the magnetic compass and a process of 'dead reckoning' whereby the ship's position would be calculated by plotting speed and direction each day starting from a known location, Christopher Columbus (1451-1506) landed at the Bahamas (off the south-east coast of Florida) in October 1492. Columbus thought that he had found a short route to the Indies (south-east Asia), and so he named this group of islands in the Gulf of Mexico the West Indies. Vasco da Gama (1460/69-1524) sailed south round Africa to land in India and pioneered the Portuguese consolidation of trade routes to the Far East. Ferdinand Magellan (1480-1521) captained a ship that achieved the first circumnavigation of the globe in 1522, although Magellan himself died before completing the voyage. He was killed in the Philippines at the Battle of Mactan by the forces of chief Lapu Lapu in April 1521, and of the 237 men who had set out with Magellan on 10 August 1519, only eighteen ever returned to the southern Spanish port of Sanlúcar de Barrameda.

The second wave of exploration at the beginning of the seventeenth century saw the British and French fleets challenge Spanish and Portuguese colonial supremacy. Many of the early settlers in what was later to become the United States were English Puritans, disillusioned with the increasing hostility between Crown and Parliament in the reign of Charles I, and by the intransigence of the Church of England to their calls for reform. Four hundred settlers, mostly Puritans, set sail from Southampton for Massachusetts Bay in 1629, followed by another seven hundred in the Winthrop Fleet that set sail in 1630. The Puritans invested their society in the 'New World' with religious significance. While still aboard the Arabella, flagship of the 1630 sailing, Governor John Winthrop preached the sermon 'A Model of Christian Charity', in which like Charlemagne before him he framed his own destiny in terms of the biblical narrative:

> We shall find that the God of Israel is among us, when ten of us shall be able to resist a thousand of our enemies; when He shall make us a praise and glory that men shall say of succeeding plantations, 'may the Lord make it like that of New England.' For we must consider that we shall be as a city upon a hill. The eyes of all people are upon us. So that if we shall deal falsely with our God in this work we have undertaken, and so cause Him to withdraw His present help from us, we shall be made a story and a by-word through the world.

The discovery of the New World was to transform not only the destiny of the European West with the rise in power of the United States throughout the nineteenth and twentieth centuries, but also of the Amerindian and African populations that were 'discovered'. The African slave trade began in the sixteenth century and ran until the nineteenth, by which time between seven and ten million black Africans had been shipped to the New World in inhuman conditions to work mining for precious metals and labouring on sugar, cotton, cocoa and coffee plantations. The discovery of the New World and the colonisation that followed ushered in for the West four hundred and fifty years' dominance of global politics and trade, a dominance that at the beginning of the twenty-first century is only now perhaps beginning to wane.

'All in doubt'

The upheaval caused in the early modern West by the Protestant Reformation and the Scientific Revolution was deeper than simply recognising the ill-foundedness of some previously held ideas. Both the Reformation's attack on the authority of the Catholic church in favour of the individual's conscience informed by the Bible and the Scientific Revolution's rejection of the sub/superlunary dichotomy in favour mathematised space challenged the 'natural order' of society, with its own supposedly eternal hierarchies and structures. The sense of disorder and confusion that this caused in many quarters is captured by the English poet John Donne (1572-1631) in a poem entitled *The First Anniversary, or, An Anatomy of the World*:

> And new Philosophy calls all in doubt,
> The Element of fire is quite put out;
> The Sun is lost, and th' earth, and no mans wit
> Can well direct him where to looke for it.
> [...]
> 'Tis all in peeces, all cohaerence gone;
> All just supply, and all Relation:
> Prince, Subject, Father, Sonne, are things forgot,
> For every man alone thinkes he hath got
> To be a Phoenix, and that then can bee
> None of that kinde, of which he is, but hee.

Donne's claim that every man thinks of himself as an autonomous individual who takes his pattern from no other looks back through the Renaissance elevation of the individual to the nominalist privileging of particulars. The thread can be traced back further, to Abelard's insistence on his own uniqueness in his autobiography *The Story of My Misfortunes*, which itself relies heavily on Augustine's pioneering of the autobiographical genre in his *Confessions*.

In the centuries that were to follow the Scientific Revolution, the West sought to resolve this sense of disorientation in terms of two contrasting and conflicting principles: reason and emotion. It was the Enlightenment of the eighteenth century that most powerfully made the case for reason, but this position was roundly rejected by the Romanticism of the late eighteenth and early nineteenth centuries, with its own premium on feeling and emotion. In our next chapter, we see how these two seemingly incompatible tendencies left the West with an irrevocably divided ethos.

6

Reason and its Limits:
The Enlightenment and Romanticism

'We are born weak, we need strength; helpless, we need aid; foolish, we need reason. All that we lack at birth, all that we need when we come to man's estate, is the gift of education.' This proclamation is emblematic of a new confidence that swept through Europe in the eighteenth century, eclipsing the disorientation caused by some aspects of the Protestant Reformation and the Scientific Revolution. The words are from *Emile, or: On Education* (1762), from the pen of Jean-Jacques Rousseau (1712-1778). Rousseau's *Emile* stands at the crossroads of the two great movements we shall consider in this chapter, two trends in the Western ethos that, in different ways, seek certainty and meaning in the modern world. It was a world that Shakespeare and Cervantes showed to be full of illusions and empty of old certainties, and a world racked by the memory of disastrous religious wars.

On one hand, Rousseau's writing looks to an age of Enlightenment for which human progress towards a perfect civilisation is slowed only by the failure to exercise reason. On the other hand, however, Rousseau also explores a way of engaging with the world that does not look primarily to reason but to a feeling and passion, harking back to a golden age of humanity unsullied by the corruption of civilisation. This did not fail to set Rousseau at odds with fellow *philosophe* Voltaire, a disagreement which allowed both men plenty of room to display their flair for invective. For Rousseau, Voltaire is 'that trumpet of impiety, that fine genius, and that low soul', to whom he writes 'if there is nothing in you I can honour but your talents, that is no fault of mine.' Voltaire was himself not one to shy away from epistolary confrontation, and when Rousseau gave him a copy of his *Social Contract* (1762), Voltaire sent the cutting reply:

> I have received your new book against the human race, and thank you for it. Never was such a cleverness used in the design of making us all stupid. One longs, in reading your book, to walk on all fours. But as I have lost that habit for more than sixty years, I feel unhappily the impossibility of resuming it.

The vitriol exchanged between these two Enlightenment thinkers no doubt has many causes, but it surely also cautions us against seeing either the Enlightenment or Romanticism as simple, coherent 'schools', and against seeing their opposition in too simplistic terms. It is these tensions that we shall seek to explore in this chapter, along with the way in which they shape the Western ethos through the eighteenth century and into the nineteenth.

The Enlightenment (late seventeenth to early nineteenth centuries)

Let us say that the Enlightenment begins with the philosophy of Baruch de Spinoza (1632-1677) in the Netherlands and John Locke (1632-1704) in England, and that it finishes with the defeat of Napoleon I at the battle of Waterloo in 1815. The term 'Enlightenment' marks both a continuity and a novelty in the Western tradition. The continuity can be appreciated when we consider that the metaphor of light has been used throughout Western history to symbolise knowledge or goodness. We think of the prisoner leaving Plato's cave and entering the blinding light; we think of Jesus proclaiming in John's gospel, 'I am the light of the world' and 'Whoever follows me will not walk in darkness, but will have the light of life' (John 8:12); and we have seen how Thomas Aquinas and Gothic architecture alike employ the symbolism of light as an ascent to the divine. Dante's *Paradiso* climaxes with a heavenly dance of lights, and of course Petrarch characterised the period from the fall of the western Roman empire until his own time as the 'Dark Ages'. So the Enlightenment (Italian: *illuminismo*; French *lumières*; German *Aufklärung*) was by no means the first moment in Western cultural history to make use of this metaphor, but in this period light became the dominant symbol for a new, modern understanding of reason.

Reason

When we say that the Enlightenment was the age of reason, what are we claiming? The question is considerably easier to pose than it is to answer. Whereas for Aquinas reason was a stepping stone to faith and for Luther it was the servant of revelation, for many Enlightenment thinkers reason was the yardstick against which all claims to knowledge, including religious claims, had to measure themselves. It is common nowadays to distinguish between the moderate Enlightenment and the radical Enlightenment. The radical Enlightenment, following in the wake of Spinoza, is more politically revolutionary and more militantly atheistic, whereas the moderate Enlightenment, traced forward from the English empiricist Locke, is more ready to compromise with existing social and epistemological structures, and more willing to settle for a position of deism as opposed to outright atheism. This division can obscure the fact that there were many thinkers in both camps who continued as more or less orthodox Christians, and it is far from the case that Christianity lost its grip on the educated classes in this period (that would come only in the nineteenth century). What we can say – and all that I want to say here – is that atheist, deist or Christian, all Enlightenment thinkers grappled in one way or another with the role of reason in establishing our knowledge.

The German philosopher Immanuel Kant (1724-1804) is among the moderates, but the privilege he gives to reason is uncompromising. In his essay 'An answer to the question: "What is Enlightenment?"', he argues that the distinctive stress of Enlightenment reason is on autonomy; it is to be exercised unrestricted by authority or tradition:

> Nothing is required for this enlightenment, however, except freedom; and the freedom in question is the least harmful of all, namely, the freedom to use reason publicly in all matters. [...] The public use of one's reason must always be free, and it alone can bring about enlightenment among mankind.

For the Enlightenment ethos, to be guided by reason is to be a 'free thinker', free from the unregulated assent of superstition, dogma and impulse. The very title of Kant's *Religion Within the Limits of Reason Alone* (1793) is testimony to this approach, and deism itself is an attempt to rethink theology within the bounds of reason, just as Abelard's invention of theology in the twelfth century was a move to bring the discussion of the Bible under the command of an external logic through the scholastic method. This emphasis on autonomy occasioned a move away from the truths of revealed religion; in stark contrast to Bacon's insistence that God has written two books (the Bible and nature), Voltaire insists that 'the one gospel one ought to read is the great book of nature, written by the hand of God and sealed with his seal'.

Despite this privilege accorded to autonomous reason, the Enlightenment was also aware of reason's limits. The Scottish empiricist philosopher David Hume (1711-1776) represents the moderate Enlightenment's awareness of reason's limits when he asserts that:

> Reason is nothing but a wonderful and unintelligible instinct in our souls, which carries us along a certain train of ideas, and endows them with particular qualities, according to their particular situations and relations. [...] All knowledge resolves itself into probability.

Nevertheless, for Hume it is still only through a careful exercise of reason that we come to see that all knowledge is probable knowledge. In other words, the limits of reason are circumscribed by an exercise of reason.

Three major Enlightenment ideas: progress, equality and freedom

In addition to the leitmotif of reason, three further themes characterise the Enlightenment project: progress, equality and freedom.

Progress

A strong trait of some but by no means all Enlightenment thinking was the notion that the history of the human race is a story of inevitable progress towards a horizon of perfection, coupled with the belief that perfection itself is a realisable goal. In 'An Essay on the History of Civil Society', Scottish Enlightenment philosopher and social scientist Adam Ferguson (1723-1816) captures both the hopes and the fears of human progress:

> Man is susceptible of improvement and has in himself a principle of progression and a desire for perfection. [...] He is in some measure the artificer of his own frame as well as his fortune, and is destined from the first age of his being to invent and contrive. [...] He is perpetually busied in reformations, and is continually wedded to his errors.

The Enlightenment notion of progress has much in common with Christian ideas of providence and of history as the stage of the working out of God's promises, but it differs markedly from the Christian eschatological view of history. Whereas the Enlightenment teleological view (from the Greek *telos*, meaning 'goal' or 'end') tends to suppose a gradual improvement towards a final state of perfection, in an eschatological frame there is an expectation that circumstances will deteriorate as the end approaches. Another contrast is the locus of change. For Ferguson man 'has in himself' a principle of progression and in some measure makes his own fortune, whereas in the Christian understanding God is the one who brings about the *eschaton*.

Equality

The ideal of political and social equality is not new with the Enlightenment. In the ancient Greco-Roman world, the Stoics are unusual in stressing the equality of all human beings – slave and free, men and women – on account of their shared rationality. Though the Bible contains the ideas of human equality in creation (all are created in the image of God, Genesis 1:27), in sin ('all have fallen short of the glory of God', Romans 3:10) and in redemption ('There is neither Jew nor Greek, there is neither slave nor free, there is no male and female, for you are all one in Christ Jesus', Galatians 3:28), by the time of the Enlightenment the state churches had become an icon of entrenched inequality. In France the clergy formed one of the three 'estates', the three unequal social strata (the other two being nobility and workers) of a rigid hierarchical society. Coinciding with the European Enlightenment and its deistic trajectory however were a number of evangelical awakenings, with Jonathan Edwards (1703-1758) in New England and with the leadership of John Wesley (1703-1791) and George Whitfield (1714-1770) in Britain. Wesley and Whitfield preached a message of repentance, faith and equality before God to a workforce often feeling downtrodden by a privileged few and, reaching out to African slaves, helped create a black Christianity, empowering the earliest black writers on both sides of the Atlantic.

For most Enlightenment thinking all human beings are equal and this equality is grounded either in a state of nature prior to the inequalities brought about by society or in a more or less deistic appeal to a Creator. For some Enlightenment thinkers, notably Jean-Jacques Rousseau, Thomas Paine (1737-1809) and Voltaire, natural or God-given equality demands to be honoured in practice. For Voltaire in his *Philosophical Dictionary* (1764) the subject of equality is traced to biology, with the curious assertion that 'all the animals of each species are equal among themselves'.

Freedom

The Enlightenment notion of freedom as autonomy – in other words the absence of constraint on an individual's capacity to make his or her own rational decisions – is but one of a number of Western ideas of freedom, and it builds on the Reformation emphasis on the individual and her freedom of conscience before the word of God. In 'An Answer to the Question: "What is Enlightenment?"', Kant pleads for the free public exercise of reason:

> A prince who does not find it beneath him to say that he takes it to be his duty to prescribe nothing, but rather to allow men complete freedom in religious matters [...] is himself enlightened and deserves to be praised by a grateful present and by posterity as the first, at least where the government is concerned, to release the human race from immaturity and to leave everyone free to use his own reason in all matters of conscience.

There is no contradiction for Enlightenment thought in the notion that freedom is found in strict adherence to reason, just as for the Christian mind freedom is found in holding to Jesus' teaching: 'If you abide in my word, you are truly my disciples, and you will know the truth, and the truth will set you free' (John 8:31-2). Both of these positions that find freedom in submission to a principle would be challenged in Romantic and in twentieth century postmodern thought. We can begin to see a drift in the notion of freedom with Rousseau, for whom the natural freedom of human beings is corrupted by an unnatural civilization, a view most eloquently summarised in the opening of the first chapter of his *Social Contract*: 'Man was born free, and he is everywhere in chains. Those who think themselves the masters of others are indeed greater slaves than they.' The emphasis here is less on freedom as the fruit of submission to reason or to God, but freedom as the absence of societal constraint.

Independence, Revolution and Terror

The ideals of progress, equality and freedom were to the fore in the two great revolutionary movements of the eighteenth century that helped shape the modern world: the American War of Independence (1775-1783) and the French Revolution (1789-1799). The American *Declaration of Independence* was issued on the fourth of July 1776 with the aim of explaining and justifying the vote, taken two days earlier, to declare the thirteen British colonies on American soil to be independent states. The body of the Declaration begins with these words: 'We hold these truths to be self-evident, that all men are created equal, that they are endowed by their Creator with certain unalienable Rights, that among these are Life, Liberty and the pursuit of Happiness.' This opening sentence is a model of Enlightenment values, concerns and outlook. First, the preamble echoes the recurring Enlightenment theme of natural law, that there is a basic law written into nature itself which can serve as the basis of human ethics and politics. This idea of a natural law, like Aristotle's final causes before it, was to be rejected by subsequent generations. Secondly, the opening of the American *Declaration of Independence* evokes an unnamed, deist god who underwrites these truths. Furthermore, the foregrounding of equality clearly carries the Enlightenment's stamp, and the 'pursuit of happiness' implies the possibility, even the duty, of social progress.

Thirteen years after the signing of the *Declaration of Independence*, France underwent its own period of revolutionary upheaval, where liberty, equality and progress were once again to the fore. The historian Thomas Carlyle (1795-1881), who hailed the French Revolution as 'the crowning Phenomenon of our Modern Time', writes in *The French Revolution: A History* that 'all things are in revolution; in change from moment to moment, which becomes sensible from epoch to epoch: in this Time-World of ours there is properly nothing else but revolution and mutation, and even nothing else conceivable'.

The storming of the Bastille prison in Paris on 14 July 1789 was but one moment in a complicated sequence of social and political events. From 1302 representatives of the three estates of clergy (first estate), aristocracy (second estate) and commoners (third estate) had intermittently met as the 'Estates General' to advise and sometimes to vote on matters of royal policy. On 17 June 1789 the deputies of the third estate unilaterally declared themselves to be the 'National Assembly' of France, and at the end of August the National Assembly drew up the *Declaration of the Rights of Man and the Citizen*, reflecting the terms of the American *Declaration* of thirteen years earlier: its basis in natural law, its deism and its emphasis on liberty and equality. The preamble to the *Declaration of the Rights of Man* evokes 'the natural, unalienable, and sacred rights of man' guaranteed 'in the presence and under the auspices of the Supreme Being', and its first article declared that 'Men are born and remain free and equal in rights'.

Alarmed by the speed and direction of events in France, surrounding nations set themselves against the new Republic and by 1793 France was at war with almost every other European state. With no sign of the tension subsiding, the National Assembly appointed a 'Committee of Public Safety' to oversee the trial and execution of internal enemies of the state. The Committee accrued increasing power and became to all intents and purposes the executive governing body of the Republic. In June 1793 the extreme Jacobin group, named after the Rue St Jacques (Latin: Jacobus) where the group originally met, took control of the

Committee and purged the National Assembly of the more moderate Girondins (named after the region of Gironde), seeking to concentrate power not with the people of France but with the Committee itself. On 27 July 1793 the Jacobin Maximilien Robespierre (1758-94) was elected to the Committee and called for 'Terror', which he defined as 'nothing other than prompt, severe, inflexible justice' and which in effect meant the ruthless and systematic execution of the Republic's internal enemies.

Many aristocratic representatives of the *ancien régime* (the old order) were efficiently dispatched with a new beheading machine introduced at the suggestion of one Dr Joseph-Ignace Guillotin (1738-1814), professor of anatomy at the Faculty of Medicine in Paris. Dr Guillotin was not himself the inventor of the guillotine, and his family became so distressed at their association with the beheading machine that they changed their name.

No symbolic moment more potently captured the feeling that France was undergoing a revolution of the mind than the installation on 10 November 1793 of the Goddess of Reason on the high altar of the Cathedral of Notre Dame de Paris in the 'Festival of Reason' (Figure 6.1), during which churches were rededicated to reason and to philosophy, and hymns were sung to liberty. The Goddess of Reason who appeared at the culmination of the festivities in Notre Dame was, by many accounts, Thérèse Momoro, wife of the printer and revolutionary Antoine-François Momoro.

The euphoric feeling of being on the brink of a new, enlightened age is summed up nowhere more vividly than in William Wordsworth's (1770-1850) famous lines from the *Prelude* (1805): 'Bliss was it in that dawn to be alive,/ But to be young was very heaven.' But these are also poignant lines, for with the onset of Robespierre's Terror, Wordsworth was moved in the same poem to curse his attachment to the French Revolution:

> Most melancholy at that time, O Friend!
> Were my day-thoughts, – my nights were miserable;
> Through months, through years, long after the last beat
> Of those atrocities, the hour of sleep
> To me came rarely charged with natural gifts,
> Such ghastly visions had I of despair
> And tyranny, and implements of death;
> And innocent victims sinking under fear,
> And momentary hope, and worn-out prayer,
> Each in his separate cell,

The Terror ended with the execution of Robespierre himself in 1794, and was followed by an imperialistic turn in France with the crowning of the Corsican-born general Napoleon Bonaparte (1769-1821) as emperor Napoleon I in 1804. Mindful of the symbolism of Charlemagne's coronation by Pope Leo III (reigned 795-815), Napoleon refused to be crowned by Pope Pius VII (reigned 1800-1823) and placed the crown on his own head, a heavily symbolic gesture speaking both of a changed understanding of

Figure 6.1. Etching of the Goddess of Reason enthroned in Notre Dame Cathedral, Paris, during the Festival of Reason (1793). Bibliothèque Nationale de France, Paris.

legitimate power and of Napoleon's own supreme self-confidence. What many perceived to be the failure of the Revolution both in the Terror and in the turn to imperial power under Napoleon I provided a severe chastening for Enlightenment thought and contributed to the Romantic challenge of the late eighteenth and nineteenth centuries.

Diderot's Encyclopaedia and Dr Johnson's Dictionary

In 1751 Denis Diderot (1713-1784) and Jean le Rond d'Alembert (1717-1783) published the first edition of their *Encyclopédie* (*Encyclopaedia, or Analytical Dictionary of the Sciences, Arts and Crafts*). No work epitomises the age of reason more than this summa of Enlightenment thought, running to no less than seventeen volumes of text and eleven of plates, comprising a total of seventy-two thousand articles compiled by over one hundred and forty named authors including Voltaire, Montesquieu, Rousseau, d'Alembert, and Diderot themselves. The project was augmented by five supplementary volumes and a two-volume index between 1776 and 1780.

The *Encyclopédie* reflects the Enlightenment's spirit of curiosity and cataloguing, as well as the boundless optimism – later Romantics would say the arrogance – of seeking to systematise all human knowledge. It is a particularly fitting literary genre for the Enlightenment age. As with Wycliffe and Luther's translations of the Bible into the vernacular, the *encyclopédistes* were also driven by the desire to democratise knowledge: everyone should have access to all that it is possible to know. Furthermore, this knowledge was by no means limited to traditional areas of learning; all aspects of human life were catalogued and commented on, and we find illustrations of everything from architecture through handicrafts and professions to clothing, fashions and various industrial machines, combining the universal curiosity of Leonardo with the systematic thoroughness of a Descartes or Bacon.

The *Encyclopédie* does have its generic precedents in the West, notably Pliny the Elder's (23-79 AD) *Natural History*, whose thirty-seven chapters range over subjects from plant and animal life to architecture and art, as well as the huge 448 chapters of Saint Isodore of Seville's (*c.* 560-636) *Origines*. Nevertheless, the *Encyclopédie* unmistakably reflects Enlightenment reason, both in its structure and its content. Diderot and d'Alembert represent the entirety of human understanding in a comprehensive 'Map of the System of Human Knowledge' which serves as an important example of the Enlightenment systematising approach. The map provides a taxonomy of knowledge under the three headings of memory, reason and imagination, with reason by far the largest. By way of example, we can trace the place of the knowledge of God on the table: it sits under the science of God, which is itself under the title of general metaphysics, which is a category of philosophy, which in turn is under the rubric of reason.

The aim of setting forth this knowledge in a 'general system' reflects a view of the world which assumes an underlying coherence to human understanding, a position that would be challenged by Romantic thought and that would come under great scrutiny in the latter half of the twentieth century. Moreover, this systematisation of knowledge is far from incidental to the genre or to the aim of the *Encyclopédie*'s editors; it is itself a Baconian mastery and possession of both nature and culture. In the words of the epigraph to the *Encyclopédie*, 'What grace may be added to commonplace matters by the power of order and connection'. Even more than this, the *Encyclopédie*'s 'Map of the System of Human Knowledge' is itself a manifesto, an attempt to alter the way people see and understand the world.

While Diderot and d'Alembert were compiling their great encyclopaedia in France, on the other side of the English channel Samuel Johnson (1709-1784) was preparing his two-volume *Dictionary of the English Language* (1755), a formidable feat of lexicographical skill which remained the primary English reference dictionary until the publication of the *Oxford English Dictionary* of 1884. Though it exemplifies the Enlightenment's desire to classify and systematise knowledge, the dictionary is also a mine of cultural information, as well as an indication of Johnson's famous wit. The entry for 'fool's errand' under *fool* reads '*see* errand', while under *errand* the reader is directed to '*see* fool', and the famous entry on 'Oats' reads 'A grain which in England is generally given to horses, but in Scotland supports the people'. Previous dictionaries had primarily been vehicles of the publishing trade to standardise English spelling and usage, but Johnson's achievement distinguishes itself by its meticulous

Figure 6.2. Jacques-Louis David, *The Death of Socrates* (1787).
Oil on canvas. The Metropolitan Museum of Art, New York.

cataloguing of the different senses of words. He lists twenty meanings of 'time' and fully one hundred and thirty-four definitions of 'take'.

Neoclassical painting

The Enlightenment was accompanied in the field of art by Neoclassicism. In the same way that the Renaissance privileged the well-proportioned nobility of classical art over the ornate proliferation of the Gothic, so also eighteenth-century Neoclassicism fashioned itself as a return, after the Baroque and the intensely ornate Rococo that followed it, to the high classical style of ancient Greece and Rome. Neoclassical painting sought to recapture the ancient aesthetic virtues of balance and expressive restraint. In France the Neoclassical style is epitomised by the noble themes and characters depicted by Jacques-Louis David (1748-1825). A revolutionary Jacobin who recoiled from the empty playfulness of the Rococo, David cultivated a style which privileged line and drawing over colour and tone, suited to promoting an ethic of stoic self-denial and public duty.

David's *Death of Socrates* (1787, Figure 6.2) is a masterpiece of rational control, both in its theme and in its form. Socrates, condemned for corrupting the youth of Athens with his teaching, prepares to drink a *kylix* (clay cup) of poison hemlock while gently chiding his emotional followers with the words given in Plato's *Apology*: 'I am not angry with my condemners, or with my accusers; they have done me no harm, although they did not mean to do me any good; and for this I may gently blame them. [...] The hour of departure has arrived, and we go our ways – I to die and you to live. Which is the better, only God knows.' Through the cup, the choice of colours, the number of Socrates' followers (twelve in total, including the three figures on the stairs in the background) and the subject, David's canvas presents itself as a reworking Leonardo's *Last Supper*, substituting Socrates for Christ and Enlightenment reason for religious faith. And who could mistake, in Socrates' upward-pointing finger, a deliberate reference to the Plato of Raphael's *School of Athens?* The English painter Sir Joshua Reynolds (1723-1792) praised the canvas in rapturous terms, claiming it to be 'the most exquisite and admirable effort of art that has appeared since the Cappella Sistina and the Stanze of Raphael. The picture would have done honour to Athens in the age of Pericles.'

The Enlightenment and music

The Classical era in music can be dated from the death of J.S. Bach in 1750 to the death of Ludwig van Beethoven in 1827; it is an era that combines the simplicity and balance of Neoclassical painting with melodic playfulness. In the course of the eighteenth century the increasingly affluent and leisured European middle class accustomed itself to the attendance of public concerts, and it demanded a music of clear melodies, expressive restraint and controlled emotion. Searching for musical clarity, composers began writing homophonic forms, rejecting the high Baroque style of polyphonic compositions. Homophony allowed a greater power of individual expression than was possible with the tightly regulated exercises of the high Baroque, a move that complemented the Enlightenment's elevation of the autonomous individual. Vienna, at the crossroads of Germany and Italy – the two great musical nations of the period – established itself as the centre of the new Classical style from around 1770 to 1789, and attracted the three greatest Classical era composers: Franz Joseph Haydn (1732-1809), Wolfgang Amadeus Mozart (1756-1791), and Ludwig van Beethoven (1770-1827).

The eldest of the three great Classical composers was the Austrian Joseph Haydn, affectionately known by his pupils as 'Papa'. One hundred and four of Haydn's symphonies survive, and for a public accustomed to new music at every performance he was the first composer whose work was regularly repeated on multiple evenings. Haydn's combination of taut craftsmanship, accessible tunefulness and compositional joie de vivre took the symphony form from its roots in the overture of Baroque era opera to the most important orchestral genre of the Classical age.

Twenty-four years Haydn's junior, Johannes Chrysostomus Wolfgangus Theophilus Mozart (to give him his full baptismal name) was to the Classical era what J.S. Bach was to the Baroque: he fully explored and perfected the potential of every type of music he composed. Mozart wrote his first composition aged only four or five, and before his early death at thirty-five with symptoms of swelling and vomiting (Mozart was convinced he was being poisoned) he had written six hundred and six individual pieces of music, at an average rate of one every nineteen days. This prodigious output was made possible by his ability fully to score an orchestral piece in his head, only afterwards 'copying' it out as manuscripts which were rarely corrected.

Beethoven provides a transition between Classical era and later Romantic music. Like Mozart he spent ten years in Vienna (1792-1802), reluctantly sent there as a pupil of the now famous Haydn by a father who wanted him to be a lawyer. Beethoven proved a petulant but brilliant pianist, later claiming that he had never learned anything from Haydn. He was only eighteen years old at the storming of the Bastille in Paris, and his dissonant, thunderous and energetic music bears the marks of that tumultuous period as well as of his own abusive childhood and the increasing onset of deafness from 1796. Even in his Viennese period, Beethoven more than Mozart distorts Classical form to suit his expressive will, conceiving works in terms of a developing narrative to which the musical form is to be bent.

Romanticism (1780-1830)

The tendency in late eighteenth- and early nineteenth-century European culture that bears the name 'Romanticism' grew in part quite naturally out of the Enlightenment and sat happily alongside it (Rousseau is prominent both as an Enlightenment *philosophe* and as an early Romantic, for example). It is also true, however, that Romanticism was in part a violent reaction against the perceived excesses and deficiencies of Enlightenment reason, in a similar way to the Renaissance humanist rejection of the fusty and turgid logic of scholasticism. The striking difference, however, is that the Romantics went much further than the humanists ever desired, rejecting the very place and privilege of reason itself. The human desire for communion with an ultimate reality that lies beyond any logical chains of reason was considered to be stifled by Enlightenment thinking, and in Germany the project of Enlightenment gained in some quarters the mocking nickname of *Aufklärerei* (enlighten-mania). Like all 'movements', to characterise Romanticism in general terms will always reduce its complexity, but there is also an equal and opposite error of stressing nuance and counterexample to the extent that one becomes blind to broader trends which, though they may rarely be overwhelming and never universal, are nevertheless often discernible and important.

The Industrial Revolution and the cult of nature

Romanticism was also in part a reaction against the increasing mechanisation of industry and society in the later eighteenth century. The term 'Industrial Revolution' was coined by the French socialist Louis Blanqui (1805-1881) in 1837 to compare the industrial change that

England was undergoing to the political change that had transformed France after 1789. Like the French Revolution before it, industrialisation was a gradual process that nevertheless produced dramatic changes in Western life and thinking. It was driven by the invention of new manufacturing machines, and began in 1768 when Derbyshire wig-maker Richard Arkwright (1733-1792) patented a water-powered cotton spinning machine called a 'water frame'. Arkwright's frame, in its later steam-powered version, was to increase cotton output in England one hundred and thirty-fold between 1770 and 1841. With the growth of the factories, Europe saw increasing urbanisation as workers were attracted to the cities to find unskilled work requiring no formal apprenticeship and uncontrolled by the medieval guilds. In the whole of the eighteenth century the population of London had grown by only around two hundred thousand, but from 1800-1850 it more than doubled in size to just under three million. By the same date, Britain was the first country in Europe to have more people living in cities and towns than in the countryside. Germany reached the tipping point in 1891, and France as late as 1931.

The Industrial Revolution exacted a price, however. Along with increased yields, the mathematisation and mechanisation of production also brought increased risks for workers and increased urban pollution. In London's 'great stink' of 1858 unusually light rainfall led to a plague of giant bluebottles as the capital's sewage lay rotting in a stagnant river Thames. Curtains soaked in chloride of lime had to be hung in Parliament to allow the business to continue amid the acrid stench. The factories also saw the birth of a new class, the industrial proletariat, often living in insanitary conditions in slum districts and condescendingly described by Edward Bulwer-Lytton in his 1830 novel *Paul Clifford* as the 'great unwashed'.

If the Greek hero is exalted for his *aretê*, if the New Testament holds up the standard of *agapê*, if medieval literature fosters the expression of *fin'amor* and if the Renaissance fashion was for gentlemanly *sprezzatura*, then the Romantic ethos exalted above all else the cult of feeling (German: *Gefühl* or *Leidenschaft*, French *sentiment*). 'Feeling alone gives to abstract terms, feet, wings' eulogised Johann Georg Hamann (1730-1788), the German philosopher and advocate of the proto-Romantic *Sturm und Drang* movement (German: 'Storm and Stress'). The Romantic ethos is powerfully portrayed in Johann Wolfgang von Goethe's (1749-1832) runaway bestseller *The Sorrows of Young Werther* (1774), the diary of a passionate young man racked by unrequited love whose agony is ended only by suicide. The slim volume made Goethe's reputation, and Napoleon himself is said to have kept a copy at his bedside.

The Romantic ethos turned to nature as its muse, an emphasis captured once more by Wordsworth, this time in *The Tables Turned* (1798):

> One impulse from a vernal wood
> May teach you more of man;
> Of moral evil and of good,
> Than all the sages can.

These lines also give an impression of the Romantic sensitivity to nature, but it would be wrong to think that the 'move' from the Enlightenment to Romanticism was like flicking a switch. Way back on 16 November 1739 the poet and Cambridge professor Thomas Gray wrote a letter from Turin in which he described one view on a walk in the Chartreuse Mountains that is: 'not a precipice, not a torrent, not a cliff, but is pregnant with religion and poetry'. Nature is here not to be mastered and possessed by humanity on the Baconian model, but it is experienced as a spiritual, even mystical reality that no rationalising description can capture. For the Wordsworth of *Tintern Abbey*, nature is 'a sense sublime of something far more deeply interfused, whose dwelling is the light of setting suns'. One notable dissenting voice to this new ethos, disturbing the Romantics' mystical evocation of nature, is that of the Marquis de Sade (1740-1814) who saw in the natural world not a religious experience of harmonious existence but a brutal kingdom where the fittest survive and any means are acceptable to fulfil one's desires at the expense of others.

Enlightenment reason came to be seen by the Romantics not as the liberating autonomy praised by Kant but as a reductive yoke on the human spirit. Whereas the Enlightenment had privileged an empirically guided reason in attaining knowledge and had devalued the imagination, authority and faith, Romanticism exulted in feeling, intuition and imagination, despising reason and empiricism along with ancient philosophical authorities appealed to for their own sake (see Figure 6.3). 'God is a poet, not a mathematician' complained Hamann, for 'what is this much lauded reason with its universality, infallibility [...] certainty, overweening claims, but a stuffed dummy [...] endowed with divine attributes?' The human spirit was not a machine in one of the new factories whose worth was to be dryly calculated and whose output was to be made ever more efficient as part of a rationalised industrial mechanism. The idea that reason reduces the mystery and rapture of existence to a series of measurements is captured in Thomas Carlyle's scorning of Diderot's 'half-world, distorted into looking like a whole', and powerfully expressed in John Keats' (1795-1821) *Lamia*:

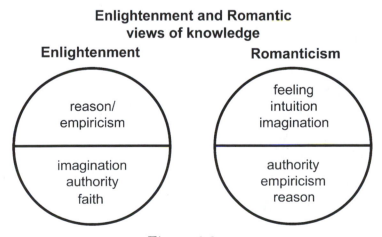

Figure 6.3.

Philosophy will clip an Angel's wings,
Conquer all mysteries by rule and line,
Empty the haunted air, and gnomed mine –
Unweave a rainbow, as it erewhile made
The tender-person'd Lamia melt into a shade.

As we have seen, Enlightenment reason by no means excludes sentiment, and we must see here in these Romantic denunciations, at least in part, what the critic Harold Bloom (born 1930) calls 'the anxiety of influence', the desire felt by every new generation of thinkers or artists to stake out its territory by exposing – or at any rate claiming to expose – inadequacies in the previous generation.

The English author, illustrator and visionary William Blake (1757-1827) was a forerunner and pioneer of the Romantic sensibility. In his strikingly illuminated books of poetry Blake portrays a dark world full of primordial powers of nurture and destruction. Rejecting the Enlightenment's idea of teleological progress, Blake saw in the Industrial Revolution an ominous, sinister and demonic power ravishing the virgin countryside with its 'dark, satanic mills'.

Similarly, his view of scientific discovery was in stark contrast to much Enlightenment thought. The poet Alexander Pope (1688-1744) had heralded Newton's scientific discoveries with the rapturous lines 'Nature and nature's laws lay hid in night./ God said: let Newton be, and all was

Figure 6.4. William, Blake, *Newton* (1795/c1805). Colour print finished in ink and watercolour on paper. Tate Gallery, London.

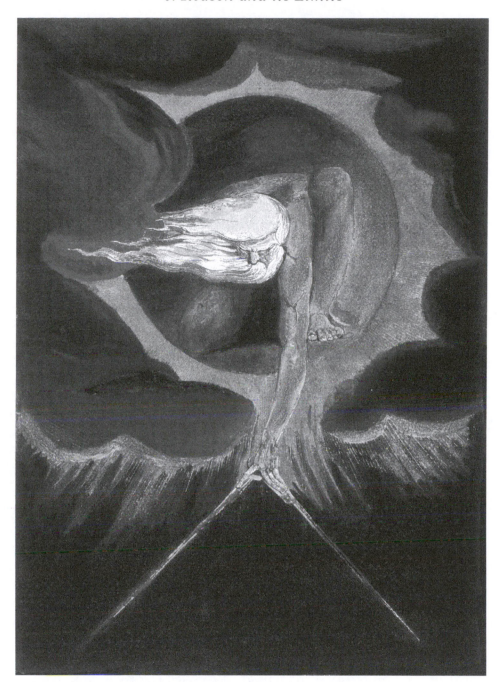

Figure 6.5. William Blake, *The Ancient of Days* (1794).
Watercolour etching. British Museum.

light', but Blake for his part had nothing but condemnation for Newton's reductive, 'single' (one-eyed) vision which, in depriving the world of mystery, was in Blake's eyes positively Satanic. In a 1795 illustration, Blake depicts a sullen and cowering Newton struggling with hesitant fingers to measure a representation of nature with a pair of compasses (Figure 6.4). The pose is in stark – and surely deliberate – contrast to his *Ancient of Days* (Figure 6.5), in which a similar pair of compasses organically and effortlessly shoot forth from the fingers of the stooping Creator.

Remade in the image of this Creator, the figure of the poet and the artist acquires a new status in Romanticism, as a priest of nature and the 'stylus of God'. The artist no longer crafts, but like God he creates, in a move that once again parallels then goes beyond the Renaissance exaltation of the figure of the artist. This exalted role for the poet was accompanied towards the end of the eighteenth century by a shift in the meaning of the term 'genius'. Up until this time it referred to a guardian spirit governing an individual's destiny, but now it took on the meaning of an individual uncommonly gifted with a quasi-superhuman mastery of a particular art or area of knowledge.

Romanticism and literature: the fragment

The very idea of fixed literary genres is, like Enlightenment reason itself, dismissed by the Romantic sensibility as a constraint on the unfettered expression of poetic genius. This rejection is famously expressed by the critic and poet Karl Wilhelm Friedrich Schlegel (1772-1829) in the journal *Athenaeum*: 'the romantic kind of poetry [...] alone is infinite, just as it alone is free; and it recognises as its first commandment that the will of the poet can tolerate no law above itself'. According to Schlegel, 'every poem is a genre unto itself', and Romantic poetry is 'the only kind of poetry that is more than a kind, that is, as it were, poetry itself'. Such poetry for Schlegel cuts across artificial boundaries, fusing poetry and prose, art and nature, and the novel is held up as the genre that, in encompassing a rich variety of types and modes of writing, both is and is not itself a genre. In truth, these thoughts are remarkably close to describing an omnibus genre, a notion that is as old as Western literature itself, but the Romantic desire to throw off all constraint was unprecedented in its fervour.

Romanticism introduces its own generic innovation into the Western canon in the form of the fragment. The fragment provides a means of literary expression that is unsystematic, impulsive, complete and direct. Fragments can present a number of different voices and a number of different topics in a single text, and in this way can be seen as both a development and a fracturing of the essay form introduced by Montaigne. The best-known collection of Romantic fragments is that written for the journal *Athenaeum* (published 1798-1800) by August Wilhelm Schlegel (1767-1845) and his brother Karl Wilhelm Friedrich, Friedrich Schleiermacher (1768-1834) and Novalis (the pseudonym of Georg Philipp Friedrich Freiherr von Hardenberg, 1772-1801). In fragment 206, Friedrich Schlegel presents the fragment form as 'entirely isolated from the surrounding world [...] complete in itself like a hedgehog', and yet also incomplete in its relation to other fragments. The unity of a collection of fragments is for Schlegel not a completed 'system' where no mystery remains, but a 'chaotic universality' of correspondences and oppositions between fragments. The fragment then is not a wholesale rejection of systems and systematising (a rejection which would itself look remarkably like a system) but rather the broad embrace of both system and rupture: 'It is equally fatal for the mind to have a system and to have none. It will simply have to decide to combine the two.'

Romantic music

There is a fundamental continuity between Classical and Romantic era music. Whereas music of the Classical era brought restrained expression to the fore, Romantic music heightened the intensity and power of expression. Whereas in Classical music clear expression served the musical form, with Romantic era music greater and greater liberties are taken with a form that was now in the service of ever more extreme emotional expression. This greater freedom of expression also meant that there is no Romantic 'period style', for in this period each composer develops his own individual style in an age when, in Beethoven's words, 'art demands that we never stand still'.

Beethoven's Third Symphony, the *Eroica* (Italian: 'heroic') composed in 1804-5, marks a watershed in the history of Western music. An admirer of the French Revolution, Beethoven originally called the symphony the 'Bonaparte', but when Napoleon was crowned emperor a disgusted Beethoven defaced his manuscript, scratching out the name so violently that he left a hole in the paper. In this Third Symphony Beethoven abandons the strict Classical form of introduction, development and recapitulation in favour of developing a single fanfare, cutting across Classical convention. Richard Taruskin in *The Oxford History of Western Music* hails the surprising and very unclassical C# at the start of the first movement's seventh bar as 'possibly the most famous single note in the entire symphonic literature'. After the Symphony's public première on 7 April 1805, Western music had entered a new era. The compositional innovation announced in Beethoven's Third Symphony was to reach its full expression three years later in the Fifth (1808), where the revolutionary upheavals of the late Enlightenment are brought together in the thunderous and Romantic form-defying self-expression of the opening 'short-short-short-long' motif of its first movement, the most recognised bars in all Western symphonic music.

While Beethoven provides the transition from the Classical style to Romantic composition, the most striking example of Romantic musical storytelling is Hector Berlioz's (1803-1869) *Symphonie Fantastique* (*Fantastic Symphony*, 1830). Like Beethoven before him, Berlioz married a powerful drive for musical innovation with an acute abruptness in social situations. Indignant at the inclusion of cymbals in a performance he attended of Christoph Willibald Gluck's (1714-1787) *Iphigenie en Tauride*, Berlioz writes in his memoirs:

> The next time the opera was played I was resolved that if these errors were repeated I would show them up. Accordingly, when the Scythian ballet began I lay in wait for my cymbals; they came in just as they had done before. Boiling with anger, I nevertheless contained myself until the piece was finished, and then, seizing the occasion of the momentary lull which

preceded the next piece, I shouted out with all my might, 'There are no cymbals there; who has dared to correct Gluck?'

Berlioz's own *Symphonie Fantastique* epitomises Romantic 'programme music', a mode of musical storytelling that seeks to convey an extra-musical narrative which, in true Romantic style, is all about the composer himself. Indeed, at the symphony's première Berlioz provided every audience member with a programme describing the narrative upon which the symphony is based. The story is built around one *idée fixe* (French: 'fixed idea'), a motif that recurs whenever the actress Harriet Smithson, the object of Berlioz's unrequited love, appears in the plot. In the five movements we follow the young lover (Berlioz himself of course) as he is first enraptured in his 'Reveries and Passions' (part 1), tormented at a ball (part 2), and then drained of hope as storm clouds gather during a 'Scene in the Country' (part 3). After he is induced through an opium overdose to see visions in his 'March to the Scaffold' (part 4), the composer's dead body becomes the parodic object of a macabre dance of old hags, including his now aged beloved, in a 'Dream of a Witches' Sabbath' (part 5). The choice of medieval and supernatural motifs as well as the unashamed prominence of the personality of the artist mark the symphony out as a quintessentially Romantic work.

Romantic art

The Romantic sensibility in art explored the sublimity and ferocity of nature and the sensitivity and horror of the human spirit. The most iconic image of Romantic art is Caspar David Friedrich's (1774-1840) *The Wanderer Above the Sea of Fog* (1818, Figure 6.6). With this brooding mountainscape Friedrich evokes the mystical religious intensity of nature. His figure is not hiking or travelling but wandering, an unsystematic pursuit outside modern society's controlling constraints and drive for productivity, implying a certain abandonment to the forces of nature. As the wanderer contemplates the dreamlike fog and the stark, upwardly thrusting rocks of this sublime landscape, the composition of the canvas invites the viewer to experience for ourselves the same communion with nature. The sublime is one of the legacies of the Romantic sensibility to the West. A sublime experience overflows the neat systematising of the rational mind, evoking both pleasure and fright as it overwhelms both intellectual or perceptual faculties. In Immanuel Kant's influential account of the sublime in his *Critique of the Power of Judgment* (1790), it seems 'to contravene the ends of our power of judgment, and to be ill-adapted to our faculty of presentation, and to be as it were an outrage on the imagination'.

For the Romantic ethos it was not only the natural world that harboured dark and menacing forces. The human imagination was also haunted by powers that disrupted the systematised world of the Enlightenment. The unconscious mind was portrayed as an inaccessible place exempt from the rule of reason, a place of dreams, visions and reveries like those

Figure 6.6. Caspar David Friedrich, *Wanderer Above the Sea of Fog*
(1818). Oil on canvas. Kunsthalle, Hamburg.

found in medieval romance. In Francesco Goya's (1746-1828) powerful
and haunting etchings in *Los Caprichos* (*The Fancies*, 1799) and *Los
Disparates* (*The Nonsense*, 1815-1823), the unconscious was privileged
both as a potential site for dark forces and as a locus for the bursting forth
of their destructive power. In *The Sleep of Reason Produces Monsters*
(*Caprichos* 43, Figure 6.7), the sleeping subject is assailed by unnamed
and uncontrollable elemental forces.

Figure 6.7. Francisco de Goya, *The Sleep of Reason Produces Monsters* (1799), from *Los Caprichos*, plate 43. Etching and aquatint.

Religion and a divided ethos

With the division between Enlightenment and Romantic sensibilities, religious expression in the West increasingly followed two opposing paths. Both paths relied on the Protestant Reformation and developed its emphasis on the importance of the individual and his personal liberty of conscience, but each did so in a different way. On the Enlightenment side, some sought to 'demythologise' and rationalise religion, getting 'behind' its myth to a kernel of historical truth. Thomas Jefferson (1743-1826), the principal architect of the *American Declaration of Independence*, produced an edition of the gospels (entitled *The Life and Morals of Jesus of Nazareth*, published posthumously in 1895) in which he omitted any passages dealing with the supernatural or with what he considered to be 'misinterpretations' of Jesus. With the miracles and overarching historical narrative of creation, fall, redemption and consummation expurgated, deistic thinking increasingly saw religion in exclusively moral terms.

For those of a more Romantic sensibility, what was needed for true worship of humankind's Creator was not an institutional church and systematised religious dogmas but a closer communion with nature. Religious experience was not to be measured in terms of rational understanding but in terms of the depth and intensity of religious feeling. The traditional scholastic 'proofs' of God's existence, which had already suffered a serious onslaught from the Enlightenment, were shunned as irrelevant. In their place, the Romantics cultivated a 'natural religion', a feeling for the quasi-divinity of the natural world and free religious self-expression. Although a clash between logic and feeling was nothing new to the West – think of Bernard of Clairvaux's vitriolic dismissal of Abelard's 'stupid-ology' – the wedge was driven deeper than ever before by the Romantics, such that we must now speak of a divided Western ethos. On the one side we find Baconian measurable, reasonable, scientific truth shorn of all meaning and final causes. On the other side there is passionate, poetic, existential meaning, floating free of any rational basis (see Figure 6.8).

The dichotomy of the modern mind

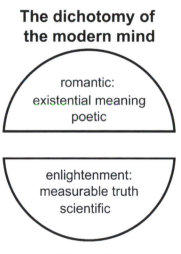

romantic:
existential meaning
poetic

enlightenment:
measurable truth
scientific

Figure 6.8.

In the religious realm, this split ethos led to a divorce of reason and faith reminiscent of Ockham's nominalism, with reason ever more dismissive of unscientific faith and religious belief ever more dismissive of the exclusive claims of a reductive reason. To the modern mind it became necessary to make what the Danish philosopher Søren Kierkegaard (1813-1855) was to call a leap of faith: an existential commitment necessarily divorced from any rational basis. Kierkegaard despised the empty formal Lutheranism he saw around him in nineteenth-century Denmark, and in *Fear and Trembling* (1843) he cites Abraham's near sacrifice of his son Isaac in obedience to God's command (Genesis 22) as a paradigm for the 'religious', which he defines as the response to an absolute demand that transcends reason. Even though Abraham knows that he should not sacrifice his son, he mistrusts his own reason and obeys the absolute call of God.

Hume and Kant on faith and reason

The gulf between reason and faith had been hollowed out by David Hume in a way that threatened to bring the whole Enlightenment edifice crashing down. Hume's problem, or 'Hume's fork' as it came to be known, has to do with Bacon's scientific or inductive method, which infers a general law or rule from repeated and careful observation of particular events or objects. The simple but devastating point that Hume made in *An Enquiry Concerning Human Understanding* (1748) was that we are never justified in thinking that we can be sure of 'matters of fact' (such as: 'the sun will rise every morning') in the same way we can be sure of 'relations of ideas' (such as: 'a triangle has three sides'):

> *That the sun will not rise to-morrow* is no less intelligible a proposition, and implies no more contradiction than the affirmation, *that it will rise*. We should in vain, therefore, attempt to demonstrate its falsehood.

In other words, we are never justified in asserting a universal law on the basis of a finite number of observations. Just because every morning of my life so far the sun has risen, nothing in that fact alone makes it necessary that it must rise tomorrow. Hume made a similar argument against the idea that we can be sure that one event causes another. When I see one billiard ball hit another and the second ball starts moving at the moment of impact, that in itself does not justify the inference that the movement of the first ball has caused the movement of the second. All I have is one sense impression after another flashing across the screen of my mind; the assumption of a causal connection between them is a product of my mind alone. In his *Treatise of Human Nature* (1739-40) Hume famously concludes that 'there is no such thing as a rational belief: If we believe that fire warms, or water refreshes, 'tis only because it costs us too much pains to think otherwise.' Hume thus reasserted and updated philosophy's age-old sceptical arguments, and this was to stimulate Immanuel Kant to bring about the greatest revolution in Western philosophy since Aristotle.

The intellectual challenge faced by Kant in the second half of the eighteenth century was a seemingly impossible one. On the one hand there was Newton and the undeniable fact that his theory of gravity can predict the movement of heavenly bodies with stunning accuracy. On the other hand there was Hume, with his critique of induction and the philosophical claim that experience could never give rise to certain knowledge. So who was correct, Hume or Newton?

Kant's epoch-making solution was to propose that scientific measurement does indeed give us reliable knowledge, but not of the world as it is. Kant claimed that the way we experience the world does not obey the structure of the world itself, but the structure of our minds. Specifically, he claimed that space and time are not things in themselves, out there in the world, but categories of human understanding, ways that we make sense of the world. In other words, the order we perceive in the world is not an order that is in the world, let alone in some higher reality of Platonic Forms, but an order that is imposed by our understanding. The human mind does not passively receive sense data but rather actively digests and structures it, and humans do not know things as they are in themselves (noumena) but merely as they appear to us (phenomena). Here we see once more the affirmation of human autonomy that comes through so strongly in Kant's 'Answer to the Question: "What is Enlightenment?"': human knowledge is autonomous because it provides its own structures and categories; it does not rely on anything outside the human mind.

Kant called this his 'Copernican Revolution', namely that our understanding does not conform itself to the world, rather our apprehension of the world is conformed to the categories and constraints of our understanding. Whereas Copernicus put the sun, instead of the earth, at the centre of the solar system, Kant insisted that the world conforms to the mind, not the mind to the world. Humankind was back at the centre from where it had been deposed by Copernicus, but it was no longer the centre of the universe; the mind was now only at the centre of *its* universe, with the possibilities of human knowledge radically restricted. I can have certain knowledge, but it is only ever knowledge of the world as it appears to me. The task of philosophy was therefore radically redefined. The philosopher's goal could no longer be to discern the reality that lies beyond our limited experience of the world, but philosophy now becomes a matter of locating and examining the limits of human reason and experience. This subjective turn ushered in the new 'critical philosophy'.

Kant's reconciliation of Hume and Newton was to prove the thin end of the wedge, propagating its own version of the West's divided ethos. If the mind determines the categories in which the world can appear to consciousness, how do we know that it does not also determine the world itself? What right do we have to maintain that the world exists independently of our minds at all? It was questions like these that preoccupied the idealist philosophers who came after Kant: Johann Gottlieb Fichte (1762-1814), Georg Wilhelm Friedrich Hegel (1770-1831) and Friedrich Wilhelm Joseph von Shelling (1775-1854). The faith/reason division of nominalism and the religion/rationality division of the modern era were now joined by a division between the human subject and the external world. In the late nineteenth and twentieth centuries this divided ethos would lead to a collapse, and it is that collapse that we shall witness in the next chapter.

Old Certainties, New Crises:
The Death of God, Modernism
and Existentialism

'It is possible to shape the picture of a person out of three anecdotes' claimed Friedrich Nietzsche (1844-1900), and indeed Nietzsche's own life is certainly not light on anecdotal detail. His father, uncle and both grandfathers were all German Lutheran pastors, and he attended the prestigious Schulpforta school near Naumberg that had served as a Cistercian monastery from 1137-1540. But 'Fritz' as he was known at home frustrated his mother's desire to follow his father into the ministry, abandoning his theological studies at Basel university in order to focus exclusively on the philology of ancient Greek. He excelled in his study and was appointed as Professor of Greek at Basel (Switzerland) at the very young age of twenty-four, before he had even begun his doctoral work.

From the 1870s onwards however Nietzsche's health began to fail, causing him to suffer from poor eyesight, acute headaches and digestive difficulties. Partly as a result of ill health, and partly following the critics' savaging of by his book *The Birth of Tragedy* (1872), Nietzsche was retired from Basel while still only thirty-four years old. It is not hard to see why *The Birth of Tragedy* received a cool reception. In its pages Nietzsche throws off academic convention, writing in a combative style full of rhetorical questions and exclamations, leading one influential review to suggest that the author might 'gather tigers and panthers about his knees, but not the youth of Germany'. It was even dismissed by a close colleague of as an exercise in megalomania. The turn in Nietzsche's style was, however, decisive, not only for his own work but – with only a little exaggeration – for the course of Western culture as a whole. From 1880-1889 the ailing Nietzsche moved between France, Italy, Switzerland and Germany, deteriorating in health as he increased in output, and in 1888, his final productive year, Nietzsche completed no less than five books. On 3 January 1889 he finally descended into irrevocable mental illness in the Piazza Carlo Alberto in Turin. The anecdote, probably apocryphal, is told of how he collapsed as he threw his arms round the neck of a horse that was being whipped by a coachman. The value of this story is more in its anecdotal open-endedness than in its truth. Like the anecdotes that Nietzsche himself so prized in his study of philosophy, it both demands interpretation and frustrates any attempt definitively to say what it means.

Although he never received more than respectful local recognition during his lifetime, with each new publication occasioning a sharpening of the critics' pencils, Nietzsche's thought takes us to the heart of a series of changes and crises that were to stamp their indelible mark on the course of Western culture in the late nineteenth and twentieth centuries. In this chapter and the next we follow two interwoven trajectories that chart the great upheavals in the West's understanding of itself and its world. The present chapter traces the thread that leads from the death of God through the disorientation of early twentieth-century modernism to the post-war existentialism that filled the fashionable cafés of the Parisian *rive gauche* in the late 1940s and '50s, and in Chapter 8 we follow changing ideas of humanity through the work of Darwin, Marx, and Freud, showing their influence on late twentieth-century feminism.

The death of God

None of the ideas Nietzsche powerfully hammers out in his writing has so imprinted the Western ethos as the 'death of God'. Throughout Western history most people believed in some sort of God or gods, from the biblical Yahweh and Homer's pantheon through Aristotle's Prime Mover and the Neoplatonic One to the Supreme Being of the Enlightenment or the divine Nature of the Romantics. Moreover, so the argument goes, even those who have denied the existence of any deity have nevertheless continued to assume in their own thinking the sort of overarching meanings that only a deity or a Platonic Form guarantees in the universe: the True, the Beautiful, and the Good. Outright professions of atheism before the eighteenth century are rare and ambiguous, and although the radical Enlightenment propagated unbelief in learned circles, atheism remained unthinkable to most people until the nineteenth century. What we see with Nietzsche then is by no means the first denial of God's existence, but rather a thinking that seeks to follow through with particular rigour the consequences of the absence of God for Western thought and the Western ethos.

Nietzsche's account of the death of God is most famously given in his *The Gay Science* (1882). In its imagery and themes this book echoes Donne's *The First Anniversary* and the crisis we saw at the dawn of the modern world. The passage in which Nietzsche deals with the death of God is only around five hundred words long and is written in the form of a parable. It opens with a madman who lights a lantern in the morning and runs into the market place crying 'I seek God! I seek God!' The people who gather round him are religious sceptics, but when they mock his frenzied search the madman pierces them with his eyes and launches into a barrage of questions:

'Whither is God?' he cried; 'I will tell you. *We have killed him* – you and I. All of us are his murderers. But how did we do this? How could we drink up the sea? Who gave us the sponge to wipe away the entire horizon? What were we doing when we unchained this earth from its sun? Whither is it moving now? Whither are we moving? Away from all suns? Are we not plunging continually? Backward, sideward, forward, in all directions? Is there still any up or down? Are we not straying, as through an infinite nothing? Do we not feel the breath of empty space? Has it not become colder? Is not night continually closing in on us? Do we not need to light lanterns in the morning? Do we hear nothing as yet of the noise of the gravediggers who are burying God? Do we smell nothing as yet of the divine decomposition? Gods, too, decompose. God is dead. God remains dead. And we have killed him.'

The parable finishes with the madman abandoning the assembled sceptics, who still fail to realise what they have done:

Lightning and thunder require time; the light of the stars requires time; deeds, though done, still require time to be seen and heard. This deed is still more distant from them than most distant stars – and *yet they have done it themselves.*

The madman knows something that the other nonbelievers do not. They seem quite relaxed at the news of God's death, laughing at the frantic fool who lights a lantern in the morning hours. However, it is not the death of God itself that animates the madman, but everything that flows from it.

So what does 'God is dead' mean for Nietzsche? In his important essay 'Nietzsche's word: "God is dead"' (1943), the German philosopher Martin Heidegger (1889-1976) explains the significance of the death of God in terms of what he calls the sensory and the suprasensory (see Figure 7.1). For Heidegger, Nietzsche's 'God' designates the suprasensory world, equivalent to Plato's world of Forms, the Christian *logos*, the Neoplatonic One or Kant's noumenal 'things in themselves': it is the world of ultimate reality. The suprasensory also encompasses ideas of the moral law, the authority of reason, progress, culture and civilisation, because these things cannot themselves be seen in the world. The suprasensory is that which is not accessible to the senses but which gives form and coherence to the changeable and merely apparent world we can see, hear and touch.

'God is dead' means that there are no Platonic Forms, no *logos*, only the change and decay of becoming; it means that 'becoming has no goal and underneath all becoming there is no grand unity'. It therefore means that Western thought and Western culture – understood as a thought and culture indebted to Platonism and Christianity – are at an end. So when Nietzsche's madman asks 'What did we do when we unchained this earth from its sun?' we are not merely to think of the Copernican Revolution but the whole Western identification of knowledge and truth with solar imagery. And when the madman asks 'How were we able to drink up the sea?', Heidegger understands that the whole objective world has been swallowed up by the Cartesian *cogito*, the 'I am thinking' that becomes the foundation of the universe. Like the hapless Wile E. Coyote in the Warner Bros. Roadrunner cartoons, the West has run off the edge

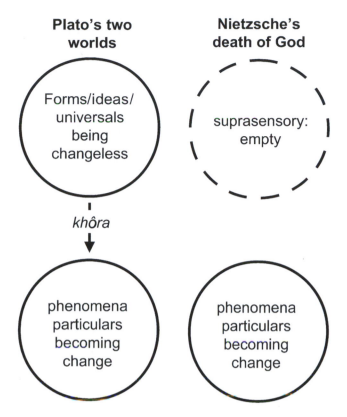

Figure 7.1.

of a cliff but is momentarily suspended in mid air before it begins to plummet, yet to realise that it has overshot solid ground.

The murder of God does not have to be a conscious act, as the uncomprehending bystanders in Nietzsche's parable amply illustrate. It is the cumulative effect of many different steps towards the modern world. The Platonic God had been dying at least since the deluded Don Quixote and the empty heavens of Shakespeare. By the turn of the twentieth century the medieval cathedral no longer dominated the skyline or the social life of the modern city, fractured as it had become into a multitude of grand buildings each representing different interests. Currents within the Scientific Revolution had sought to account for the order in the universe without recourse to God or to Aristotelian final causes, and the Enlightenment had sought to wrest ethics and morality from the control of God and bring them under the purview of human reason.

The consequences of the death of God

So what are these consequences of the death of God that Nietzsche's madman so fears? The author Fyodor Dostoyevsky (1821-1881) is often misquoted as saying that 'If God is dead, everything is permitted'. What Ivan Fyodorovich in Dostoyevsky's *The Brothers Karamazov* (1880) in fact says, as he draws attention the consequences of a loss of faith in God and immortality, is that:

the whole natural law lies in that faith, and that if you were to destroy in mankind the belief in immortality, not only love but every living force maintaining the life of the world would at once be dried up. Moreover, nothing then would be immoral, everything would be lawful, even cannibalism.

For this strand of Western thought at least, then, the death of God necessitates a wholesale rethinking of our notions of morality and law. God and Platonic Forms, particularly the Form of the Good, had been understood as both the origin and final court off appeal in matters of law and morality, but if we can no longer appeal to this court then we are deluded to think that we can simply carry on as if nothing has happened.

Nietzsche himself draws our attention to a second consequence of the death of God when he argues that the way in which the West understands language relies on God. The God of the Bible is a speaking God, and as his Words are divinely effective – 'God said "let there be light", and there was light'. Human words are humanly effective because they participate in or reflect the divine *logos*. Without this *logos*, what is there to guarantee the suitability of language to be effective in describing the world? 'I am afraid we are not rid of God', warned Nietzsche, 'because we still have faith in grammar'.

Thirdly, in 'Truth and Lies in an Extramoral Sense' (written in 1873 but unpublished in his lifetime) Nietzsche seeks to expose the superficiality of the West's faith in truth:

What then is truth? A mobile army of metaphors, metonyms, and anthropomorphisms: in short, a sum of human relations which have been poetically and rhetorically intensified, transferred, and embellished, and which, after long usage, seem to a people to be fixed, canonical, and binding. Truths are illusions which we have forgotten are illusions – they are metaphors that have become worn out and have been drained of sensuous force, coins which have lost their embossing and are now considered as metal and no longer as coins.

As well as mounting this critique of truth, Nietzsche also argues for the unreasonableness of reason. Like the Romantics before him, Nietzsche accused reason of being an iron cage, and in his *Thus Spoke Zarathustra* (1885) he opposes the 'logic of reason' – reductive, stifling and systematising – to the 'logic of life' – free, affirmative and joyous. But Nietzsche goes further even than the Romantics in subjecting the very choice between 'reason' and 'life' to critique. The choice for reason cannot itself be reasonable, he argues, unless it is question-beggingly so (for any reasons offered will inevitably assume the reason for which they are supposed to be arguing). There can be no rational or emotional criteria for the choice between the 'logic of life' and the 'logic of reason', and so Nietzsche insists on the unavoidable human responsibility to choose for oneself, in the absence of any adequate criteria. Thus, for Nietzsche, the self is the origin of meaning, and 'man is what man can make of himself.' In thus driving the Enlightenment and Romantic accent on autonomy to its logical conclusion, Nietzsche gives us a fore-echo of twentieth-century existentialism.

Given these claims about truth and reason, it would make no sense for Nietzsche himself to go on philosophising in the old way of Aristotle or of Kant, stringing together arguments and reaching conclusions by careful logical steps in order to build an overarching philosophical system. So he forges a new philosophical style more fitting to its content, a style he describes in the subtitle to *Twilight of the Idols* as philosophising 'with a hammer'. With a rhetorical sensibility combining aphorism, satire and irony, Nietzsche bludgeons out his philosophy in what he considers the only way possible after the death of God.

Modernism

The crisis in Western culture that Nietzsche's madman prophesies, the crisis which is 'still more distant from them than most distant stars', was the crisis of modernism. The movements in the Western ethos starting with the Enlightenment and finishing with modernism can be likened to the swinging back and forth of a pendulum. As Romanticism swung away from what it perceived to be an Enlightenment excesses of reason, so in turn the philosophy of positivism rejected Romanticism's own excesses and swung back in the latter half of the nineteenth century to a reliance upon reason and scientific measurement. Returning to Descartes' confidence in reason and the Baconian and Lockean conviction that human understanding comes through the senses, Auguste Comte (1798-1857) sought to establish the new philosophy of positivism on a rigorously scientific basis. Positivism held that all true knowledge was to be gained from sense experience, with logic and mathematics accounting for the relations between the ideas ascertained empirically.

Positivist ideas found expression in nineteenth-century literary realism. With shades of Cervantes's puncturing of medieval myths, Gustave Flaubert's (1821-1880) realist novels sought to relate the details of everyday life in all their wonder and horror, refusing to present a romanticised or idealised account of human life. The American realist novelist Henry James sums up the spirit of this literary realism in his essay 'The Art of Fiction' (1884):

> There is no impression of life, no manner of seeing it and feeling it, to which the plan of the novelist may not offer a place; you have only to remember that talents so dissimilar as those of Alexandre Dumas and Jane Austen, Charles Dickens and Gustave Flaubert, have worked in this field with equal glory. Don't think too much about optimism and pessimism; try and catch the colour of life itself.

Nevertheless, just as Romanticism had rejected what it saw as a reductive Enlightenment rationalism, so the positivist (and to a lesser extent realist) failure to take full account of the intuitive, the emotional and the non-measurable led by the 1890s to a further pendulum swing. The scientific certainty of positivism finally collapsed with the First World War, and by 1918 the international popularity of Comte's philosophy had all but evaporated, its confidence in reason shot to pieces in a shell-shocked Europe whose conscience was now heavy with the technology-assisted slaughter of the trenches. Positivist certainty increasingly seemed like naive and dangerous arrogance, and the compass of scientific reason alone was no longer thought fit to guide humanity towards the horizon of perfection.

By contrast with the positivist's objective and scientific mastery of his surroundings, the individual human being increasingly appeared alone and alienated in an incomprehensible world vacated by the gods who had vanished in a puff of Nietzschean metaphor. Science itself seemed to reinforce these ideas. The four articles of Albert Einstein's (1879-1955) 'annus mirabilis' (Latin: 'wonderful year') published in the journal *Annalen der Physik* in 1905 moved physics definitively away from Newton's clockwork universe and towards a new reality where even time and space are relative to the viewer. Einstein spent his early life working as a patent clerk, and when he obtained his doctorate in 1900 from the Swiss Federal Institute of Technology he failed to impress his tutors. Einstein was characterised by one particularly acerbic – and monumentally mistaken – examiner as a 'lazy dog' who did not care at all for mathematics. A misjudgement second only perhaps to the dismissal of a young Thomas Aquinas as a 'dumb ox'.

The West's notion of history also underwent a fundamental change in the aftermath of the First World War. Judeo-Christian eschatology and Enlightenment teleology sought to explain events in terms of an overarching purpose that makes sense of the sweep of world history. To a Europe still on its knees from the slaughter of the trenches, Oswald Spengler's (1880-1936) *Decline of the West* (1918) presented history neither in terms of Greek fate, nor Christian providence, nor Enlightenment teleology, but as the cyclical rise and fall of a series of civilisations, each with its own values and goals. For Spengler 'there are no eternal truths; each philosophy is an expression of its own time and only of its own time'. The early twentieth century stripped history of any overarching purpose or sense just as, three hundred years before, Francis Bacon had stripped the natural world of Aristotelian final causes.

Modernism itself is not simply another swing of the pendulum but a crisis brought about by the entrenched dichotomy of reason and imagination itself, a dichotomy between (Romantic) deep existential meaning and (Enlightenment) verifiable and quantifiable truth. Modern man finds himself in a bewildering world of bureaucratic systems that is free from any overarching cosmic and ethical order that he can understand. All previous sensibilities – Greek *aretê*, Christian *agapê*, medieval *fin'amor*, Renaissance *sprezzatura*, the Romantic cult of feeling – are replaced for modernist man by the overriding sensibility of alienation, the individual disorientated in an impenetrable system he can neither escape nor understand. The poet

7. Old Certainties, New Crises

William Butler Yeats (1865-1939) brings this sense of alienation to acute expression in his poem 'The Second Coming': 'Things fall apart; the centre cannot hold; mere anarchy is loosed upon the world'. It was a mood prophesied by Karl Marx (1818-1883) in his *Manifesto of the Communist Party* (1848):

> Constant revolutionising of production, uninterrupted disturbance of all social conditions, everlasting uncertainty and agitation distinguish the bourgeois epoch from all earlier ones. All fixed, fast-frozen relations, with their train of ancient and venerable prejudices and opinions, are swept away, all new-formed ones become antiquated before they can ossify. All that is solid melts into air, all that is holy is profaned, and man is at last compelled to face with sober senses, his real conditions of life, and his relations with his kind.

What Yeats and Marx are expressing is a crisis of freedom, the crisis that Nietzsche prophesied when his madman asked 'Who gave us the sponge to wipe away the entire horizon?'

Art from positivism to modernism

Modernism's crisis of freedom is echoed in the world of art by a gradual but definitive move toward abstraction and a tendency for art to become more and more overtly about itself, its own conventions and systems of representation. We will begin to trace this trajectory by considering the realist art that flourished alongside philosophical positivism, an art that suffers from no crisis of identity. In a way that recalls Rembrandt's focus on everyday life as a worthy object of representation, the self-taught realist painter Gustave Courbet (1819-1877) dignified the ordinary realities of daily life in a style that sought to represent a secular objective reality stripped of artificial artistic grace and painted from direct observation. In *The Meeting, or 'Bonjour, Monsieur Courbet'* of 1854 (Figure 7.2) the artist's intention is one of Aristotelian mimesis; he sets out simply to represent the objective world, without drawing undue attention to the means through which that is achieved.

With the onset of modernism, however, confidence that such an objective reality can be 'simply represented' is thrown increasingly into doubt. In addition, the desire for objective representations of reality was increasingly satisfied, without any need for a painter, by the newly invented photograph. The earliest surviving glass 'heliograph' was taken in 1826 by Joseph-Nicéphore Niepce, and required an exposure time of eight hours. It is likely (if impossible to say) that art would still have taken an abstract turn without the invention of the photograph, but the new medium did provoke painting to enter a period of self-reflection and may have hastened its rapid move to increased abstraction in the late nineteenth and early twentieth centuries.

The Impressionism of the late nineteenth century is an important moment in Western painting's increasing self-consciousness. The name

Figure 7.2. Gustave Courbet, *The Meeting, or 'Bonjour, Monsieur Courbet'* (1854). Oil on canvas. Musée Fabre, Montpellier.

of the movement comes from Claude Monet's (1840-1926) *Impression: Sunrise* (1872), an ethereal blending of oranges, blues and greens that give an 'impression' of the harbour in Le Havre, France. Impressionism seeks to do away with line and form; it does not seek to represent third-person objective solid objects but to render the plays of light that strike the artist's retina as he views the world. The purpose of this painting is not only faithfully to convey the effects of natural light but also to communicate the emotions that are stirred by perceiving different conditions of light. Between 1892 and 1894 Monet painted a view of the west façade of Rouen cathedral over thirty times (see Figure 7.3) at different times of day and in different light conditions, employing a wide variety of colours and tones. What is important in Monet's canvases is not the 'objective reality' of the stone edifice but the way in which each artistic encounter with the cathedral is a new experience.

The Cubism of Pablo Picasso (1881-1973) and Georges Braque (1882-1963) seeks once more to transcend this subjective viewpoint, but not with a return to the objective ideology of realism. Cubism continues on the path begun by Impressionism by making art at least as much about its own means of representation as about what is represented, doing so through increased abstraction. Abstraction is, of course, not a new feature of twentieth-century art. All art is necessarily abstracted from the flux of life, if only by its context as 'art'. The story is told (in a number of different versions!) of a conversation between Picasso and an American soldier who professed a dislike for the artist's 'abstract' paintings. Picasso let the comment go but later, when the GI showed him a photo of his wife, the artist made his point by remarking with surprise 'is she really that small?'

All art may well be abstracted from life to some extent, but even so some styles are more abstract than others. Nevertheless, in the trajectory begun with Impressionism we see an abstraction that is unlike anything

Figure 7.3. Claude Monet, *Rouen Cathedral* (1893-1894).
Oil on canvas. Louvre, Paris.

153

Figure 7.4. Pablo Picasso, *Les Demoiselles d'Avignon* (1907).
Oil on canvas. The Museum of Modern Art, New York.

previously attempted in Western art. It is not, like the idealised hulks of Michelangelo's Sistine Chapel, a Neoplatonic gesture to convey the truth of what is represented and it is not, like the wide-eyed saints of Byzantine mosaics, symbolic of an invisible truth. It is rather a deliberate attempt to make the production of art part of the theme of art, to question and explore the notion of a point of view and of artistic representation itself. Pablo Picasso's *Les Demoiselles d'Avignon* (*The Young Ladies of Avignon*, 1907, Figure 7.4) seeks, like realist painting, to depict all of life – the five young ladies are prostitutes and Avignon is a street in Barcelona famous for its brothel – but the mode of representation marks a rupture in Western art. Reality is no longer represented but reconstructed from geometric forms and points of view that cut across previous theories of mimesis and perspective.

The single point perspective developed in the early Renaissance puts the viewer in the position of an ideal, disembodied (or at least one-eyed) observer, splendidly detached in god-like self-sufficiency from the scene he observes. It is a disembodied, divine standpoint, a 'view from nowhere' that, with the demise of Western theism, becomes artistically hypocritical. If there is no God, how can you justify painting from a God's-eye view? The lack of depth suggested on Picasso's canvas is similarly revolutionary, breaking with artistic practice set down and followed since Leon Batista Alberti's (1404-1472) *On Painting* (1435), according to which a painting is a 'picture-window' onto the world. What is represented in *Les Demoiselles d'Avignon* is not a real or imaginary scene but how a scene is reconstructed by the viewer from a combination of perception, memory and extrapolation. What Picasso paints is not merely the result of representation, but representation itself.

The trend towards abstraction in Western art intensified after Cubism. In the Netherlands Piet Mondrian (1872-1944) jettisoned mimesis altogether for the white backgrounds, flat geometric forms and neutral titles of Neoplasticism, and in 1940s New York Jackson Pollock (1912-1956) and Mark Rothko (1903-1970) pioneered the style of Abstract Expressionism. Pollock's 'action paintings' (see Figure 7.5)

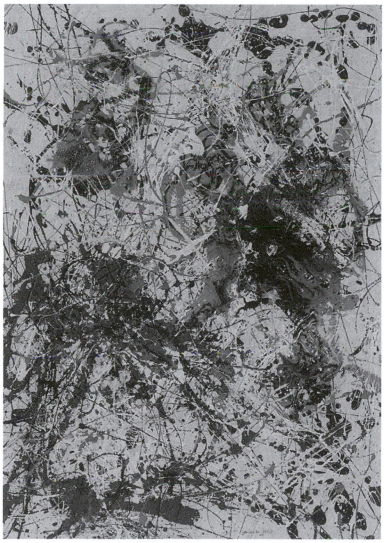

Figure 7.5. Jackson Pollock, *Number 12, 1949* (1949). Enamel on paper, mounted on fibreboard. The Museum of Modern Art, New York.

were produced by laying a large canvas or sheet of paper on the studio floor and dripping paint onto it from a brush or squirting from a syringe. They have no subject matter (they are not *about* anything) and make no attempt to distinguish between foreground and background. Pollock's action paintings are not a window onto a world but are themselves objects in this world. In a development of the Enlightenment theme of individual autonomy, the art critic Harold Rosenberg understands action painting in terms of freedom: 'The gesture on the canvas was a gesture of liberation from value – political, aesthetic, moral'. In 2006 Pollock's drip painting *No. 5* (1948) became the most expensive canvas ever auctioned, selling to an anonymous buyer for a reputed $140 million.

The highpoint of the move to abstraction was the Suprematism of Kasimir Malevich (1879-1935), intended to throw aside 'art-ideas, concepts and images' in favour of a 'desert in which nothing can be perceived but feeling'. This feeling could only be expressed through pure geometric forms set against pure emptiness. Commenting in *The Manifesto of Suprematism* (1926) on his *Black Square*, a solid black square on a white ground hung in the corner of a room like a Russian icon in its first exhibition of 1905, Malevich insists that 'this is no "empty square" which I had exhibited but rather the feeling of non-objectivity'. At the end of this journey of abstraction, God's-eye view objectivity has vanished and been replaced by an extreme abstraction that occupies the empty place left by the departed deity.

Modernist literature: Joyce and Kafka

The move from realism to Cubism in painting is shadowed in literary modernism by both a growing subjective inwardness and increasing artistic self-reference. Even the title of James Joyce's (1882-1941) *Ulysses* suggests a self-aware literary reference in its nod to Homer's foundational text of Western epic poetry. Joyce's modernist epic is not the heroic story of a warrior returning from the Trojan War but twenty-four hours in the life of a bourgeois Dubliner by the name of Leopold Bloom. Two of the book's eighteen chapters are written as a 'stream of consciousness', a device characteristic of literary modernism that directly inscribes the often haphazard and loosely connected inner thoughts of a character without systematisation or sometimes even without punctuation. The modernist author and critic Virginia Woolf (1882-1941) said that the technique should 'make us feel ourselves seated at the centre of another mind'. The intense and demanding punning and rhythmical word-play of *Ulysses* is indicative of a modernist desire to burst the bounds of customary classifications, blurring the distinction between poetry and prose. It is also indicative of the modernist trend to shun 'low' art in favour of a highly challenging literature that makes few concessions to its reader, a trend amusingly illustrated in the 'Calypso' chapter of *Ulysses* when Bloom uses a page from the popular magazine *Tit Bits* as toilet paper. On 16 June every year, on the anniversary of Joyce's first walk through Dublin with his future wife Nora Barnacle, Joyce aficionados celebrate the 'Bloomsday' pilgrimage, touring the parts of the city that feature in Joyce's book.

We can trace the trajectory of modernist alienation back through the Romantic artist, through Enlightenment autonomy and the Cartesian *cogito*, through the Reformation emphasis on individual conscience and back, once again, to Augustine's *Confessions*. In twentieth-century high modernism, this trajectory of increasingly alienated inwardness reaches a crisis, and it is nowhere more powerfully epitomised than in the novels and short stories of Franz Kafka (1883-1924). Whereas the isolated Romantic self is a heroic and potent Creator, the modernist individual is alienated, alone and lost in a the technological and bureaucratic machine of the modern urban labyrinth. Kafka's antiheroes inhabit nameless places and exist dislocated from their families, from any working normality and from reality itself. The sudden irruption into the narrative of inexplicable events suggests the working of some unnamed and menacing primeval power haunting the modern world, a power that is rarely if ever questioned within Kafka's writing. His novella *The Metamorphosis* begins with the line 'One morning, as Gregor Samsa was waking up from anxious dreams, he discovered that in his bed he had been changed into a monstrous verminous bug'. The sense of unease in the novella comes as much from Gregor's failure to question the normality of such an event as from the grotesque nature of the metamorphosis itself. The transformation is, to be sure, inconvenient, and Gregor must seek to find ways round it, but in a world of modernist alienation there is nothing to be done but to cope with his new identity as best he can.

Modernist music: Debussy, Stravinsky, Schoenberg

The development from Romanticism to modernism in music is a story of increasing freedom and experimentation. Beethoven had already begun to subordinate musical form to expressive intent and, at the close of the nineteenth and beginning of the twentieth centuries, composers sought freedom from the diatonic tonal system, the fundamental grammar of Western music since Bach. Diatonic tonal compositions are given a key signature, meaning that one pitch or harmony is central to a given piece (for example Beethoven's Symphony No. 3 <u>in E flat major</u>, key signature underlined). The key lends the piece coherence and, so to speak, an identity. However, late nineteenth and early twentieth century music sought to free itself in ever more dramatic ways from this diatonic system.

In Richard Wagner's (1813-1883) opera *Tristan and Isolde* (1859) the tonal system is manipulated by the introduction of series of chords which are tonally ambiguous (that is to say, they do not privilege any one note), and further innovations are introduced by Claude Debussy (1862-1918) and Igor Stravinsky (1882-1971). Debussy's *Prelude to the Afternoon of a Faun* (1894) elevates timbre to an organising principle of music equivalent to rhythm, harmony or pitch. He creates structure by introducing and sustaining certain instrumental combinations, at the same time disobeying diatonic rules of harmony that prescribe the resolution of dissonance. This innovation was not to everyone's taste. Composer and pianist Ferruccio Busoni wrote of *Prelude to the Afternoon of a Faun* that 'It is like a beautiful sunset; it fades as one looks at it', and writer and critic Louis Schneider dismissed Debussy's *La Mer* (*The Sea*) with the words: 'By dint of looking through the end of his opera glasses, Debussy gives us the impression not of the ocean but of the basin at the Tuileries Gardens'. Debussy's style has been called a musical impressionism (though he disliked the term intensely), a style that renounces the fierce contours of Romantic self-expressive programme music like Berlioz's *Symphonie Fantastique* in favour of a musical tone akin to the soft and subtle plays of light rendered in Impressionist painting. Stravinsky's *The Rite of Spring* (1913), which unleashed not a rite but a riot at its Paris première in 1913, introduces unheard-of experimentation with asymmetric rhythm and harsh 'primitive' dissonances, freeing the music from any customary conformity to regular time signatures. Through transgressing rhythmical norms, Stravinsky harnesses rhythm in a new way to serve his dramatic and expressive purposes.

As with modernist art, this trajectory of freedom reaches its climax with the move from Impressionism to Expressionism, and with the project of the German expressionist composer Arnold Schoenberg (1874-1951) to 'emancipate' dissonance. Schoenberg's *Pierrot Lunaire* (*Moonstruck Pierrot*, 1912) is a setting of twenty-one poems by the Belgian poet Albert Giraud composed in an atonal style, that is to say, without privileging any particular harmony or tonal key. The ensemble of five instruments Schoenberg required for *Pierrot Lunaire* (piano, clarinet, flute, violin and cello) has become so standard in Western music that it is simply called the Pierrot ensemble. The work also experiments with the human voice, employing the *Sprechstimme* technique (German: 'speech-voice') in which the pitch of sung notes is raised and lowered in a way that replicates the tonality of speech.

The frenzied experimentation and paralysing alienation of modernism both opened new horizons for the Western sensibility and also threatened, in the words of Nietzsche's madman, to wipe away those horizons. This trajectory of freedom was both liberating and incapacitating for the high modernism of the first decades of the twentieth century, leading the sociologist Zygmunt Bauman in his *Intimations of Postmodernity* (1992) to characterise modernity as 'a long march to prison'. After Malevich's Suprematism it is difficult to see how the drive to ever greater abstraction can be sustained, and in his later compositions (after 1923) Schoenberg introduced the artifice of twelve-tone composition, in which each of the twelve notes on the chromatic scale (the black and white keys in an octave range on the piano) has to be played once before any can be repeated. Such an arbitrarily imposed constraint is indicative of the need for some system or structure, even if it is an artificial one, in order to mitigate the abyss of freedom proclaimed by Nietzsche's madman. One powerful way of re-thinking freedom after God was celebrated in the chic cafés and bistros of post-war Paris, and it went by the name of existentialism.

Existentialism

The cultural context into which existentialism arrived was one of bleakness and fatigue. The Second World War had exacted somewhere near sixty million casualties, and the sense of pointlessness that existentialism sought to overcome is nowhere more vividly seen than in the plays and novels of Samuel Beckett (1906-1989). Beckett holds the peculiar record of being the only Nobel prize-winner to appear in the Wisden Almanac, the authoritative yearly record of the cricketing world. A left-hand opening batsman, Beckett represented Dublin University in matches against Northamptonshire in 1925 and 1926. Off the field, Beckett's plays paint a humorously pessimistic picture of a society limping forward, disorientated and exhausted, after two World Wars, shorn of its guiding values and anticlimactically failing to enjoy a pointless freedom. Vladimir and Estragon, the two main characters in *Waiting for Godot* (première 1953), are free to speak, come and go as they will, but there is 'nothing to be done'. Throughout the play these two tramp-like characters seek to pass the time (though 'it would have passed in any case') putting off and on their shoes and hats and amusing themselves with endless misunderstandings and wordplays. It is a theatre of exhaustion where the only remaining *logos* is to be found in the structures and conventions of language that spins like a frictionless wheel in midair. The critic Vivian Mercier gently teased Beckett for having 'achieved a theoretical impossibility – a play in which nothing happens, yet that keeps audiences glued to their seats. What's more, since the second act is a subtly different reprise of the first, he has written a play in which nothing happens, twice.' The rhythms and resolutions of Aristotelian tragedy and comedy can no longer be used to represent a world without any certain *telos* or *logos*. The death of God and the exhaustion of a war-ravaged humanity may have brought freedom, but not in a way that can be welcomed. Freedom from structure and the suprasensory yields a life drained of meaning, so that for Beckett the human condition is that 'they give birth astride a grave, the light gleams an instant, then it's night once more'.

Beckettian exhaustion is not the only response to the twentieth century's abyss of freedom, however. Playwright, novelist and philosopher Albert Camus (1913-1960) sought to find meaning and purpose through elaborating an understanding of human existence as absurd (Figure 7.6). The state of 'absurdity' for Camus is a tension between two irreconcilable things. On one hand there is the human desire for meaning, clarity and wholeness, a futile desire that does not correspond to anything in the world (hence the broken line in the diagram). On the other hand there is the irrational silence of a world that frustrates this desire, a world

Camus' absurd

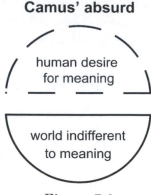

Figure 7.6.

that won't shed a tear when we die. It is a tension present already in Cervantes, a tension that in fact structures the experience of Western modernity as a whole.

We can best appreciate how Camus intends the absurd to be understood by looking at the way he rewrites the ancient myth of Sisyphus. In the Greek myth, King Sisyphus is condemned by the god Tartarus for trying to trick his way out of Hades, and his punishment is that he must unendingly try to roll a great stone up to the top of a mountain, only to see it roll down again just as he reaches the top. Returning to the foot of the mountain, Sisyphus must start all over again in a futile and never-ending cycle. Thus far the story could be Beckettian, but Camus turns Sisyphus' torture into his dignity and turns Sisyphus himself from a figure of despair into a hero of the absurd. For Camus, Sisyphus transforms his torment into a victory through realising and accepting the absurd nature of his existence in Hades. Sisyphus does not seek to make his task somehow supernaturally meaningful, rather he effects a change within himself, an internal acceptance of the appalling truth of his fate. He does not confront the gods but works to make their imposed torture the very basis of his dignity. Camus' summary of Sisyphus' condition strikes a modestly triumphal note:

> I leave Sisyphus at the foot of the mountain! One always finds one's burden again. But Sisyphus teaches the higher fidelity that negates the gods and raises rocks. He too concludes that all is well. The universe henceforth without a master seems to him neither sterile nor futile. Each atom of that stone, each mineral flake of that night-filled mountain, in itself forms a world. The struggle itself towards the heights is enough to fill a man's heart. One must imagine Sisyphus happy.

In time this 'one must' would be unpicked and the Camusean manner of negotiating a godless universe through acknowledging the absurdity of the human condition would be broadly rejected, but in the Paris of the 1950s it provided for many a compelling new ethos, a new way of coping with life for a world that had long since lost faith in both Enlightenment reason and Romantic heroism.

In *L'Etranger* (1942, variously translated *The Stranger* or *The*

Outsider) Camus developed a new style of fiction to reflect the condition of human absurdity. It is a style that breaks both with a nineteenth-century realism that still maintains a traditional 'literary' style and also with the high-minded sophistication of Joyce's modernism. Camus' style in *L'Etranger* is described by the literary theorist Roland Barthes (1915-1980) as 'writing degree zero', a 'basic speech' that 'achieves a style of absence which is almost an ideal absence of style; writing is then reduced to a sort of negative mood in which the social or mythical characters of a language are abolished in favour of a neutral and inert state of form'. The modernist's alienated individual is replaced by the existentialist's cool and neutral impassivity.

The most famous Parisian existentialist of the 1950s and 1960s, and one of the twentieth century's most influential philosophers of freedom, was Jean-Paul Sartre (1905-1980). For Sartre, human existence simply is freedom. A stone cannot choose how to be a stone; it is self-identical, it simply is what it is. A human being however is not self-identical but self-conscious, and must choose how it is to be in the world. For Sartre, we cannot avoid this free choice; in *Existentialism and Humanism* (1946) he argues that 'we are a freedom which chooses, but we do not choose to be free. We are condemned to freedom'.

With no God from whom to seek guidance as to the meaning of our lives, we must each choose our destiny and our identity for ourselves. We can either choose to abdicate our responsibility by simply assuming the roles and identities presented to us by our circumstances – Sartre calls this 'bad faith' – or we can assume the responsibility of our freedom and choose our own destiny. For Sartre this responsibility to choose is not dependent on our circumstances. Even under torture, he argues, the victim is free to choose to speak or to remain silent: 'it is necessary to understand this: the limit imposed does not come from the action of others [...] even torture does not dispossess us of our freedom; when we give in, we do so *freely*'. In 1959 Sartre's complete works were put on the Catholic index of prohibited books, and his commitment to freedom led him to be one of only two people ever voluntarily to refuse a Nobel Prize (Sartre was offered the Nobel Prize for literature in 1964) with the words 'a writer must refuse to allow himself to be transformed into an institution'. The other refusal was the 1973 Peace Prize, offered to Le Duc Tho (1911-1990) for his work on the Paris Peace Accords, intended to stop the fighting in Vietnam. He refused on the basis that there was no real peace in Vietnam. For the record, the 1958 Prize for Literature was almost refused by Boris Pasternack, but his own refusal was refused by the Nobel committee and the prize was eventually received posthumously by his son Yevgeny Pasternak in 1989.

By the 1960s the West had discovered that freedom was both an emancipation and an incarceration, and the long process of finding a way to live in the world after the death of God had begun. We shall pick up this thread again in the final chapter when we turn to consider postmodernism. Before that, however, we need to trace one further thread that fundamentally shaped the culture and life of the West in the twentieth and twenty-first centuries: the changes in the understanding of human beings brought about by Charles Darwin, Karl Marx, Sigmund Freud, and twentieth-century feminism.

Evolving Ideas of Humanity: Darwin, Marx, Freud and Feminism

The size of Darwin's nose almost prevented him from making the famous voyage that led to his theory of evolution. Captain of HMS Beagle, Vice Admiral Robert FitzRoy was a physiognomist, believing that he could judge a person's character from the relative size and position of his facial features. As Darwin recounts in his autobiography, FitzRoy 'doubted whether any one with my nose could possess sufficient energy and determination for the voyage'. Happily, the nose finally passed muster and Darwin took his place on the Beagle. Afterwards, a tongue-in-cheek Darwin records of FitzRoy that 'I think he was afterwards well satisfied that my nose had spoken falsely.' In this chapter we begin with the fruit of the observations Darwin made on his Beagle voyage and follow a path that runs parallel to the story of the death of God, considering how the West's understanding of humanity underwent a series of profound changes in the nineteenth and twentieth centuries. The journey will take us from Darwin's biology through the political economy of Karl Marx and the psychoanalysis of Sigmund Freud, all the way to late twentieth-century feminism.

Charles Darwin (1809-1882)

After abandoning medical training in Edinburgh and studying in preparation for ordination in the Church of England in Cambridge, in 1831 Charles Darwin set sail on HMS Beagle to survey Cape Horn, off the southern coast of Chile. During the voyage Darwin filled fourteen small notebooks with information concerning the animals he observed during excursions from the ship. The ideas that matured in Darwin's mind during the twenty years following his return in 1836 were systematically set down in *The Origin of Species* (1859) and *The Descent of Man* (1871). Darwin's ideas and their subsequent reception produced a number of important challenges to Western humanity's view of itself and its world, alike in their impact to Copernicus' *De revolutionibus* or Einstein's three 'golden year' papers of 1905.

The Origin of Species (1859)

Charles' father Robert Darwin married Susannah Wedgewood, daughter and heiress of the Josiah Wedgewood who made his fortune pioneering the manufacture of premium 'Jasperware' porcelain known for its signature blue matte finish and white cameo work. On Josiah's death Susannah's inheritance of £25,000 (equivalent to over £2.5 million today) was to secure for Charles the freedom to pursue his scientific interests without the need to earn a living. Thus it was that, after more than twenty years' of thought and research, Darwin was able to publish his *On the Origin of Species by Means of Natural Selection, or the Preservation of Favoured Races in the Struggle for Life* (1859). The book stamped its mark from the beginning, the twelve hundred and fifty copies of its first edition selling out on the day of publication. In the *Origin of Species* Darwin builds his central idea of natural selection on four observed tendencies in the natural world, none of them absolute but all verifiable:

- First, animals reproduce at an exponential rate that often exceeds the amount of food available and that far exceeds the ratio needed to maintain the species at a constant population.
- Secondly, despite this level of reproduction populations do not increase exponentially because, while some offspring survive, others perish.
- Thirdly, there appear in the offspring of every species minor variations (differences in height, colour and so on). Some of these variations will provide the individual with a slight advantage in the struggle for survival, and if that individual breeds its advantage will be passed to its own offspring.
- Fourthly, animals with variations that offer a slightly better chance of survival will pass those variations down the generations slightly more often than those without the advantage, and over time these variations will spread through the population. Individuals less suited to survive will gradually be replaced.

So by 'natural selection' Darwin means that, as a result of environmental conditions, some individuals in a given generation are slightly more likely to survive and reproduce than others. Over time, and owing to the tendency of those individuals in a species who are most different from each other to diverge further, this can result in the evolution of new species.

Perhaps the major provocation to Western thought in the *Origin of Species* was, like Nietzsche's death of God, its challenge to the idea that there exists a suprasensory realm of Platonic Forms and, by extension, its challenge to the idea that constancy and Being is more fundamental than change and becoming. For Plato, the Forms are eternal and unchanging: to participate in the Form of a dog is the same at any moment in history. Darwin's gradualism, however, makes it very problematic to hold to such a theory of essences in the case of living organisms, and the way in which terms like 'dog' are to be understood must fundamentally change. In the biological domain change is primary, and perceived constancy is only an illusion created by very slow change. Whereas for Plato Being was the primary ontological category and becoming was derivative of Being, the theory of evolution sees the 'being' of different species as a transitory effect of their gradual becoming. Thus Darwinism as a philosophy performs an overturning of Platonism. Darwin is well aware of this in the *Origin of Species*, where he refers to species as 'merely artificial combinations made for convenience'. In stressing the primacy of becoming over Being, evolution strikes one of the major emphases that would be central to late twentieth-century postmodern thought.

As for broader philosophical implications of evolution, the picture is more complicated. Natural selection can be pressed into serving a number of different Darwinisms that use it as a frame for different philosophical positions. Sir Julian Huxley (1887-1975) is the exponent of one such position, maintaining in the *Rationalist Annual* of 1946 that 'after Darwin it was no longer necessary to deduce the existence of divine purpose for the facts of biological adaptation'. In his *Chance and Necessity* (1971), the French biologist Jacques Monod maintains that 'chance alone is at the source of every innovation, of all creation in the biosphere', and that this is 'the sole conceivable hypothesis', where 'conceivable' means 'the only one that squares with observable and tested fact'. Similarly, evolution has led to both positive and negative assessments of human freedom. On the positive side, Sir Julian Huxley writes that 'man's destiny is to be the sole agent for the future evolution of this planet'. A more cautious position is voiced in Darwin's autobiography, with reference to the 'grand conclusion' of the evolutionary hypothesis: 'But then arises the doubt: can the mind of man, which has, as I fully believe, been developed from a mind as low as that possessed by the lowest animal, be trusted when it draws such grand conclusions?'

The Descent of Man (1871)

Partly as a result of the heated polemic that was unleashed by the *Origin of Species*, in 1871 Darwin published *The Descent of Man*, a volume with a threefold aim:

> The sole object of this work is to consider, firstly, whether man, like every other species, is descended from some pre-existing form; secondly, the manner of his development; and thirdly, the value of the differences between the so-called races of man.

In *The Descent of Man* Darwin seeks to counter arguments for the uniqueness of human reason and ethics by seeking to show how human reason, sympathy and an appreciation of beauty are present to a much lesser degree in other species, arguing that 'the difference in mind between man and the higher animals, great as it is, certainly is one of degree and not of kind'. He combines this with a catalogue of the anatomical similarities between humanity and other species and concludes that, despite all his 'noble qualities', man 'still bears in his bodily frame the indelible stamp of his lowly origin'.

Figure 8.1. Cartoon entitled *Man is But a Worm*, from
Punch's Almanack (6 December 1881).

It can be argued that the account of human evolution had a more profound effect on the West's view of itself than the Copernican Revolution. Darwinian evolution takes away from humankind its place as the inevitable *telos* of the natural world (though Julian Huxley can still talk of man's 'destiny' in the quotation above). This was well understood by Adam Sedgwick (1785-1873), Darwin's former biology professor at Cambridge, who in an unfavourable review of *The Descent of Man* complained that the book 'utterly repudiates final causes, and thereby indicates a demoralised understanding on the part of its advocates'. 'Demoralised' here means free of morals: Sedgwick is arguing that there is no morality, no natural goodness in evolution, as there was with Aristotle's final causes.

The Descent of Man was received with mockery in some quarters. A cartoon from the English satirical magazine *Punch* from 1881 pictures a bearded Darwin surrounded by apes with the caption 'Man is but a Worm' (Figure 8.1). It would be a mistake to think that Christians from the first set themselves against Darwin's position. Early Christian reception of Darwin's findings was rather unremarkable. Darwin records in the *Origin of Species* itself that

> a celebrated author and divine has written to me that he has gradually learned to see that it is just as noble a conception of the Deity to believe that he created a few original forms capable of self-development into other and needful forms, as to believe that he required a fresh act of creation to supply the voids caused by the action of his laws.

By the early 1870s the overwhelming majority of American Protestant zoologists and botanists accepted some form of evolution, and the historian James Moore in *The Post-Darwinian Controversies* concludes that 'with but few exceptions the leading Christian thinkers in Great Britain and America came to terms quite readily with Darwinism and evolution'. The tide turned for some in the early 1920s, however, and an increasing hostility developed between Darwinism and many religious commentators, particularly in the United States. Darwinism was increasingly seen by believers and nonbelievers alike as an alternative and rival to the biblical account of creation in Genesis 1.

The deepest implications of philosophical Darwinism for the Western ethos are not, however, in the nature and extent of the contradictions between evolution and Genesis, but in the way in which philosophical Darwinism rewrites the story that humanity tells about itself. Instead of seeing itself in terms of a narrative with a definite beginning, a period of meaningful progress and an end, humanity now contemplates its status as one moment in a process of constant becoming, imperceptibly evolved from 'other lower animals' and eventually to be surpassed by descendents more suitably adapted to their environment than we are. Evolution progresses not as a teleological line but a 'bush' (in the *Origin of Species* Darwin called it the tree of life), with any number of false starts and dead ends. Darwinism challenges the teleological view of history that places humanity necessarily at the centre of its own story.

One way found to reinstate humankind as the hero of its own narrative is to use its evolved intellect in order to take the process of evolution into its own hands. Julian Huxley first used the term 'social Darwinism' to describe this development in his *Evolution: The Modern Synthesis* (1942). *The Descent of Man* broaches what would become the central themes of social Darwinism when, in the chapter on 'Civilised Nations', Darwin notes that:

> There is reason to believe that vaccination has preserved thousands, who from a weak constitution would formerly have succumbed to small-pox. Thus the weak members of civilised societies propagate their kind. No one

who has attended to the breeding of domestic animals will doubt that this must be highly injurious to the race of man.

Nevertheless, Darwin explicitly distances himself from any proactive eugenic implications of this line of thinking, contenting himself with the more passive position that 'there should be open competition for all men; and the most able should not be prevented by laws or customs from succeeding best and rearing the largest number of offspring'. More problematic implications were embraced by other thinkers who drew Darwin's theories in the direction of social engineering. The philosopher and biologist Herbert Spencer (1820-1903) coined the term 'survival of the fittest' in his theory of social evolution, according to which society should allow the strongest to survive and the weakest to be consumed by poverty and disease. Eugenicists like Darwin's cousin Francis Galton (1822-1911) argued for measures to discourage the breeding of less fit human beings and to promote the breeding of the more fit.

Karl Marx (1818-1883)

The second lens through which we shall contemplate changing views of humanity in the late nineteenth century is given to us by Karl Marx. For Darwinian evolution humanity is no longer the hero of its own story in the same way as before, but Marx by contrast does develop a linear and teleological account of human history. Nevertheless, it is an account in which the human is under threat of being de-centred by overarching structures of social change. Marx's three-volume work *Das Kapital* (*Capital*, published 1867-1894) was written during long hours in the reading room of the British Museum in London, a regime that did not slacken even when Marx suffered a bout of haemorrhoids. He wrote in a letter of 1857 that, expecting a revolution in the near future, he was 'working madly through the nights', the task absorbing its author to such an extent that Marx was observed to neglect his personal hygiene. Unlike Darwin, Marx did not have an inheritance to support him, though he received financial support from Friedrich Engels, son of a Prussian textile manufacturer and co-author with Marx of the *Communist Manifesto*.

Hegel, Marx and historical progress

Before we can understand Marx's philosophy of history we first need to consider one major influence on his thinking: the dialectical idealism of the German philosopher Georg Wilhelm Friedrich Hegel (1770-1831). Hegel has done as much as any thinker to shape the modern world, and his dialectical view of history is fundamental to much later twentieth-century thinking. In his youth Hegel read both Enlightenment writers like Kant and Romantic poets like Klopstock and Hölderlin, and in his own philosophy of history he seeks to give an account of the final and inevitable reconciliation of such opposite tendencies in a way that challenges Nietzsche's later position that we must simply make a free choice between the 'logic of reason' and the 'logic of life'. In his *Lectures on the Philosophy of History* (given 1822-30, first published 1837) Hegel conceives of history as a progressive and evolving 'dialectic' that challenges Aristotelian logic, in particular Aristotle's law of non-contradiction. There are three stages in the Hegelian dialectic:

1. The stage of understanding. Two concepts are accepted as fixed and mutually exclusive (for example: 'being' and 'nothingness').
2. The stage of dialectical reason. The concepts are seen to harbour contradictions (if 'being' and 'nothingness' are absolute, how can anything ever come into being or cease to be?)
3. The stage of speculation or sublation (resolution in a higher unity). The two former categories are 'sublated' or 'passed over' and a new, higher category embraces them and resolves the contradiction uncovered at stage two ('becoming' embraces both 'being' and 'nothingness', and accounts for the seeming contradictions in those two lower categories).

The three stages are sometimes labelled 'thesis', 'antithesis' and 'synthesis', but Hegel uses these terms only in his critique of Kant, never in relation to his own thinking. Secondly, history for Hegel is the self-realisation of 'Spirit' (German: Geist), where Spirit is the force that controls the development of human society and culture. Spirit, because it is infinite, can endure contradictions (if it could not be both itself and its opposite it would not be infinite but would have a limit). The goal of world history is the unity of concept and reality, achieved as Absolute Spirit dialectically sublates everything lower than itself. To take one example, Hegel sees the move from Greek and Roman to Christian civilisation as a sublation of the Form/matter dualism of Plato into the motif of incarnation. According to this theory, world-historical figures (Alexander the Great, Julius Caesar, Napoleon I) are manipulated unknowingly by Spirit's 'cunning of reason' into bringing about the goal of Absolute Spirit. Hegel is in fact said to have declared, on meeting Napoleon I in Jena, that he had seen 'the World Spirit on horseback'.

The implications of Hegel's philosophy of history for the West are profound. As opposed to the Spenglerian model discussed in the previous chapter according to which history has no goal, Hegel's dialectical view of history preserves a sort of providence; history can be said to have a meaning, and a definite goal. But the progress of history is now dialectical, not merely linear. As with Darwin, a blow is struck here at the Platonic notion of Forms; the (moral, political, social) truths in any society are not eternal but part of the dialectical process of Spirit revealing itself in history. We see once more that the primacy of static Being and essence is replaced with becoming and existence.

Just as the Enlightenment had its moderate and radical wings, so also Hegel's followers split into two camps. 'Right-wing Hegelians' sought to combine Hegel's understanding of history with a broadly theistic view, whereas 'Left-wing Hegelians' understood Hegel's thought to be a fundamental assault on all religion. Marx, a Left-wing Hegelian, accepts Hegel's dialectical structure but rejects the idealism of Hegel's Spirit. In Marx's own dialectical materialism, historical change is not brought about by Spirit but by material conditions and relations of production (that is: who owns the means of production in a society, who does the producing, and what the relationship is between the two groups). History is a class struggle in which the proletariat (the working class) is destined to overthrow the control of the bourgeoisie (the middle class) through a revolution leading to a classless society, just as surely as, for Hegel, Spirit is destined to realise itself in history. This pattern of revolutionary history resembles the Christian shape of creation-fall-redemption, and in *The Opium of the Intellectuals* French philosopher and sociologist Raymond Aron (1905-1983) identifies a 'secular religion' of Communism in which 'Marxist eschatology attributes to the proletariat the role of a collective saviour'.

The Communist Manifesto

For Marx it is material conditions that determine what, in previous centuries, would have been called 'human nature', and this focus on the material contributes to the displacement of Being by becoming in the West. For Marx human nature is not ahistorical, nor is it geographically universal. Rather, what Marx calls human 'species-being' is a function of both biological and social factors. Marx drew inspiration from the nineteenth-century atheistic philosopher Ludwig Feuerbach (1804-1872), and in the sixth of his *Theses on Feuerbach* (1845) he insists (against Feuerbach himself) that 'the essence of man is no abstraction inherent in each single individual. In reality, it is the ensemble of social relations'. In fact, history bears witness to 'a continuous transformation of human nature'.

Against the background of this view of history and humanity, the *Manifesto of the Communist Party* (1848) which Marx co-wrote with Friedrich Engels (1820-1895) is a call to the international proletariat to join together in overthrowing the rule of the bourgeoisie and bringing about the common ownership of property and the means of production. The *Manifesto* begins with the statement that 'the history of all hitherto existing society is the history of class struggles', and it climaxes with the rallying cry:

> The Communists disdain to conceal their views and aims. They openly declare that their ends can be attained only by the forcible overthrow of all existing social conditions. Let the ruling classes tremble at a Communistic revolution. The proletarians have nothing to lose but their chains. They have a world to win. Working Men of All Countries, Unite!

The nature and extent of this 'forcible overthrow' was to cause tensions among the Western inheritors of Marxism in the twentieth century. As opposed to the more peace-seeking socialists, the Russian Communists became intent on altering relations of production by force. Marx argued (in a Hegelian way) that history had to pass through a number of stages before the arrival of the classless society, stages including the rise and dominance of capitalism and then its inevitable collapse. For Vladimir Ilyich Lenin (1870-1924) and the Russian Bolshevik party however, this historical process could be short-circuited by a revolutionary vanguard who would seize power on behalf of the proletariat. The March 1917 Revolution in Russia saw the rise to power of Lenin's Bolsheviks and the creation of local 'soviets' or workers' councils. Lenin declared that the country was entering the Dictatorship of the Proletariat, and in the years following the First World War power was concentrated in the hands of the Bolsheviks, now renamed the Communist party. The division between the Communist East and capitalist West would be the defining axis of twentieth-century Western international relations. With the revelation of the brutalities of Joseph Stalin's (ruled 1924-1953) Communist regime, faith in the Communist hypothesis waned.

Marxism and culture

In Communist countries there developed a distinctively Marxist understanding of cultural production and cultural critique. Starting from the position that economic conditions determine consciousness and human nature, it is natural that a Marxist approach to art and literature should seek also to understand and critique the social structures that inform the production of texts. Perhaps the greatest Marxist cultural critic was the Hungarian Gyorgy Lukács (1885-1971), who denounced the alienated individual of Kafka's modernism and the Joycean stream of consciousness as decadent and politically impotent, preferring Honoré de Balzac's (1799-1850) realist novels that reflected his time and recent history. In his *History and Class Consciousness* (1923) Lukács gives primacy not to the individual consciousness but rather to 'class consciousness', an aspiration towards which a particular social class strives. Only the proletariat can in fact achieve class consciousness; the bourgeoisie have a 'false consciousness', mistakenly thinking that capitalism will last indefinitely and is not simply a stage on the way to socialist revolution.

Religion for Marx is also a form of false consciousness. In *A Contribution to the Critique of Hegel's Philosophy of Right* (1843) – where he also calls religion 'the opium of the people' – Marx argues that:

> The abolition of religion as the *illusory* happiness of the people is the demand for their *real* happiness. To call on them to give up their illusions about their condition is to call on them to give up a condition that requires illusions. The criticism of religion is, therefore, in embryo, the criticism of that vale of tears of which religion is the halo.

From 1929 onward the Russian Communist party called for a 'Socialist

Figure 8.2. Vera Mukhina, *Worker and Kolkhoz Woman* (1937).
Stainless steel. Russian Exhibition Centre, Moscow.

Realism', an aesthetic that exalts the power and achievements of the Revolution and of the Communist state. What Socialist Realism has in common with the realism of nineteenth-century writers like Flaubert and Balzac is a desire to provide a faithful reflection of the whole of lived reality, rather than a sanitised or partial view. It was also expected to endorse the Marxist aspiration of a classless society and to be accessible to the proletariat which would bring that society about. Art was not to distract from social realities but to illuminate them. The 24.5 metre high statue *Worker and Kolkhoz Woman* (Figure 8.2) is an icon of Socialist Realism, made to stand atop the Soviet pavilion at the 1937 World's Fair in Paris. The worker and the woman together hold the Soviet hammer and sickle emblem as they thrust energetically forward toward the Communist eschaton of the classless society.

Sigmund Freud (1856-1939)

Marx's insistence that the ownership of the means of production is an important factor in the sculpting of human nature, and his position that this ownership can be controlled and made to serve humanity, were rejected by the psychoanalyst Sigmund Freud. Freud took an altogether gloomier view of the human condition. Unlike other theories of the mind in the early twentieth century, Freud's Austrian school of psychoanalysis chose to base its study on mental illness, wagering that an understanding of how the mind breaks down will also yield a template for its proper working. Two distinctives characterise Freud's approach, his focus on child sexuality and the importance he ascribes to the unconscious mind.

The Oedipus complex

In *The Interpretation of Dreams* (1899) Freud sought to account for the neuroses and psychoses in adult patients in terms of traumatic sexual encounters they had experienced as children. Although the book was published in 1899 it appeared with a publication date of 1900 in order to signal its importance for the new century, an importance which was not immediately apparent as the book sold only three hundred copies in its first six years of publication. Nevertheless, its importance for the development of Western thought in the twentieth century is now securely established and its explanation of the 'Oedipus complex' has become one of the most influential of Freud's ideas. Freud begins by asking why the Greek myth of King Oedipus – who unknowingly murders his father and marries his mother – still has such a strong hold on the modern mind. Answering his own question, he argues that:

> His destiny moves us only because it might have been ours – because the oracle laid the same curse upon us before birth as upon him. It is the fate of all of us, perhaps, to direct our first sexual impulse towards our mother and our first hatred and our first murderous wish against our father.

What the Oedipus complex explains, Freud continues, is that male children are attracted to their mothers and jealous of their fathers. Freudians normally date the beginning of the Oedipus complex to the age of three to five years, when the child stops having an almost incestuous relationship with the mother and begins to see his father as a threat. At first the Oedipus complex was a theory only of male child sexuality, and in his early work on the idea Freud assumes a primal state in which only maleness exists. Females have been 'symbolically castrated' and are constituted by a fundamental lack of male genitals, causing them to suffer from 'penis envy'. Freud's attitude to the 'dark continent' of the female psyche is the cause of much heated debate, some of which we shall consider below in relation to feminism.

The unconscious

After child sexuality, the second important focus of Freudian psychoanalysis is the unconscious. Freud was not the first to evoke the unconscious; Nietzsche in *The Will to Power* (published posthumously from Nietzsche's notes) makes use of the term in his description of dreams. In turn, Freud hailed dreams as the 'the royal road to the unconscious', arguing that they represent, in disguised form, the fulfilment of unconscious wishes, usually of a sexual nature. In the unconscious we find everything that has been repressed (shut out) from the conscious mind but that nevertheless still manifests itself in slips of the tongue, memory lapses and some jokes.

Freud elaborated two topographies – or maps – of the human mind. His first contains the elements 'unconscious', 'preconscious' and 'conscious', and Marcel Gauchet (born 1946) has argued in *The Cerebral Unconscious* (1992) that this first topography draws on Romantic roots. In Figure 8.3 I have sought to represent Freud's unconscious as a modified Romanticism, with the repressed unconscious providing the ultimate, arational, inexpressible significance of the human mind, and the everyday conscious mind containing rational meanings of only secondary significance. In Freud's second topography of the mind, he identifies three elements, usually translated into English as ego, id and superego.

**Freud's
unconscious**

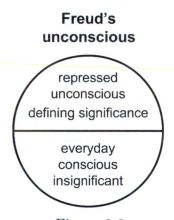

Figure 8.3.

- 'Id' translates the German 'das Es', literally 'the it'. It is a reservoir of libido and energy, described by Freud as 'the dark, inaccessible part of our personality' and 'a chaos, a cauldron full of seething excitations'.
- The ego, in German 'das Ich' ('the I'), sits in between the id and the superego, constantly threatened by both of them. It is the conscious, thinking part of the mind, the 'I am thinking' of Descartes' *cogito*. Freud describes the ego in its relation to the id as 'like a man on horseback, who has to hold in check the superior strength of the horse'.
- The superego becomes important when a child emerges from the Oedipus complex. It is an inner policeman that internalises the

prohibitions on sexual relations with the mother, and is often associated with law and commandment.

Freud's second topography of the psyche is an important factor contributing to the change in the West's understanding of humanity in the twentieth century because it destroys a Cartesian understanding of the self as a thinking thing. The *cogito* requires a thinking that is transparent to itself, in other words the 'I' who is thinking and the 'I' who exists must be the same 'I'. But this is not what we find in Freud's second topography, where the conscious ego is only one fragment of the psyche: the 'I am thinking' can no longer be equivalent to the 'I exist'.

This is part of what Freud sees as an ongoing humbling of humanity. In his *Introductory Lectures on Psychoanalysis* (1915) he argues that the 'naïve self-love of men' has suffered 'two major blows' at the hands of science. The first is associated with Copernicus, when Western man realised himself to be 'not the centre of the universe, but only a tiny speck in a world-system of a magnitude hardly conceivable'; the second is associated with Darwin, who 'destroyed man's supposedly privileged place in creation and proved his descent from the animal kingdom and his ineradicable animal nature'. Freud considers his own psychoanalysis to deliver a third blow, as he 'seeks to prove to the ego that it is not even master in its own house, but must content itself with scanty information of what is going on unconsciously in its mind'.

In *Civilisation and its Discontents* (1930) Freud delivers a gloomy account of Western society, rejecting the utopian hope of Rousseau or Marx that a change in society can bring about a change in human nature. Men are not gentle creatures, and aggressiveness was not created by property, Freud argues. Rather, aggressiveness 'forms the basis of every relation of affection and love among people (with the single exception, perhaps, of the mother's relation to her male child)'. Human culture for Freud is the acceptable expression of repressed sexuality and aggression, and 'the existence of civilisation presupposes the non-gratification (suppression, repression or something else?) of powerful instinctual urgencies'. Energy that cannot be expended sexually is channelled into secondary pursuits like art, literature and philosophy. During the First World War Freud's own family underwent severe deprivation; Freud even demanded payment for one of his academic papers in the currency of potatoes. His daughter Sophie died in 1920 of the 'Spanish influenza', numerically the worst epidemic in recorded history. The Spanish flu that ripped through a war-wearied Europe in 1918 and 1919 killed between twenty and forty million people, more than the Great War itself.

Like Marx, Freud's approach includes an attack on religion, which for Freud is the illusion that projects the human desire for a fatherly superego onto an imaginary 'Heavenly Father'. Striking again the Enlightenment note of autonomy, Freud argues that religion is a mental illness whose sufferers fail to leave behind their childhood dependency on a surrogate father figure. In *Moses and Monotheism* (1939) he expands on Ludwig

Feuerbach's (1872) argument that 'it is not, as in the Bible, that God created man in his own image. But, on the contrary, man created God in his own image.'

Freud considered psychoanalysis to be a strict science, and in his *New Introductory Lectures to Psychoanalysis* (1933) he argues for the exclusivity of what he calls the scientific worldview. This worldview asserts:

> that there is no other source of knowledge of the universe, but the intellectual manipulation of carefully verified observations, in fact, what is called research, and that no knowledge can be obtained from Revelation, intuition, or inspiration. [...] The bare fact is that truth cannot be tolerant and cannot admit compromise or limitations, that scientific research looks on the whole field of human activity as its own, and must adopt an uncompromisingly critical attitude towards any other power that seeks to usurp any part of its provenance.

Freud had a similar disdain for the scientific pretensions of philosophy, which 'must needs fall into pieces with every new advance in our knowledge'. Freud's position here is indicative of the growing marginalisation of a religious approach to knowledge in mainstream twentieth-century Western culture, along with growing claims that what Freud is calling here the scientific worldview is the solution to human problems in every sphere, the net to catch every fish.

Art, literature and the unconscious

The idea that the unconscious is the ultimate explanation for human behaviour is echoed in the artistic and literary movements that take inspiration in part from Freud. The use of Western rationality and technology in the service of the industrial slaughter of the First World War, coupled with the dehumanising bureaucracy of modern life portrayed so vividly by Kafka, led early twentieth-century avant-garde movements in Europe to turn away from reason in favour of emotion, the a-rational, the shocking and the violent.

Dada

Of all the early twentieth-century avant-garde movements, the most radical was 'Dada', named (so the story goes) after its originators opened a French dictionary at random and stuck in a penknife that happened to fall on the word *dada*, a child's term for a rocking horse or 'horsie'. For the Dadaists, all previous culture was decadent and dying, and had to undergo an apocalyptic destruction in order to clear the way for an eschatological new age. In making 'art' from garbage, writing nonsense poems and producing works created by chance rather than by the expressive intention of an artist, Dadaists sought to hasten this eschatology of Western reason and culture. With a strange Trinitarian echo, Dadaist Francis Picabia

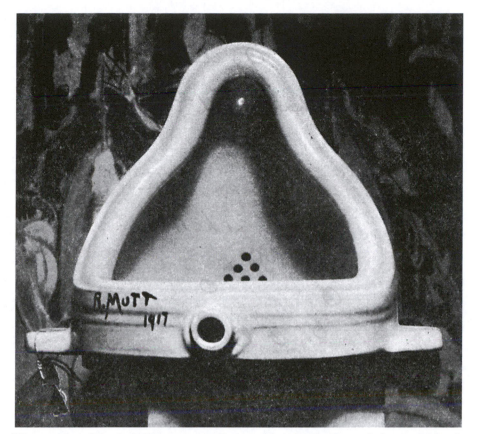

Figure 8.4. Marcel Duchamp, *Fountain* (1917). Porcelain and black paint. The original no longer exists.

(1879-1953) insists that 'the Dadaists are nothing, nothing, nothing and they will surely succeed in nothing, nothing, nothing'. An exhibition by Dadaists Hans Arp (1887-1966) Johannes Theodor Baargeld (1892-1927) and Max Ernst (1891-1976) in Cologne in 1920 featured a sculpture that the public was invited to destroy with an axe and an installation with urinals and obscene poetry. Following complaints, the exhibition was temporarily closed by the police.

In his early years Marcel Duchamp (1887-1968) was a painter in the Cubist mode, his most famous piece from this period being the *Nude Descending a Staircase, No. 2* of 1912. However, in part through his friendship with Picabia he renounced 'retinal art' that engages only the sense of sight, and began producing three-dimensional works that challenged the boundaries of what was considered as 'art'. His 'ready-mades' were mass-produced objects exhibited as works of art with little or no modification.

The most famous of Duchamp's ready-mades is *Fountain* (1917), a gentleman's urinal signed 'R Mutt' (Figure 8.4). Duchamp's ready-mades question and parody the norms and taboos of institutionalised art, rejecting the traditional understanding of art as the mimetic representation of reality and attacking conventions of taste and aesthetics. However, there is a danger inherent in this sort of avant-garde protest, and Duchamp fell into it. In time the very art world Duchamp was seeking to scandalise came to 'appreciate' and 'value' his rebellious work. In Hans Richter's *Dada* (1962), Duchamp laments that:

> When I discovered ready-mades I thought to discourage aesthetics. In Neo-Dada they have taken my ready-mades and found aesthetic beauty in them. I threw the bottle rack and the urinal in their faces and now they admire them for their aesthetic beauty.

In fact, time and again the gestures of destruction made by twentieth-century avant-garde movements like Dada become absorbed into the culture they were seeking to reject or destroy. This was a lesson that the postmodernists attempted to learn, when later in the century they sought not to oppose and destroy but rather to dislocate and disrupt.

Surrealism

The disruption of rational and aesthetic norms also plays an important part in the self-theorising of the Surrealist movement. Founded by André Breton (1896-1966) in 1924, Surrealism is notorious for a series of high-profile spats between its leading lights, including Breton himself, Louis Aragon (1897-1982), Antonin Artaud (1896-1948), Georges Bataille (1897-1962) and Salvador Dalí (1904-1989). When Dalí agreed to create Surrealist window displays in New York department stores and endorsed themed ashtrays and playing cards, Breton was so incensed that he anagrammatically renamed the treacherous Dalí 'Avida Dollars'.

Breton, who came to his understanding of Surrealism from his work as a psychiatrist involved with soldiers traumatised by the First World War, defined Surrealism in the following way:

> SURREALISM, n. Pure psychic automatism, by which it is intended to express, verbally, in writing, or by other means, the real process of thought. Thought's dictation, in the absence of all control exercised by the reason and outside all aesthetic or moral preoccupations.

As with William Blake a century previously, reason for Breton is an iron cage that stifles human freedom, the bars of which must be broken. Surrealism is a revolt against all forms of realism, against rationality itself, in an attempt to liberate unconscious creativity.

The Surrealists sought acceptance from Freud, but he was never as well disposed towards them as they were to him. They share Freud's interest in dreams, but for the Surrealists the unconscious is in more of a dialectic relationship with the rational mind than it is for Freud. Striking a rather Hegelian pose, Breton declares, 'I believe in the future resolution of those two apparently contradictory states, dream and reality, in a kind of absolute reality, of surreality.' This overcoming of contradiction as a means to a new, broader understanding can also be seen in the strange juxtapositions that the Surrealists were fond of making, juxtapositions that Breton described as 'beautiful as the chance meeting on a dissecting-table of a sewing-machine and an umbrella!' There is both an acknowledgment and a parodic rejection of the Hegelian dialectic in the way that such a juxtaposition of opposites produces a startling new effect, yet without being part of any overarching rational progress, either of the Spirit in history (as for Hegel) or of the overthrow of capitalism for the classless society (as for Marx).

Surrealist aesthetics sought to bypass the stifling control of the rational mind. The Surrealists practised 'automatic writing', the production of text in a state of trance or loss of rational control, as a way of achieving Breton's 'pure psychic automatism'. Another means to bypass the censorship of the rational mind was chance. The story is told of how a group of Surrealists would gather at 54 Rue du Château, in the 14th arrondissement of Paris and play parlour games, the most famous of which was named 'the exquisite corpse', known to many children as the game of 'consequences'. Each participant in turn would write one phrase of a sentence, fold over the paper, and pass it to the next contributor, not knowing what the others had written before. Apparently, the first time the game was played the final sentence read 'Le cadavre exquis boira le vin nouveau' ('The exquisite corpse will drink the new wine'), and the name stuck. For Breton, 'with the Exquisite Corpse we had at our command an infallible way of holding the critical intellect in abeyance, and of fully liberating the mind's metaphorical activity'.

Twentieth-century feminism

Twentieth- century feminism both reinforced and reacted against many of the positions we have sketched so far in relation to Hegel, Darwin, Marx and Freud. Feminism shadows Marx's account of the inevitable overthrow of the bourgeoisie by the proletariat, substituting oppressed women for the oppressed proletariat and the oppressive masculine order for Marx's bourgeois ownership of the means of production. Broadly, feminism asserts two premises: (1) that throughout the history of Western culture there has been an inequality of the sexes, with women suffering economic, sexual, vocational or cultural oppression at the hands of men and the structures of society made by men, and (2) that this oppression is unjust. Feminism seeks to emancipate or liberate women from various forms of oppression, and so it can be understood as one more example of the broader movement in twentieth-century Western culture against hierarchical or fixed structures: the overturning of Being and Platonic essences in favour of becoming. In the discussion below we shall seek to understand twentieth-century feminism in terms of what have come to be known as its three 'waves'.

First-wave feminism

The concerns expressed in twentieth-century Western feminism are by no means absent in previous eras. In England Mary Wollstonecraft's

(1759-1797) *A Vindication of the Rights of Woman* (1792) is an attack on Rousseau's educational philosophy and in particular on *Emile* (1762), his treaty on education. Rousseau insists that 'a woman's education must be planned in relation to man' such that 'she will never be free to set her own opinion above his'. Wollstonecraft replies that 'if women be educated for dependence, that is, to act according to the will of another fallible being, and submit, right or wrong, to power, where are we to stop?' In post-revolutionary France, Olympe de Gouges (1748-1793) penned the *Declaration of the Rights of Woman and the Female Citizen* (1791), claiming that if 'women have the right to mount the scaffold, they should also have the right to mount the tribune'. She was guillotined in 1793.

First-wave feminism refers to the campaign in the early decades of the twentieth century for the democratic enfranchisement of women. Most iconically, first-wave feminism is associated with the female suffragists, nicknamed 'suffragettes'. In Britain, suffrage for women householders over the age of thirty was granted in 1918, with the age lowered to twenty-one and granted to all women over that age in 1928. Only in 1970 was the age further lowered to eighteen for both sexes. Suffrage was granted to women in France in 1944 (although before that time suffrage had nevertheless, and rather problematically, still been called 'universal'), and in the USA the nineteenth amendment to the Constitution, passed in 1920, confirmed and formalised the trend whereby 'the right of citizens of the United States to vote shall not be denied or abridged by the United States or by any state on account of sex'.

It is no coincidence that the granting of female suffrage coincides in many cases with the end of the two world wars. Women had 'manned' the factories and offices during the wars, gaining a new freedom that did not evaporate with the return of peace. The First World War brought about a great social revolution, with the state requiring women to leave the family home and to leave their jobs serving the middle and upper classes in order to take on work which they had previously been considered unfit or incapable of performing. As well as working in munitions factories, women undertook heavy labour on farms.

In 1903 Emmeline Pankhurst (1858-1928) and her three daughters formed the *Women's Social and Political Union*, campaigning for adult female suffrage in the UK and the USA. The group rose to the forefront of British national consciousness through heckling political speeches, violently resisting arrest and maintaining hunger strikes when imprisoned, leading in some cases to episodes of violent force feeding. On 22 May 1914 suffragist Mary Richardson damaged five paintings in the National Gallery in London. In response to similar attacks, the National Gallery and British Museum closed their doors until further notice, and the British Museum announced that it would only in future admit women who could produce a letter from a man 'willing to be responsible for their behaviour'. In June 1913 suffragist Emily Davidson threw herself under the King's horse Anmer at the Epsom Derby, dying of her injuries four days later, and in 1914 a performance in His Majesty's Theatre attended by King George V was interrupted by one suffragist shouting 'you Russian Tsar!' and another climbing onto the stage to make a speech.

Second-wave feminism

With adult female suffrage secured in the West, feminism moved on. The second wave was the 'women's liberation movement' of the 1960s and 1970s, with its iconic media images of bra burning and slogans 'the personal is political', 'sisterhood is powerful' and 'rights not roses!' for Mother's Day. With Germaine Greer (born 1939), Betty Friedan (1921-2006) and Juliet Mitchell (born 1940) among its leading spokeswomen, second-wave feminism increasingly stressed cultural issues in addition to legal rights. In *The Feminine Mystique* (1963) Betty Friedan argued that Western culture forces women to acquire recognition through their roles as wives and mothers; it is the culture as a whole that is 'patriarchal'. It was second-wave feminism that secured reproductive rights, with the spread of the contraceptive pill (first approved in 1960 for use in the USA) and the widespread legalisation of abortion, allowing women – in the language of the Boston organisation 'Our Bodies Ourselves' – to take control of their own bodies.

One crucially important figure for second-wave feminism was Simone de Beauvoir (1908-1986), described by critic Carol Ascher as 'the mother of us all'. De Beauvoir was the intellectual companion of Jean-Paul Sartre, sharing Sartre's existentialist orientation. Sartre and de Beauvoir were also close personally, having met while Sartre was a student at the prestigious École Normale Supérieure in Paris and de Beauvoir was at the more modest Sorbonne. Their fifty-year open relationship allowed for 'contingent' lovers on both sides, as Sartre explains: 'To have such freedom, we had to suppress or overcome any possessiveness, any tendency to be jealous. In other words, passion. To be free, you cannot be passionate.' Sartre and de Beauvoir were also together in condemnation, her work finding its way onto the Catholic Index alongside his. Abortion was not legalised in France until 1974, but in 1971 de Beauvoir signed the 'Manifesto of the 343', a list of well-known women claiming to have undergone a termination.

In 1949, de Beauvoir published the first volume of her best-selling *The Second Sex*, sometimes called the Bible of feminism. She did not, however, conceive *The Second Sex* as a feminist text. In 1949 she still pinned her hopes for sexual equality on a Marxist revolution, with no need for a separate women's struggle, but this would change when, in 1974, she became president of the *Ligue du Droit des Femmes* (*League for Women's Rights*).

For de Beauvoir, there is no 'feminine human nature' or feminine essence that is different from a 'masculine human nature' or essence. Gender is, on the contrary, socially constructed. In other words little boys grow up as boys and little girls as girls because of the way they are treated and because of the expectations laid upon them by a society that conditions them to act in certain ways. This is summed up in the most widely quoted line from all of de Beauvoir's oeuvre: 'One is not born, but one becomes, a woman', in which we hear echoes of Sartre's own existentialist mantra 'existence precedes essence'. Both Sartre's and de Beauvoir's positions reinforce further the attack on Platonic Forms and the privileging of becoming over Being that has been a constant theme of the thinkers discussed in this chapter.

The first volume of *The Second Sex* opens strikingly with a single word question: 'Woman?' ('La femme?' in French), and in its argument de Beauvoir examines woman as 'other' to man:

> she is defined and differentiated with reference to man and not he with reference to her; she is incidental, the inessential as opposed to the essential. He is the subject, he is the absolute – she is the other.

Despite this subordination of the female 'other', de Beauvoir looks forward to a time when the drama of conflict between the sexes will be overcome by 'the free recognition of each individual in the other, each posing at once himself and the other as object and as subject in a reciprocal movement'.

Third-wave feminism

By the third wave of the 1980s and 1990s, feminism had also become a more established feature in the Western academic landscape. In the 1980s women's studies and gender studies courses multiplied on both sides of the Atlantic, and feminist publishing houses prospered. Linda Noclin's (born 1931) 'Why have there been no great women artists?' (1971) and Sandra Gilbert and Susan Gubar's *Madwoman in the Attic: The Woman Writer and the Nineteenth-Century Literary Imagination* (1979) are two milestones in the burgeoning field of feminist criticism or 'gynocritics', as Elaine Showalter (born 1941) called the sustained investigation of women's writing. If first-wave feminism focuses on legal discrimination, and second-wave feminism broadens the struggle to include cultural discrimination, then the third wave widens feminism's concerns in two further directions. It more fully includes considerations of race and class, and it scrutinises the very categories of Western thought and the very structure of Western languages. It was also in this third wave that feminism turned back to Freud, whose ideas about female infant sexuality had long made him the object of feminist distaste. While critics like Germaine Greer saw psychoanalysis as a manifestation of patriarchal ideology, Juliet Mitchell argued in *Psychoanalysis and Feminism* (1974) that Freud's ideas could be a tool of female emancipation if they are used not to confirm but to analyse patriarchy.

Mindful of the way in which direct opposition to dominant theories could easily be swallowed up the system it was trying to oppose (remember Duchamp's ready-mades), third-wave feminists increasingly saw the battle for equal rights as a necessary but insufficient basis upon which to further the feminist cause. In setting herself up against man, woman was accepting the terms of debate given to her by man, with all the binary, antagonistic structures embedded in its Aristotelian logic and in the grammar of Western languages. Far from merely opposing masculine logic, the very logic of opposition itself was seen to be oppressive of femininity. In other words, simply to oppose patriarchy was to accept patriarchy's liking for oppositions. In this vein, Julia Kristeva (born 1941) criticised feminism's 'phallic competition' with men, and Hélène Cixous (born 1937) saw feminism as little more than 'ideological transvestism'.

Feminism and literature: écriture féminine

For third-wave feminists, language itself was put under the spotlight. Grammar categorises, makes distinctions, and forces either/or choices, and for Cixous and other third-wave feminists all these are typically masculinist traits. The charge is made that language and logic are 'phallocentric': they have been devised by men to suit the way that men think and see the world, paying no attention to any difference that women might have. The desire to disrupt the very logic of phallocentric language and the patriarchal culture it reinforces led third-wave French feminists to elaborate an *écriture féminine* (French: 'feminine writing', though the term is usually left untranslated). Cixous writes:

> It is impossible to *define* a feminine practice of writing, and this is an impossibility that will remain, for this practice can never be theorised, enclosed, coded – which doesn't mean that it doesn't exist. But it will always surpass the discourse that regulates the phallocentric system.

Écriture féminine escapes all theorising and all definition because to define it would be to place it back within phallocentric logic. The position that Cixous takes up in relation to phallocentric logic is not one of strict opposition, putting woman in the position of dominance where man has been, because once again this would keep the fundamental masculinist structure of dominance but just swap round the places that women and men occupy within that structure; it would shuffle the deck but continue playing the same game. *Écriture féminine* seeks not just to play a new move in an old game but to frustrate the game itself, and thereby it seeks to avoid the problems of the early twentieth-century avant-garde in not directly opposing masculinist logic but cutting across it (see Figure 8.5).

Third-wave feminism's oblique approach to the binary oppositions that structure masculinist logic was part of an attempt to rethink the concepts that undergird Western thought. In her essay 'About Chinese Women', the philosopher and psychoanalyst Julia Kristeva acknowledges this need and offers a response: 'if there is no "absolute", what is truth, if not the unspoken of the spoken?' This is a rich sentence that bears careful analysis, because it reveals a great deal about third-wave feminist thinking and also about the postmodernism we shall consider in the final

The rejection of masculinist logic

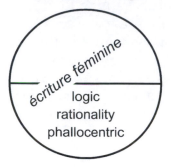

Figure 8.5.

chapter. First of all, there is no 'absolute' in the sense now familiar to us from Nietzsche, namely that the Platonic Forms or the suprasensory *logos*-God who guarantees the unchanging truth of the universe is considered never to have existed. Secondly, without such 'absolutes', it makes no sense any longer to talk about truth in a way that relies on unchanging Forms or an unchanging God. Thirdly, truth cannot now be reduced to (masculinist) language and logic; truth is what language always aims at capturing, but what it can never completely contain because there is always more to say. Note also that truth is the unspoken 'of the spoken'; language is not rejected, but neither is truth reduced to language. We will pick up the threads of this concern for rethinking truth in the final chapter on postmodernism.

Assault on hierarchies

Darwinism, Marxism, psychoanalysis and important currents within feminism each seek to question and disrupt hierarchical or logical structures that have run through Western culture from its Greco-Roman and Judeo-Christian origins. Until the nineteenth century, these hierarchies – between God and humanity, between different classes of society in the feudal system, between humanity and the animal kingdom, between men and women – held the West together and gave it its identity. Each of the thinkers and movements we have considered in this chapter finds liberation from certain social, theoretical or linguistic structures, seeking new understandings of human nature and human society that tend to privilege becoming over Being. In the process they find new ways of conceiving art and writing that reflect these new orientations. The latter decades of the twentieth century saw a broader effort to find new ways of understanding that did not assume or rely on the structures and concepts of a previous age. It was an effort to understand a world that was, in Nietzsche's terms, cut away from its moorings. It is to this effort to find a new way of understanding and living without the old hierarchies that we now turn in our final chapter.

9

What Comes After the New?
Postmodernism and Postmodernity

The awarding of an honorary degree by an academic institution rarely makes the 'news in brief' in the national press, let alone create a scandal in the letters pages. But when in 1992 the University of Cambridge floated the idea of bestowing such a degree on the French philosopher Jacques Derrida the pages of *The Times* and *The Guardian* fizzed with invective and indignation. On 9 May 1992, seven days before the Cambridge ballot to decide whether to award Derrida his doctorate, a group of nineteen philosophers headed by Professor Barry Smith, editor of the academic journal *The Monist*, added their signatures to a letter in *The Times* that protested in the strongest terms against Derrida's 'tricks and gimmicks similar to those of the Dadaists' which had reduced 'contemporary French philosophy to an object of ridicule'. Derrida's writing was 'little more than semi-intelligible attacks upon the values of reason, truth, and scholarship' that 'does not meet accepted standards of clarity and rigour'. In the end the Cambridge vote was not swayed by the letter, and it was decided by a narrow majority that Derrida should receive his honorary doctorate.

The 'Cambridge affair', as it came to be known, doubtless illustrates a great many things, but one of them is the capacity of so-called 'postmodern' philosophy to polarise opinion. To its supporters, postmodernism merely points out that the assumptions of the West going back to Plato and Aristotle – assumptions about truth, logic, being and ethics – have always been more problematic than the West was willing to admit. To its most fervent detractors, postmodernism is a terroristic wrecking exercise intended to tear down the edifice of culture itself. In this chapter we shall leave aside these rapidly ageing debates and consider how postmodernism continues the story of the West after Nietzsche and the death of God, after Darwin, Marx and Freud, and after the trauma of two World Wars.

In taking this path, it is important to point out that not everyone followed Nietzsche's repudiation of the suprasensory. One branch of Western thought, the heir of Comte's positivism, rejected Nietzsche's conclusions and reasserted the claims of reason in twentieth-century logical positivism and the Anglo-Saxon linguistic philosophy that followed. In his early thought Ludwig Wittgenstein (1889-1951) held that both reality and language share a logical structure. Like the mechanistic approach of the seventeenth century, this philosophy proceeded by analysis, breaking down its object into its smallest possible components. The object in question for this Analytic Philosophy was linguistic statements and propositions, and its 'logical atomism' saw the world as the sum of true propositions or logical states of affairs. In his later work, Wittgenstein was central in the movement that came to be known as ordinary language philosophy, for which sense was not now considered to be logically determined but to be a result of how words are used in any number of 'language games'.

It is our intention in this final chapter, however, to follow the branch of Western thinking that finds itself in the direct lineage of Nietzsche, Freud and Marx, seeking to find a new way of orientating itself in a world where old certainties are, as Marx said, melting into air. Postmodernism does not try hastily to erect new certainties to replace the old, but rather seeks to develop new ways of thinking that take account of the breakdown of hierarchies that we see in the modern age.

Five snapshots of postmodern thought

As we begin our exploration of the postmodern, it will help us to distinguish between 'postmodernity' and 'postmodernism'. 'Postmodernity' is a word to describe a whole society, and thus 'the postmodern West' is used in the same way as 'the Renaissance West' or 'the West of the Enlightenment'. 'Postmodernism', on the other hand, describes the philosophy that is characteristic of postmodernity. Like other such sweeping terms, 'postmodernism' is too broad a designation to have much specific meaning. It groups together a number of very different thinkers who disagree with each other strongly on some important matters. The best way to approach postmodern thought will be through a series of intellectual snapshots.

Michel Foucault: the death of man

Our first two snapshots of postmodern thought seek to comprehend the consequences of the 'death of God' for our understanding of human beings. The West's answer to the question 'what is a human being?' was from the earliest times tied up with an understanding of God or the gods. Philosophically, the birth of modern man can be traced to Descartes' *cogito* ('I am thinking'), and the *cogito* is thought by many scholars to rely on the existence of a non-deceiving God, to whom Descartes himself appeals:

> Thus I see plainly that the certainty and truth of all knowledge depends uniquely on my awareness of the true God, to such an extent that I was incapable of perfect knowledge about anything else until I became aware of him.

For the drafters of the *Declaration of the Rights of Man and of the Citizen* in France and the *Declaration of Independence* in the former American colonies, humanity's status is proclaimed 'in the presence and under the auspices of the Supreme Being' and human rights are 'endowed by their Creator'. If, then, God disappears from the picture, the modern Western understanding of humanity and human rights finds itself, at the very least, under threat.

This consequence of the death of God was followed through in the structuralism that eclipsed post-war existentialism in 1960s Paris. Structuralism sought to understand meaning and human society by analysing underlying structures and relations between ideas, rather than by analysing its object to find its smallest constituent parts. It was structuralism that proclaimed both the death of man, with Michel Foucault (1926-1984), and the death of the author, with Roland Barthes.

Like so many French philosophers of the twentieth century, Foucault passed through the prestigious École Normale Supérieure in Paris, but the young Michel failed the entrance exam at his first attempt in 1945. Stung by the failure, he tried again after further education at the renowned Lycée Henri IV in Paris, and second time round he was ranked fourth in the entire cohort, drawn from the whole of France. Foucault's proclamation of the death of man comes in his preface to *The Order of Things* (1966):

> it is comforting, however, and a source of profound relief to think that man is only a recent invention, a figure who is not yet two centuries old, a new wrinkle in our knowledge, and that he will disappear again as soon as that knowledge has discovered a new form.

For Foucault, 'man' is dependent not on a timeless human essence or Platonic Form; he is rather the effect of a historically changeable 'episteme'. An episteme for Foucault is a set of categories for thought and language that determines what is knowable and thinkable at a particular moment in history. Each episteme makes sense of the world and our place in it through different categories. So for example in *Madness and Civilisation* (1961) Foucault charts the different ways in which the 'mad' have been understood over the history of Western thought: from being thought of as demon possessed, as witches, as the insane to be locked away in Dickensian madhouses, to the contemporary category the mentally ill. None of these categories is essential and timeless; each one reflects the way that knowledge is constructed in a particular historical period. Foucault robustly sought to question supposedly timeless categories, calling them 'totalisations', or attempts to treat changing epistemes as if they were changeless Platonic Forms. The Cartesian 'man' of 'I am thinking therefore I exist', bound as it is for Foucault to the modern episteme, was passing away.

Roland Barthes: the death of the author

At the age of fifteen the young Roland Barthes (1915-1980) dreamed of being a Protestant pastor, but instead he grew up to be one of the most influential critics and theorists of structuralism. Barthes had an eye for analysing the myths and structures of mass culture, and his *Mythologies* (1957) included essays on how soap powder advertisements invent the dimension of depth in fabric to show off their 'deep cleaning', and how all-in wrestling reflects back to society its own concepts of good and evil, suffering and justice. Perhaps Barthes' best-known article is his short polemic piece 'The Death of the Author' (1968) in which, in a way similar to Foucault, he launches a critique of the modern West. The notion of the author, like that of man, is not a timeless notion in the Western tradition. Barthes dismisses the approach according to which 'the explanation of a work is always sought in the man or woman who produced it, as if it were always in the end, through the more or less transparent allegory of the fiction, the voice of a single person, the author "confiding" in us'. We must instead realise, he insists, that just writing 'I' does not make the 'author' the final authority on their writing, any more than just speaking 'I' provides the unproblematic foundation for personhood that Descartes thought it did in his *cogito*:

> Linguistically, the author is never more than the instance writing, just as 'I' is nothing other than the instance saying 'I': language knows a 'subject', not a 'person', and this subject, empty outside of the very enunciation which defines it, suffices to make language 'hold together', suffices, that is to say, to exhaust it.

What Barthes is saying here is that the Cartesian 'I' of the 'I am thinking, therefore I exist' is nothing more than the subject of the verbs 'think' and 'exist', not a person existing and thinking independently of and 'behind' the little story 'cogito ergo sum'. Instead of assuming that a 'person' exists before any language, Barthes is arguing that a 'person' is an effect of language: 'I' is only the subject of the verb 'to think'.

Barthes proclaims the death of the author insofar as he or she is the origin and explanation of the text, and privileged authority over it. We see here a further echo of the death of God. God was the origin and explanation of the universe, with authority to declare what is 'good' and what is 'evil', what is 'true' and what is 'false' in the universe he has made. When this idea of supreme authority is taken away, then other, smaller structures of authority lose their legitimacy, including the author's authority to say what his or her text means. For Barthes, the death of the author is the price to pay for the birth of a reader who no longer has to rifle through an author's diary and personal correspondence for the key to her or his writing.

Gilles Deleuze: the overturning of Platonism

1968 in Paris was a time of overturning. In May that year, the student and workers' street protests threatened to bring the government of the war hero General Charles de Gaulle (1890-1970) to its knees, and the universities were bubbling hotbeds of political ferment. Maoist student groups vied with the Communists for leadership of the student revolt, and well-known authors and intellectuals came out in support of the student cause. In the aftermath of 'May 68' a group of breakaway academics founded the University of Vincennes in Saint-Denis, ten kilometres from the centre of Paris, with an ethos of greater student freedom. One of the philosophers to teach at the new university was Gilles Deleuze (1925-1995), whose packed seminars at Vincennes gained a cult following among students. One of Deleuze's most important contributions to twentieth-century thought was his overturning of the hierarchy implied by Plato's notion of the Forms.

For Plato there is a strict hierarchy moving down from the eternal Forms through objects in this world to the representations of objects. Think of a bed. There is a perfect, unchanging Form of a bed, of which any bed made by a carpenter is a copy. If an artist should choose to paint that carpenter's bed, then his art is a copy of a copy. But in the first appendix to his *Logic of Sense* (1969) Deleuze argues that there is a problem with Plato's thinking, namely that the division between the Form, the copy and the copy of a copy (or simulacrum) itself relies on a simulacrum, namely an artistic myth. The reasoning goes like this:

- The myth of the cave in *Republic* book 7 is the basis for understanding the difference between the reality of intelligible Forms (the sun outside the cave) and the shadow existence of this sensory world (life in the cave).
- Artistic works including poetry and myth, because they are copies of things in this world, have the lowest place in the hierarchy.
- But this distinction between the intelligible and the artistic is drawn only by virtue of a myth: the myth of the cave itself.
- So the whole idea of privileging the intelligible over the mythic relies on a myth: myth is the source both of both the category of 'intelligible' and the category of 'mythic', and of the privileging of the first over the second.
- The hierarchy between Form and copy has been subverted, or turned against itself. The 'lower' term is seen to be the origin of the 'higher' term.

Furthermore, the aim of Plato's account of Forms, Deleuze argues, is not only to distinguish Form from copy, but to distinguish two sorts of image: icon (the carpenter's bed) and simulacrum (the artist's bed). An icon is an image which 'participates in' the Form (a wooden bed is indeed a bed), whereas a simulacrum is an image which does not (a painting of a bed is not a bed, but a painting). So the copy is limited, precisely because it has to copy the Form (the bed has to participate in the Form of a bed, otherwise it isn't a bed), but the simulacrum is unlimited (it does not have to resemble a bed at all; think of the numberless ways a bed could figure in abstract painting). What Platonism seeks to do, Deleuze concludes, is to set a limit on the endless becoming of the simulacrum by making it subordinate to the copy.

For his part, Deleuze proposes an account which inverts the order of the simulacrum and the copy. Plato's thinking can be characterised as 'only resemblance differs' (only the carpenter's bed is a copy of the Form of the bed, because it resembles the Form), but Deleuze instead proposes that 'only differences resemble' (difference precedes resemblance and resemblance relies on this preceding difference). In proposing this re-reading of Plato he is closely shadowing and continuing the move that we saw in Nietzsche, in existentialism, in Darwin, in Marx and in de Beauvoir's feminism, namely that 'becoming' and difference is shown to precede Being or sameness. In all this, Deleuze is seeking to think in a way that does not rely on the foundations and structures underwritten by God.

In *Rhizomes: An Introduction* (1976), Deleuze and his collaborator Félix Guattari (1930-1992) contrast the predominance of what they call 'arborescence' in Western thought with their own 'rhizomatic' account of meaning (Figure 9.1). Arborescences are like trees, having one thick central trunk with lots of roots splitting off from it; they systematise knowledge by prescribing a limited number of connections (like Diderot and d'Alembert's 'Map of the System of Human Knowledge' in their *Encyclopédie*). Rhizomes, on the other hand, are non-hierarchical and have no centre and no constant overall structure. Meanings understood rhizomatically need no central origin or god-like authority to underwrite them.

**Deleuze: arborescent meaning (left)
and rhizomatic meaning (right)**

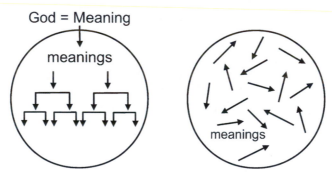

Figure 9.1.

There is an important difference between this understanding and the existentialism that comes before it. For Camus and Sartre, as for early twentieth-century modernism before them, there is a stubborn desire for the sorts of truths and meanings that were traditionally supplied by religion or Platonism, a desire for the knowledge of ultimate reality that we have been representing in the top half of our circle diagrams. For existentialism these meanings are absent (hence the dotted line in the diagram of Camus' absurd on p. 160), but there is still an empty place where they should be. According to the Heidegger of 'Nietzsche's Word: God is Dead', this is also Nietzsche's problem: Nietzsche doesn't realise

190

that if you get rid of the 'suprasensory' then you cannot hold onto the 'sensory' as it was previously, because it only has meaning as part of the pair of sensory and suprasensory. If you knock off the top storey of a two-storey house, it no longer makes sense to refer to the one remaining storey as the 'lower storey'. This is what postmodernism realises: if there is no Being then becoming is no longer one half of a picture with the other half missing; becoming is itself the whole picture.

Jean-François Lyotard: incredulity toward metanarratives

The best-known philosophical use of the term 'postmodern' is found in Jean-François Lyotard's (1924-1998) *The Postmodern Condition* (1979). The postmodern for Lyotard describes not only what comes after the modern but also what made the modern age possible in the first place; it names the difficulties that the modern age tried to subdue and master with its mathematised reason (Descartes and Newton) and with teleological stories about its own eventual triumph. Lyotard describes the postmodern in terms of no longer believing in this sort of overarching historical story, or metanarrative. A metanarrative is a story that makes sense of history and legitimates certain actions in it, like Marx's story of the inevitable triumph of the proletariat or Charlemagne talking of his court at Aachen as the 'New Jerusalem' in a way that is supposed to legitimate his forced conversion of the surrounding nations. As the prefix *meta-* (Greek: 'beyond') suggests, these stories stand beyond our everyday experience of the world, making sense of that world from above. For Lyotard, postmodernism can be defined as 'incredulity towards metanarratives'.

Lyotard's point is both that people cannot believe in these big stories any more (think of the way that two world wars bring the idea of the incremental march of human progress to a juddering halt) and also that these big stories often turn into tools of oppression used by those in power to legitimate their own position in society. Metanarratives are not simply unwarranted but also dangerous. Lyotard showed his own suspicion of metanarratives in his membership of the French left wing group *Socialism or Barbarism* from 1950-1963. The group rejected not only capitalist bureaucracy but also the Leninism that insisted that an elite vanguard had to bring about the Revolution, even spurning Marxist ideas about the overarching historical stages leading to Revolution in favour of a focus on the real lives of workers.

The Postmodern Condition closes with Lyotard declaring war on totality:

> We have paid a high enough price for the nostalgia of the whole and the one [...] The answer is: let us wage a war on totality, let us be witnesses to the unrepresentable; let us activate the differences and save the honour of the name.

Totality, as Lyotard is using the term here, is the idea that we can know all there is to know about any given thing, that the world is transparent to our reason. It echoes Foucault's denunciation of totalisation and Deleuze's rejection of arborescence: the postmodern decades saw a concerted attack on closed or self-sufficient systems of knowledge.

Jacques Derrida: deconstructing the Western logos

Like Foucault, Jacques Derrida (1930-2004) failed his entrance exam to the École Normale Supérieure (Derrida in fact failed twice, before finally gaining admission in 1951). Like Foucault, Derrida also questions the overarching structures that the modern West uses to make sense of the world. In *Of Grammatology* (1967) he turns his attention to the Western notion of the *logos*, the rational principle or glue holding the universe together, whether it be Plato's Form of the Good, the Word of God in John chapter 1 in the Bible, or Enlightenment Reason. Derrida calls any way of thinking that assumes the existence of such a glue 'logocentric'.

In the same way as Jackson Pollock's action paintings call attention to paint and traditional theories of perspective by playing with normal artistic conventions, so also Derrida seeks to draw attention to the philosophical ideas that the West has assumed for so long. These ideas have acted like a pair of spectacles the West has looked through, often without realising it, to bring into focus everything that we see, and Derrida is seeking to stop looking *through* and start looking *at* the spectacles, showing that the way we see the world is not as self-evident as we may have thought. In *Of Grammatology* he argues that the *logos* is a fiction, wedded to a second fiction: that things can be absolutely present to our understanding, in other words understood completely. There is no absolute presence because such a notion of presence piggybacks on the notion of a God's-eye view from which nothing is absent. At this point Derrida introduces a number of key terms – onto-theology, parousia, trace, self-identicality, *différance* – and in order to understand what he is saying we need to take a deep breath, drink a strong coffee and take the terms one at a time.

- The notion of absolute presence is an onto-theology, that is to say an understanding of being (ontology) that relies on a God's-eye view (theology) from which nothing is absent.
- Absolute presence is also a parousia, the theological term for the moment at the end of time when all secrets will be revealed, when nothing is hidden.
- And absolute presence has no 'trace', no mark of absence in it (like a footprint in the mud is a trace, a mark that shows the absence of the foot that made it).
- The idea of 'self-identicality' is best understood in terms of Descartes' *cogito*. Descartes assumes that the 'I' that thinks and the 'I' that exists are one and the same, that the two 'I's are self-identical.

- Finally, whereas the *logos* is a fixed and authoritative origin of everything there is (think of the opening of John's gospel: 'In the beginning was the word ...'), Derrida uses the term *différance* (spelled with an 'a', whereas the French word for 'difference' is usually spelled with an 'e') to denote a very different sort of origin, one that is not self-identical, that always has a trace of its 'outside' on its 'inside' – just like the *cogito* when the 'I am thinking' and the 'I exist' are not the same 'I'. We will come back to *différance* and explain it further below, but that's enough to get us going for now.

In our ideas and experiences things are never completely present to us in an onto-theological way; we see only one side of a thing at once, and think about a thing only imperfectly, not with all its secrets uncovered in some sort of intellectual parousia. Neither we nor our concepts are self-identical, without any trace of distance or absence. This sort of divine self-identical presence, Derrida argues, has never existed, but philosophy has always needed to pretend that it does. Let's now look at how Derrida himself expresses these ideas:

> The subordination of the trace to the full presence summed up in the logos, the humbling of writing beneath a speech dreaming its plenitude, such are the gestures required by an onto-theology determining the archaeological and eschatological meaning of being as presence, as parousia, as life without différance: [...] the name of God, at least as it is pronounced in classical rationalisms, is the name of indifference itself.

What does Derrida mean? Presence as parousia, without any difference or trace of absence, he is arguing, never existed; it was always just a twinkle in the philosopher's eye. Instead, in the same way that Deleuze shows how Plato's privileging of the Forms over myth is itself based on a myth, Derrida sees the origin of thought and knowledge not as a self-identical presence (as Descartes assumes in his *cogito*) but as *différance* spelled with an 'a'. The idea of *différance* is that there is no stable, self-identical origin from which everything else flows, be it God or 'the One' or reason or whatever else philosophers have suggested it might be. For Derrida, if you go right back to the beginning, you don't come to a single stable origin and full presence, but to *différance*, which is always both different from itself (like the difference between the two halves of the cogito) and deferred with relation to itself (its completion is always to come; it is never full and complete here and now).

To help us understand this more concretely, let's follow a little thought experiment. Imagine a group of people shipwrecked on a desert island. They dry themselves off and come together to form a community. After some discussion they all sit down and sign an Island Constitution that lays out what will be legal and what will be illegal on the island. Now, the signing of the constitution itself is neither a legal act nor an illegal one, because it is the constitution being signed that sets out what will be within and what will be outside the law. The signing itself can't be either in conformity with or in contradiction to the law, because that distinction hasn't been decided yet. If the law decides what is legal and illegal, then the origin of law cannot itself be properly considered either legal or illegal. The foundation of the island law has been deconstructed, and its origin is not a firm *logos*-like foundation but a moment that is itself neither fully inside nor outside the law it brings into being.

Now Derrida is not suggesting that this is the case only with desert island constitutions, but with our whole Western logic and our way of thinking. Opposites like true and false, inside and outside are built on foundations that disrupt these very distinctions, just as the origin of the desert island law is neither legal nor illegal. This then is Derrida's 'deconstruction' of the Western *logos*, and we must not confuse it with 'destruction'. To deconstruct something is not to destroy it but to show – as Derrida has done here with the *logos* and as Deleuze did with the Platonic distinction between intellect and myth – that its supposed self-identicality or solid foundation is in fact suppressing a difference that, once attention is drawn to it, destabilises the foundation itself. In other words, to deconstruct something is to show how it cannot be itself without something that it tries to suppress or expel outside itself. Deconstruction does not show that something is useless or meaningless, but that it lacks the sort of foundation we tend to assume it possessed, the sort of foundation that assumes a God's-eye view of things.

Postmodernity and postmodern society

If modern society is characterised by capitalism then postmodern society, true to its ambiguous relation to the modernity that it deconstructs, is characterised by what is known as late capitalism. Ever since the first Industrial Revolution in the eighteenth century, the Western national economies have been increasingly dependent on trade, but the second half of the twentieth century saw a dramatic explosion in trade. In the years from 1500 to 1820 world GDP increased at an average rate of 0.3% per year; from 1820-1950 it grew at an average of 1.6% a year, but in the period from 1950-1998 world GDP grew at an average of 3.9% a year, leaving it in 1998 six times larger than it was in 1950.

From the 1950s onwards the West has developed a 'consumer society', a society increasingly organised around the consumption (or purchase) of goods and services, rather than around the production of materials. Those who in previous periods may have been called peasants, comrades or burghers gain the new identity of 'consumers'. Jean Baudrillard (1929-2007) argues in *The Consumer Society* (1970) that consumption, rather than production, is the main engine of late twentieth-century capitalist society, reliant on the availability of cheap credit and the satisfaction of wants, rather than the meeting of needs. Consumption in itself, regardless of what is consumed, becomes a necessary and important element of Western society, with a person's identity increasingly rooted in their purchasing power. In *The Theory of the Leisure Class* (1899) the economist Thorstein Veblen (1857-1929) coined the term 'conspicuous consumption' to describe the purchase of goods or services intended to advertise the buying power of the purchaser. Veblen writes:

> The basis on which good repute in any highly organised industrial community ultimately rests is pecuniary strength; and the means of showing pecuniary strength, and so of gaining or retaining a good name, are leisure and a conspicuous consumption of goods.

Goods consumed become a means to the end of making a public show of one's consumption.

Along with the consumer society, the second half of the twentieth century was characterised by globalisation, the process whereby increasing deregulation and improvements in communication technology allow for an expansion of trade in international markets. Globalisation in the production of goods means that parts of a single item can be manufactured in many different countries and sold in others still, and with the globalisation of the service industry call centres and other services were increasingly located off-shore. Some have sought to give globalisation a cultural meaning, using the term to refer to the worldwide spread of north American culture (largely through television and cinema) and north American consumer brands.

Though globalisation has brought great prosperity to the West and elsewhere, it has many detractors. In *The McDonaldisation of Society* (1993), sociologist George Ritzer (born 1940) argues that globalisation brings about a cultural sameness and monotony along with an 'irrational rationality' where the efficiency of globalised consumption becomes the end to which human beings are the means: 'irrationality means that rational systems are unreasonable systems', he says. 'By that I mean that they deny the basic humanity, the human reason, of the people who work within or are served by them'. We can see here a postmodern recycling of Kafka's portrait of the modernist individual's alienation in the midst of a bureaucratic society.

Finally, the condition of postmodernity has grown along with the rise of the 'information society', a society which primarily produces and distributes not material goods but data. It has been estimated that anyone who watches or listens to a news programme for one hour today will receive more news information than a medieval peasant would hear in the whole of his or her life. The growth of the information society in the West was accompanied and fostered by the 'third Industrial Revolution', the rapid telecommunications and computing advances of the second half of the twentieth century. At the beginning of the twentieth century it is estimated that there were around 2 million telephones worldwide, 1.4 million in the USA alone. By 1910 the number was estimated at 10 million, which doubled by 1922; the milestone of 50 million was passed in 1939. By the end of 2008 there were 4 billion mobile phone users worldwide, in addition to 1 billion fixed line telephones. Whereas by 1930 40% of US households owned a radio, by 1940 it was more than 80%, and the number of households with at least one television rose from 11% in 1950 to 88% by only 1960. The invention of the world wide web in 1991 by the British engineer and computer scientist Sir Timothy Berners-Lee (born 1955) has proliferated the information sources available to the Western consumer, with nearly two billion internet users worldwide by 2010. By 2011 there were well over one trillion unique URLs (web addresses), with the web itself growing at a rate of millions of new pages each day.

According to some analysts, the information society comes to dominate the consumer society when physical goods become only one of a range of signs that can manipulated to construct individual or corporate identity. This is the view taken by Baudrillard in his book *Simulation and Simulacra* (1981), where he argues that the division between reality and representation has collapsed in the 'simulacrum', a sign that is no longer a copy of reality but that exists and circulates in its own right in a 'hyperreality' in which the experiences offered by information technologies are more intense and immediate than everyday life's 'desert of the real'. These ideas are captured in Baudrillard's famous analysis of Disneyland:

> Disneyland exists in order to hide the fact that it is the 'real' country, all of 'real' America that is Disneyland (a bit like prisons are there to hide the fact that it is the social in its entirety, in its banal omnipresence, that is carceral). Disneyland is presented as imaginary in order to make us believe that the rest is real, whereas all of Los Angeles and the America that surrounds it are no longer real, but belong to the hyperreal order and to the order of simulation.

Postmodernity's awareness of its world as a simulacrum contributes to placing irony at the centre of the postmodern ethos. Where Achilles is lauded for his *aretê*, Christianity is distinguished by *agapê*, the high medieval period is known for its chivalry and *fin'amor*, the courts of the Renaissance prized Castiglione's *sprezzatura* and Romanticism burned with its cult of feeling, the attitude characteristic of postmodernity is an ironic subversion. It is a subversion because the certainties by which the West previously lived are no longer available, and this subversion is ironic because we knowingly continue to live with them ringing in our ideas. To take the example of Derrida and law, we know that the law has no self-identical foundation, that its origin has been subverted, but we carry on using it and (for the most part) being thankful for it. For Lyotard, a decreasing ability to believe the 'big stories' of modernity was coupled with an inability to jettison those stories altogether, and irony provides a mode of detachment that neither forgets the old stories nor continues relating to them in the same way as before. The postmodern ethos does not pine for divine meaning like the man of Camus's absurd, but rather sets about trying to understand meaning anew using the tools, the logic and the language bequeathed to it by a bygone onto-theological age.

Postmodern architecture

In relation to the arts, the term 'postmodern' was first used to describe a new style of architecture which emerged in the second half of the twentieth century. Modernist architecture was epitomised by the 'International Style' developed after the First World War and was at its most influential in the early 1930s. The International Style was characterised by an austerity expressed in severe right-angled corners, a preponderance of concrete and steel and a heavy emphasis on functionality. The aesthetic of the movement is epitomised in Ludwig Mies van der Rohe's (1886-1969) adage that 'less is more', while for the modernist Swiss architect Charles-Édouard Jeanneret (1887-1965), better known as Le Corbusier, houses were functional 'machines for living'. One of the most famous buildings designed in accordance with these modernist principles is the Bauhaus school in Dessau, Germany (Figure 9.2).

The term 'postmodern' was coined in relation to architecture by Joseph Hundt in *Architecture and the Spirit of Man* (1949), and came to describe the rejection of the implied ideology of progress, rationality and functionality that characterised the International Style, often in favour of incorporating historically and geographically disparate influences and styles in a single building. In *Complexity and Contradictions in Architecture* (1966), Robert Charles Venturi (born 1925) argued for a

Figure 9.2. Walter Gropius, The Bauhaus building in Dessau (1925-6).

Figure 9.3. Philip Johnson, AT&T (Sony) Building, New York (1984).

style characterised by ambiguity and complexity in contrast to the pared-down forms of the International Style, rewriting Mies van der Rohe's 'less is more' as his own 'less is a bore'. Philip Johnson (1906-2005) and John Burgee's (born 1933) AT&T Tower (now the Sony Tower, Figure 9.3), completed in 1984 on Madison Avenue, Manhattan, ruffled modernist feathers with its seven-storey triumphal arch entrance, its paraphrase of an open-topped pediment (sarcastically called the Chippendale roof), and its non-orthogonal angles. Serving no immediate functional end, the entrance and the roof usher in a new aesthetic of pastiche that would increasingly see buildings bringing together a broad range of historical references and allusions.

Pop Art and after

In visual art, the postmodern reaction was against the high and austere modernism of the Abstract Expressionists. The modernist obsession with creative novelty and with ever greater abstraction exhausted itself after Malevich's *Black Square*, and one direction taken by art was to turn to popular culture. Whereas high modernist art had disdained the popular, the new 'Pop Art' would blur the boundaries between 'high' and 'low' artistic production. Whereas modernism strove for ever more innovative forms of expression, Pop Art re-worked, quoted and pastiched existing modes. Whereas Abstract Expressionism sought the transcendent and noumenal, Pop Art embraced a new playfulness and worked with everyday consumer objects. Pop Art was the Aristotelian particular to high modernism's Platonic universal, the crowd-pleasing Classical Haydn to high modernism's Baroque Bach.

The most famous practitioner of Pop Art was Andy Warhol (1928-1987), almost as notorious for the wild parties in his Manhattan 'Factory' studio as for his art. Warhol's drug-fuelled parties were frequented by the 'Warhol Superstars' who helped produce his silk-screen art and star in his films, which included *Sleep* (1968), an eight-hour feature of a man asleep, and *Empire* (1964), a shot of the Empire State Building from sunrise to sunset. Warhol's public life was curtailed after he was shot in the stomach in 1968 by the feminist Valerie Solanas, founder (and sole member) of the Society to Cut Up Men (SCUM). Though Warhol's intellect was not universally appreciated – the author Truman Capote called him 'a sphinx without a secret' – the movement of which he was part left a profound impression on the twentieth-century West.

Warhol's work reuses and explores the images and icons of the mass media which are both fleeting and to be found everywhere. In *The Philosophy of Andy Warhol* the artist makes a famous boast about his rate of production:

> When Picasso died, I read in a magazine that he had made four thousand masterpieces in his lifetime and I thought, 'Gee, I could do that in a day.' So I started. And then I found out, 'Gee it takes more than a day to do four thousand pictures.'

The silkscreen print *Marilyn Diptych* (1962, Figure 9.4) was produced in the months following Marilyn Monroe's death, and according to the critic Thomas Crow presents 'a stark and unresolved dialectic of presence and absence, life and death', bringing together the ubiquity of the mass-

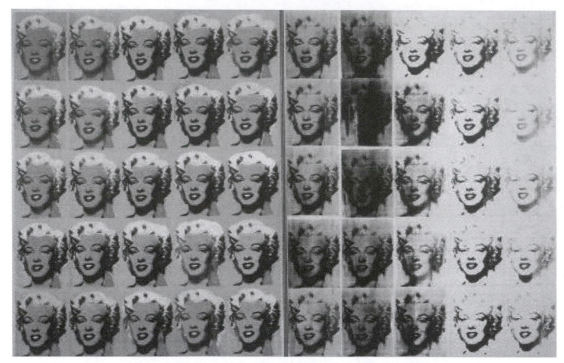

Figure 9.4. Andy Warhol, *Marilyn Diptych* (1962). Acrylic on canvas.
Tate Gallery, London.

produced image and the cult of celebrity with a meditation on mortality in the fading and blackened images on the right-hand panel.

Warhol also challenges the conventions of artistic authorship. Artists had for centuries been using apprentices to help complete their works and to paint the less important parts like stonework, sky or grass, but Warhol's technique of photo processing and screen printing meant that, once conceived, his works could be produced in large quantities in his Factory with no need for his personal intervention. The painter is no longer the Romantic Creator forging his unique vision in his works but one more instance of repetition in the circulation and reproduction of images. This comes as a challenge to originality and authenticity; with the reproduction of prints from photographic negatives it makes no sense to ask which print is the 'authentic' one.

After Pop Art, the late twentieth and early twenty-first centuries saw a proliferation in artistic forms, pushing further the horizons already broadened by Duchamp's Dada ready-mades. Installations, performance art and 'happenings', multimedia art and conceptual art all found their place in Western galleries and challenged the West's understanding of art. One early milestone in this proliferation of forms was produced by Richard Long, at the time a student of St Martin's School of Art and Design in London. *A Line Made by Walking* (1967, Figure 9.5) is the photographic record of a line that Long made by walking up and down in a field. It is a piece of 'land art' that explores the relationship between humans and their environment. Since the 1960s, Western art has continued, like early twentieth-century Cubism, to turn in on itself, using art to explore the nature of art itself and its own place in society. Some artists have

Figure 9.5. Richard Long, *A Line Made by Walking* (1967).
Photograph and pencil on board. Tate Gallery, London.

also continued seeking, like the early twentieth-century avant-garde, to shock the viewer, though this has proved increasingly difficult as each new shocking gesture becomes one more page in the story it was seeking to interrupt.

This proliferation of postmodern art forms, many of them blurring the boundaries between 'art' and 'life', is confusing and frustrating to many, but it perhaps becomes a little clearer to understand when we see it as an attempt to think and to practise what it means to make art after the death of God, after Darwin, Marx, Freud and Nietzsche. If the art of Rubens was appropriate for an age that believed in a transcendent God whose light infused the whole of creation, and if Cubism reflected an age increasingly aware of the limits of its own awareness, then we must not expect postmodern art merely to hawk ideas of beauty and form from a previous century, rather than come to terms with the disorientation and breakdown in structures of which Nietzsche spoke. Yes, there are charlatans, but every age has its charlatans. Art, as we have seen throughout this story of the West, reflects and dialogues with the ideas in the society of which it is part; to do anything less would be a stubborn deafness.

Music: experimentation, indeterminacy, pastiche

The proliferation of postmodern art forms finds its parallel in the world of music which, after the modernism of Schoenberg, follows a number of different and irreconcilable directions. The music of John Cage (1912-1992) stands on the threshold of the postmodern, bearing many of the characteristic traits of modernism while also gesturing beyond them. The modernist desire for ever greater novelty and ever more radical experimentation can be seen in Cage's *Sonatas and Interludes* (1946-48), composed for a 'prepared' piano into which objects or 'preparations' are inserted in contact with its strings. These insertions alter the timbre and decay of its notes, with the aim of yielding complex, multi-toned sounds from pressing a single key. In the case of *Sonatas and Interludes*, forty-five notes are 'prepared' with a combination of nuts, bolts, screws, pieces of plastic and rubber and one eraser. The effect for Cage was 'to place in the hands of a single pianist the equivalent of an entire percussion orchestra'.

In the original version of Cage's work *4'33": for any instrument or combination of instruments*, the score contains the single word 'tacet' (Latin: 'it is silent'). It was given its first performance at the Woodstock festival in New York on 29 August 1952, with David Tudor at the piano. Tudor indicated the beginning of each of the piece's three 'movements' by opening and closing the piano's keyboard cover at times chosen by him. During the four minutes thirty-three seconds of the performance not a note was played. In Cage's record of his early thoughts about the piece, it is called 'silent prayer', and the idea that the 'music' is created by the natural sounds of the audience during the performance seems to be an alien attempt to try to make sense of the piece in a way Cage may not have intended. Nevertheless, the piece challenges conventions of musical authorship in the way that its 'movements' are signalled at moments not prescribed by the composer. In its austere minimalism *4'33"* bears affinities with the conceptual purity (and exhaustion) of Malevich's *Black Square*.

Steve Reich (born 1936) and Philip Glass (born 1937) reject both the indeterminacy of Cage and the 'emancipated dissonance' of Schoenberg with a minimalism that focuses on the a-teleological repetition of simple pulses or notes, often electronically reproduced on a recorded loop. In *Music as a Gradual Process* (1968), Reich sounds quite Beckettian as he sets out his understanding of minimalist 'process music':

Performing and listening to a gradual musical process resembles: pulling back a swing, releasing it, and observing it gradually come to rest; turning over an hour glass and watching the sand slowly run through the bottom; placing your feet in the sand by the ocean's edge and watching, feeling, and listening to the waves gradually bury them.

As with Warhol's screen printing in his Factory studio, it is not the 'authenticity' of a live performance that is important to Reich, but the way in which, with a gradual process, 'all the cards are on the table' and there is no compositional structure hidden by the composer that the listener has to chase and reconstruct. Minimalism found a certain popularity among followers of rock music and influenced the 'art rock' of songwriters like David Bowie (born 1947) and Kate Bush (born 1958).

Other directions in music included the rise of the popular genres of blues, jazz, rock and pop, the pastiching of a wide range of different musical influences in pieces by John Zorn (born 1953) and William Bolcom (born 1938), or experiments in electronic music such as Charles Wuorinen's (born 1938) *Time's Encomium*, the first electronically composed piece to win the Pulitzer Prize for Music, which Wuorinen was also the youngest composer ever to be awarded at the age of thirty-two.

The postmodern novel

The problematic question of authorship and the end of belief in metanarratives find their echoes in the postmodern novel, an important precursor of which was the French 'new novel'. In *For a New Novel*, Alain Robbe-Grillet (1922-2008) rejects a teleological understanding of novelistic plot, insisting that his ambition is not to 'do better' than Flaubert, Proust, Kafka and Joyce but rather 'to situate ourselves in their wake, now, in our own time.' The new novel breaks with the realism of Balzac and Flaubert by rejecting the realist conceit of providing a window onto reality; it 'is not a testimony offered in evidence concerning an external reality, but is its own reality for itself'. In working through the implications of such a textual reality Robbe-Grillet and other new novelists abandoned linear plot in favour of a fragmented string of episodes whose temporal sequence the reader is ultimately frustrated in reconstructing. For Robbe-Grillet, the new novel is a bid for honesty, for exposing the conceit by which the novel for centuries has told a lie that the reader has chosen to believe:

> A tacit convention is established between the reader and the author: the latter will pretend to believe in what he is telling, the former will forget that everything is invented and will pretend to be dealing with a document, a biography, a real-life story.

With the new novel there is no longer any effort to make the reader believe in the 'reality' of the novel, and all previous such attempts are exposed as exercises in deception. The new novel makes the world strange through extended descriptions of familiar objects in mathematical and geometrical terms. The description of a quarter tomato encountered in a self-service restaurant in Robbe-Grillet's *The Erasers* (1953) is purposefully purged of the metaphors that make the world falsely comfortable and familiar:

> The peripheral flesh, compact and homogenous, of a fine chemical redness, is uniformly thick between a band of shiny skin and the semicircular area where the seeds are arranged, yellow, of uniform calibre, held in place by a thin layer of greenish jelly lying alongside the swelling at the heart. The latter, of a diluted and slightly granular pink, begins, near the lower hollow, in a network of white veins, one of which stretches out towards the seeds, in a somewhat uncertain manner.

'Characters' are similarly stripped of their customary depth and often also of their names, reduced to a series of perceptions and senses held together by a fragile narrative 'I'.

The new novel stands half way between modern and postmodern literature, however, requiring just as much of its reader as modernist writing by Joyce or Kafka. Later postmodern novels follow the trajectory of Pop Art in disrupting modernism's dichotomy of high and low culture. One such novel is Italo Calvino's (1923-1985) *If on a Winter's Night a Traveller* (1979), and it displays many of the traits that have come to be associated with the postmodern novel. First, the reader is required to participate to a large degree in making sense of Calvino's novel, and finds him or herself represented within it. The two main characters in the novel are most frequently referred to as Lettore and Lettrice ('Male Reader' and 'Female Reader') and the novel's twelve chapters describe how Lettore and Lettrice try to complete their reading of a book they have purchased. These chapters are interspersed with the opening pages of ten different novels, each supposedly with a different author and each parodying a genre of novel writing. The story of Lettore and Lettrice's frustrated reading, combined with the frustration of the incomplete stories of the ten novels, become Calvino's completed novel *If on a Winter's Night...* The book ends with the two readers married and in bed. The female reader (named Ludmilla, we find out) asks the male reader (still unnamed) if she can turn out the light and he answers, in the final sentence of the novel 'Just a moment, I've almost finished *If on a Winter's Night a Traveller* by Italo Calvino'. In his essay 'Cybernetics and ghosts', Calvino situates this fictional self-reference at a moment in literary history when 'the process of literary composition has been taken to pieces and reassembled', and when 'the decisive moment in literary life is bound to be the act of reading'.

The novel has always been an omnibus genre, but the postmodern novel foregrounds its borrowings and pastiches with a new boldness. It blurs and intentionally subverts generic boundaries in a way that resonates with philosophies in postmodernity that question identity and presence. In a deconstructive move with which we are now familiar, Jacques Derrida's 'The Law of Genre' seeks to show how generic labels like 'novel' and 'romance', while they both verify and create divisions between what is 'inside' and what is 'outside' a particular genre, cannot themselves be thought of in terms of the 'inside' and 'outside' they create. As with authorship, readership, reason and writing, genre distinctions become a problem around which postmodern thought and literature circle and a question which they explore.

With postmodernism's disruption of the ideology of teleological progress, its incredulity towards overarching stories that make sense of the world and of the place and humans in it, its exhaustion of modernist innovation and novelty and its uneasiness with the structures and assumptions upon which the Western world and its culture have largely relied, the question of what we are to make of the West's 3,000 years so far is both pressing and problematic. It is to this 'so what?' question that we turn next, for some brief concluding thoughts to our journey through Western culture.

Concluding Thoughts

To provide any definitive conclusion to a survey of Western culture from Plato to postmodernism would be folly, and only slightly better than refusing to make any concluding remarks at all. A conclusion might lament the brevity of this survey, challenging the reader to take up the threads offered and explore further the rich tapestry of Western thought, art, literature and music. I certainly hope that the each reader will be spurred on to delve more deeply into Western philosophy, literature and art, but such a conclusion seems to say too little. I could finish by stressing the importance of a knowledge of our cultural and intellectual history, warning along with George Santayana that 'those who cannot remember the past are condemned to repeat it'. Or perhaps I might remind the reader that the future remains to be written and that it is now our turn to pen the next chapter and find our own place in the story. A particularly foolhardy conclusion could seek to give a sense of where things are going in the next twenty or one hundred years, but the twists and turns in the story of the West teach us to be humble about our predictions of the future. On this matter, I can do no better than pay heed to the anecdote told about the British Prime Minister Harold Macmillan (1894-1986). When, early in his premiership, Macmillan was asked by a young reporter what he thought would most define his time in office, he is said to have answered 'Events, dear boy, events'.

In lieu of a conclusion I offer here some brief thoughts, thoughts that have kept returning to me throughout the period of researching and writing this book, and thoughts that I offer to the reader in the spirit of encouraging further reflection. They are simple, perhaps, but I hope not simplistic. The first thought is a haunting question. Have we made progress? The notion of progress itself is, of course, at stake in the history of Western thought and culture, so the question cannot be innocent. Furthermore, the notion of 'progress' applies differently in different fields. You can be a great physician if all you know is the current state of surgery, and a biology lecturer will rarely refer to Hippocrates' account of the four humours other than out of historical curiosity. But that is not the case in philosophy. Philosophers still engage with Plato as a philosophical (if not cultural or chronological) contemporary, and it is almost certainly true that you cannot be a good artist without knowing the history of art. For the orthodox Christian believer, the notion of moving on from 'the faith that was once for all delivered to the saints' (Jude 1:3) is quite the opposite of progress. With apologies to Tolkien's Tengwar inscription in *The Lord of the Rings*, it would be unwise to seek one theory of progress 'to rule them all'. Perhaps all we can say is that it is progress to realise that any measure of progress will itself be situated in the story it seeks to judge. Do we measure progress by increased happiness, increased wealth, reduced warfare, longer life spans, increased care for the most vulnerable, or better quality of relationships? Each yardstick is possible, and each comes with its own assumptions and weaknesses. To realise that – I am aware of the irony as I write this – is progress.

The second thought is that, over these past three millennia, Western humanity has achieved wondrous heights of aesthetic beauty, complex feats of philosophical contemplation and actions of great ethical prowess. Almost every century of Western history is studded with glittering achievements almost unimaginable just a hundred years previously. But a third thought follows quickly on the tail of the second: for each chapter of triumph there is an episode of disaster, cruelty or destruction. Three thousand years of history leave us reaching for that old and unfashionable word 'evil' to describe the worst of which human beings are capable. Wonder and disgust, rejoicing and shame are both in order when we contemplate who we are and what the West has become.

Finally, I hope to have shown the reader that the concepts and ideas we assume in order to live daily lives have histories and genealogies, that not everyone has thought as we think now, nor felt as we feel, and nor will everyone in the future live as we live now. Our great-grandchildren are just as unlikely to look back with nostalgia to our generation and wistfully long to return to the good old days as are we to think that everything our great-grandparents thought and did was a yardstick for us to aspire to today. The concepts of 'love', 'freedom' and 'the individual' have their histories (as does 'history'!), just as much as do England, France or the United States. With chronological as well as ideological separation, the dictum *audi alteram partem* (Latin: 'hear the other side') is a good starting point in order to avoid what the medievalist and Christian apologist C.S. Lewis (1898-1963) called a 'chronological snobbery'. Just think what people in a hundred years' time might be writing about us!

Glossary

Abstract Expressionism. An art movement that reached its height in the 1940s and 1950s in the USA. Intense artistic emotions are expressed in abstract forms. Examples include Jackson Pollock's action paintings and Mark Rothko's blocks of colour.

absurd. A term in Albert Camus's **existentialism** that designates the tension between (1) a world which is impassive to human emotions, dreams and hopes (expressed in sentiments such as 'the universe will not shed a tear when I die'), and (2) the persistence of human longings and desires for meaning in the face of this impassive world.

ad fontes (Latin: 'back to the sources'). In **Renaissance humanism**, *ad fontes* acted as a rallying cry to study the texts of ancient antiquity and the Bible themselves, rather than relying on subsequent commentators and **scholastic** manuals.

aesthetics/an aesthetic. That branch of philosophy that considers beauty or taste. 'An aesthetic' is a particular way of understanding and representing beauty and form, as in 'the aesthetic of Christian art' or 'Picasso's aesthetic'. As an adjective, the term usually denotes a pleasing sense of beauty, as in 'an aesthetic scene'. See also **epistemology**, **ontology**.

agapê (Greek: love, charity). The word is given a particular meaning in the Christian New Testament, where it denotes the self-sacrificial love shown by Christ in dying on the cross to **redeem sinners**, and by extension the self-sacrificial love for other people that is supposed to characterise the Christian community. It is at the heart of what is distinctive about the Christian **ethos** in Western history.

alienation. For Karl Marx, the condition in which, under **capitalism**, a worker is detached from the meaning of his own nature through losing the power to determine his own destiny. In early twentieth-century **modernism**, alienation is the condition of an individual lost in and threatened by a bureaucratic world the workings of which remain impenetrable. Alienation is seen acutely in the **novels** and short stories of Franz Kafka.

alogon (Greek: without reason). In ancient Greek thought, that which does not conform to a regular proportion or form is *alogon*. Irrational numbers are *alogon*. For Pythagoras, discovering such disproportion in the natural world was scandalous. See also *logos*.

antitype, see **typology**.

apeiron (Greek: without limit). For the **pre-Socratic philosopher** Anaximander, *apeiron* is the limitless material out of which everything is formed. It is the earliest recorded philosophical term in the Western world.

archê (Greek: beginning, origin). In ancient Greek thought, the ultimate origin or principle of all things. See also **pre-Socratic philosophers**.

aretê (Greek: excellence, goodness). In ancient Greek thought, *aretê* is the virtue or excellence of a thing or person in performing their purpose (*telos*) or **final cause**. A hammer has *aretê* if it performs well its function of hammering; a person has *aretê* if he or she performs well the purpose of his or her existence. Needless to say, there is more confusion among the Greeks about the purpose of human life then there is about the purpose of hammers.

Aristotelian logic. The system of logic first formalised by Aristotle. It includes principles fundamental to Western thinking such as the 'law of the excluded middle' (every proposition is either true or false), and the 'law of non-contradiction' (a thing cannot be both itself and its opposite at the same time and in the same way). It is sometimes known as Greek logic. Some scholars contrast it with Hebrew 'block' logic. Its adequacy is challenged by the mystical tradition and its sufficiency comes under attack in twentieth-century **postmodern** philosophy.

atheism. The belief and doctrine that there is no god, or gods. Early Christians were called atheists because they denied the existence of the Roman **pantheon**. The ancient **atomists** Epicurus and Lucretius seem to have believed in the existence of gods, but thought them irrelevant to human existence. Many modern scholars argue that true atheism is not seen in the West before the nineteenth century. In the eighteenth century, Hume and Kant paved the way for modern atheism, and the nineteenth- and early twentieth-century philosophies of Marx, Freud and Nietzsche are on many counts atheistic.

atomism. From the Greek *atomos*: uncuttable. In philosophy, the position according to which all that exists is atoms (very small indivisible particles of matter) and the void in which the atoms move. The first important atomist was Democritus in the fourth century BC, and the doctrine was later spread by Epicurus, and by Lucretius in his poem *De rerum natura* (*On the Nature of Things*). Atomism was eclipsed by Aristotle in the **medieval** universities, but bears significant similarities to the thought of Descartes in the seventeenth century. The 'logical atomism' of early twentieth-century linguistic philosophy uses the term in a different sense, to refer to the analysis of language to its simplest, indivisible parts.

atonal. In twentieth-century music, a composition is atonal if it is not written in any particular key, that is to say, if it does not have a dominant tone or tones. Atonal music was pioneered by the composer Arnold Schoenberg's 'emancipation of **dissonance**'.

autonomy. From the Greek *autos* (self) and *nomos* (law), an individual or a state is autonomous if it is self-governing, making its own laws. The term is of great importance in **Enlightenment** thought, which asserts the autonomous exercise of human reason, free from constraints of tradition or authority. Perhaps the most influential expression of the Enlightenment ideal of autonomy is Immanuel Kant's essay 'An Answer to the Question: "What is Enlightenment?"'

avant-garde. A very loosely connected group of artists and writers in the early decades of the twentieth century, characteristic for their unconventionality, violence and the shock produced by their work. Avant-garde movements include **Dada** and **Surrealism.**

Baroque. A broad term that describes the style, predominantly in art, music and architecture, that followed the **Renaissance** (*c.* 1600-1750). The word is thought to come from the Spanish *barocco*, a rough or imperfectly shaped pearl. In art, the Baroque is characterised by dramatic emotional expression and movement, as in the canvases of Rubens or Caravaggio, and intense contrasts of light and dark, often seen in Rembrandt and Vermeer. In architecture, the style often features complex flowing curves and exaggerated ornate features, epitomised in the chapel of the Palace of Versailles, outside Paris. In music, the Baroque period runs from 1600 until the death of J.S. Bach in 1750. It is characterised by the **polyphonic** complexity of forms like the **fugue**, and is superseded by the **homophony** of the **Classical** period. The term is used less precisely in literary studies, but can denote the ornate, artificial style that characterised some work in the late seventeenth and eighteenth centuries.

binary. A binary opposition (sometimes shortened to 'a binary') is any pair of terms which are contrasting and mutually exclusive, and which (at least in principle) allow no third term. Examples include good/evil, inside/outside, male/female.

bourgeoisie. In the sixteenth century, the bourgeoisie were the freemen of a *bourg* or market town, usually artisans or people working in crafts or trades. For Karl Marx, the bourgeoisie is the class of people in a **capitalist** society that has ownership of the **means of production**.

Byzantine. Art and architecture relating to Byzantium. Byzantium was the eastern division of the Roman empire, dating from when Constantine I founded the city of Byzantium (or Constantinople, modern-day Istanbul) in 330 AD until the capture of Constantinople by the Turks in 1453. Byzantine art is usually two-dimensional and depicts sacred subjects, representing saints with wide-open penetrating eyes. Its most common forms are the mosaic and the icon.

capitalism. The economic and political system that emerges with the rise of the Florentine merchant class in the fifteenth century, and that characterises the modern West. In capitalism, the **means of production** are owned not by the state but by private individuals, who run them for profit. See also **bourgeoisie**, **proletariat**.

catharsis. In Aristotle's theory of tragedy, catharsis is the release and purification of the audience's emotions of pity and fear which takes place when they experience the fate of the tragic hero. Critics disagree over the term's precise meaning for Aristotle.

church fathers, see **patristic**.

Classical. In music, the period from the end of the **Baroque** era (dated to the death of J.S. Bach in 1750) to the **Romanticism** of Beethoven's middle symphonies. It is characterised by an emphasis on **homophonic** melody and had great popular appeal to an increasingly **bourgeois** eighteenth-century Viennese public. The three greatest Classical composers are Haydn, Mozart and Beethoven.

coenobitic, **coenobite**. One of the two branches of monasticism. Eremitic monks live in solitary isolation, often in caves or deserts, whereas coenobitic monks live a communal life. Coenobitic monasticism is by far the form most frequently encountered in the West.

cogito (Latin: I think/I am thinking). Used as a noun, 'the *cogito*' refers to the formula from Descartes' *Discourse on the Method* 'cogito ergo sum', 'I am thinking, therefore I exist'. The *cogito* is often taken to be one of the most important milestones in the birth of the modern age, as it seeks to make the thinking self and not God the foundation of all true knowledge. See also **modernity**.

consumer society. A term applied to twentieth-century Western society to suggest that its economy is increasingly driven by the consumption of goods and services, rather than by the production of materials. For Baudrillard, in the consumer society consumption is considered as a social good in itself. See also **globalisation**, **postmodernity**.

Copernican Revolution. The change in thinking brought about by Nicolaus Copernicus, who, in *On the Revolutions of the Heavenly Spheres*, hypothesised that the sun is at the centre of the solar system, and not, as had been previously thought, the earth. By extension, it denotes any fundamental change in thinking. Used later by Immanuel Kant to describe his own critical philosophy.

courtly love. The high **medieval** sensibility of *fin'amor* or courtly love is a code of chivalric etiquette first expressed by the troubadour poets of the twelfth century. The term describes the ecstatic suffering induced by the love of a knight for a beautiful and yet inaccessible lady.

Cubism. A movement in pre-First World War twentieth-century art that rejects single viewpoint **perspective** and presents its subjects with geometric shapes and interlocking planes. Pioneered by Pablo Picasso and Georges Braque.

cubit. The measurement from the elbow to the tip of the middle finger. In ancient measurement, the cubit was commonly 18 inches (44 centimetres) long.

cult of feeling. A characteristic sensibility of **Romanticism**, the cult of feeling is a privileging of spontaneous and self-expressive passion in one's engagement with the world. It is important in the writing of Rousseau in France, Goethe in Germany and the English Romantic poets: Wordsworth, Coleridge, Shelley, Keats and Byron.

Dada. An early twentieth-century **avant-garde** artistic movement that favoured an **aesthetic** of shock to scandalise a **bourgeois** public. Prominent Dadaists included Max Ernst, artist and photographer Man Ray, and Marcel Duchamp for a period.

Duchamp's ready-mades are among the best-known examples of Dada art.

Dark Ages. A term first coined in the fourteenth century by the poet Petrarch to refer to the period from the fall of the western Roman empire in 476 AD to his own day. Petrarch intended the term to be a derogatory designation for a period lacking the radiance of ancient Roman literature and culture.

death of God. In *The Gay Science*, Nietzsche asserts that God is dead and that we have killed him. He means that the West finds itself no longer able to believe in the existence of any reality beyond that of our senses to which we can appeal to arbitrate questions of truth, goodness and beauty. For Nietzsche, though we have killed God we are yet to realise the consequences of our action.

deconstruction. A term used to describe the late twentieth-century philosophy of Jacques Derrida. Among other meanings offered by Derrida, to deconstruct something is to show how the distinctions it uses or assumes (for example: inside/outside) are made possible by something that cannot itself be reduced to either term of the distinction (for example: a wall separating inside from outside).

deesis (Greek: petition). In **Byzantine** art, a deesis is a composition with Christ flanked by the Virgin Mary and John the Baptist who raise their hands towards him in petitionary prayer. Christ is often depicted in glory, carrying a book.

deism. The belief and doctrine that there exists a Supreme Being that has created the universe, but a rejection of Christian ideas of **revelation** and the miraculous. Deists may believe in an active **Providence** guiding history, but refuse to believe in a God who personally intervenes in the natural world. Deism became popular among certain members of the **Enlightenment** intellectual elite, including Voltaire, Rousseau, and (more controversially) Hume and Locke.

dialectic. The term has two distinct meanings. For Plato, dialectic describes the way that Socrates argues in the dialogues, by means of question and answer. By implication, dialectic means the art of argument or debating opinions. For Hegel, dialectic describes the process of change in thought or in the world, where opposite terms are overcome or **sublated** into a new term which neither extinguishes nor fully embraces them. For example: being and nonbeing are dialectically sublated into becoming.

dialectical idealism. The philosophy of history, held by Hegel, according to which the final goal of historical progress is the self-realisation in history of Absolute Spirit.

dialectical materialism. The view, held by Karl Marx, that the dialectical progress of history is driven not by an Absolute Spirit, as in Hegel's **dialectical idealism**, but by the material conditions of a society.

diatonic. Music is diatonic if it is written in a major or minor key. Western music is diatonic from the early **Baroque** until the **atonal**

experiments of Arnold Schoenberg in the early twentieth century.

différance. A term coined by philosopher Jacques Derrida to suggest that meaning is an effect of differences between terms and ideas rather than the result of one foundational *logos*, and that full or ultimate meaning is never fully present in any single sign or concept, but always deferred. Think of using a dictionary to find out what a word means: each definition is also a sequence of words which themselves need to be defined, and then those definitions are also sequences of words, and so on. The *-ance* ending, though differing from conventional French spelling, is intentional.

dissonance. In musical theory, combinations of pitch are dissonant if they transgress rules of harmony and resolution adhered to during the 'common practice period' in music from the **Baroque** to **Romanticism**.

ecphrasis. The literary description of a non-verbal work of art such as a goblet or a painting. A frequent feature of **medieval** literature.

écriture féminine. In third wave **feminism**, a kind of writing that cuts across the **binary oppositions** and **Aristotelian logic** that are deemed to be characteristic of masculinist writing. The term is first coined by Hélène Cixous in her essay 'The Laugh of the Medusa' (1975).

ego. In Freud's second map of the human mind, the ego is the largely conscious part of the mind; it is the mind that thinks, wills and reasons, the *cogito* of Descartes. See also **id**, **superego**.

Egyptian gold. When Moses leads the Hebrews out of slavery in Egypt towards the promised land, **Yahweh** commands them in Exodus 3:22 to ask the Egyptians for items of gold jewellery to take with them. In *On Christian Doctrine*, Augustine uses the Egyptian gold as an image of those aspects of a pagan culture – its philosophy, literature and art – that Christians should gratefully accept and put to their own use.

ellen, see *þrym* **and** *ellen* (with *þ* transliterated as 'th').

elegy, elegiac. In ancient Greek and Roman poetry, an elegy is usually a first person poem, frequently portraying the tormented passion of a male poet whose love enslaves him to a mistress who does not return his affections. Elegies are often mournful or lamenting in tone. See also **lyric**.

Elohim (Hebrew: God). A generic ancient Hebrew word for God. *Elohim* is plural of *el*, a 'plural of majesty' that exalts the one being spoken of. Christians have often seen the plural as an early indication of the Christian **Trinity**.

empiricism. The philosophical doctrine according to which all knowledge is derived from sense experience. Empiricists deny the **rationalist** claim that certain ideas are innate in our minds at birth. The British Empiricists Locke, Berkeley and Hume form an influential current of **Enlightenment** thought. See also **logical positivism**, **positivism**, **rationalism**.

Enlightenment. An eighteenth-century intellectual and social movement characterised by the **epistemological** privilege of experience and reason at the expense of tradition and **revelation**. Contemporary scholarship tends to distinguish between the 'radical Enlightenment' and the 'moderate Enlightenment'. The radical Enlightenment, in the wake of Spinoza's **pantheism**, is considered the more **atheistic** and politically revolutionary wing, and the moderate Enlightenment, looking to Sir Isaac Newton and the British **empiricist** John Locke, was politically more conservative and more willing to sit alongside traditional **theistic** or **deistic** beliefs.

epic. A long poem, typically telling of heroic exploits and adventures. Epics are usually written in a grand style, and often tell of battles and gods. The greatest epics of the ancient world are Homer's *Iliad* and *Odyssey* in Greek, and Virgil's *Aeneid* in Latin. Other notable epics in Western literary history are the Anglo-Saxon *Beowulf* and John Milton's *Paradise Lost*.

episteme. A term used by mid twentieth-century philosopher Michel Foucault to designate the set of conditions that make it possible for something to be known. Foucault distinguishes between the classical and modern epistemes: the classical episteme organises knowledge by analogies, and the modern episteme by a reason that classifies into categories. One episteme or regime of knowledge recognises the category of 'demon possession', whereas in another regime that category is simply unthinkable, replaced for example by 'mental illness'. See also **postmodernism**.

epistemology. The branch of philosophy that considers the conditions and extent of knowledge, and that seeks to answer the questions 'what can we know?' and 'how do we know it?' See also **aesthetics**, **ontology**.

epithet. An adjective that designates something characteristic of the person or thing it describes. Epithets are an important part of Homer's style, and famous Homeric epithets include the 'wine-dark sea', 'rosy-fingered dawn' and 'swift-footed Achilles'.

eschatology, *eschaton*. From the Greek *eschatos* (adjective: last or extreme), eschatology is the part of Christian theology that considers the 'last things': death, final judgment, heaven and hell.

ethos (Greek: character, disposition, way of life). An ethos is the way of life or 'spirit' that typifies a particular community or society. Broader than 'worldview', it includes that society's customs, rituals, behaviours, aspirations, beliefs, values and fears. In this book, the term is used to describe those dispositions and ways of being in the world that are broadly characteristic of a particular period or movement. See also *aretê*, *agapê*, **courtly love**, *sprezzatura*, *virtù*, **cult of feeling**, **subversion**.

exegesis. The careful, critical explanation of a passage of text, commonly used in relation to the Bible.

existentialism. A twentieth-century French philosophical movement with its roots in the thought of Pascal, Kierkegaard and Heidegger. In Sartre's brief formulation, a central notion of existentialism is that 'existence precedes essence', in other words there are no **final**

causes in nature and therefore humanity is 'condemned to be free', to choose its own destiny. Albert Camus did much to popularise the philosophy through his **novels** and through his notion of the **absurd**. Other prominent existentialists are Simone de Beauvoir and Maurice Merleau-Ponty.

fate. For much Greek thought, a person's fate (share, or portion) is determined at birth. This always includes the person's death, and may also encompass the salient events of their life. It is the fate of Oedipus to murder his father and marry his mother. See also **providence**, **teleology**.

feminism. The twentieth-century movement that advocates women's equality and women's' rights. Feminism is commonly understood to have three waves in the twentieth century. The first wave is the women's suffrage movement of the late nineteenth and early twentieth centuries; the second wave brings the women's liberation movement of the 1960s to 1980s, with the focus now on equality for women in employment and reproductive law, and in the arts and culture. Third-wave feminism turns its attention to **Aristotelian logic** and the structure of Western languages, arguing that they are **phallocentric** and need to be **subverted** by practices such as *écriture féminine*.

feudalism. The hierarchical organisation typical of Western **medieval** societies. The feudal hierarchy has three main levels, excepting the monarch. Landowning lords (first level) grant tenure of pockets of land (called fiefs) to vassals (second level), in exchange for the vassals' military service. The land is worked by peasants, or serfs (third level), who give a proportion of their crops to the lord, as well as paying taxes. Feudalism began to be superseded, around the time of the Florentine **Renaissance**, with the rise of **capitalism**. In France, the final vestiges of the feudal system were abandoned by the National Assembly in the revolutionary year of 1789.

final cause. In his *Metaphysics*, Aristotle identifies four different types of cause. The 'material cause' is the matter out of which a thing exists (in the case of Michelangelo's statue of David, this is the marble). The 'formal cause' is the form or model of the thing (the model who poses for Michelangelo). The 'efficient cause' is that which imparts form to matter (Michelangelo's chisel blows), and the final cause is that which is finally realised in time (Michelangelo's idea of what the finished sculpture should look like). For Aristotle, final causes exist in the world; everything that exists has its particular purpose, something that it is 'good for'. The notion of actually existing final causes is criticised by Francis Bacon and lost in the science of the modern era.

fin'amor, see **courtly love**.

first-wave feminism, see **feminism**.

flying buttress. A characteristic feature of **Gothic** architecture. An exterior arch supporting the wall of a building, taking the weight of the roof and allowing the wall to be thinner and built with larger windows.

Forms. In Plato's philosophy, Forms (upper case 'F', sometimes called Ideas) are abstract universals that really exist in another world, what Plato calls a 'heavenly place'. All particular things in the world participate in these Forms. For example, every table in the world participates in (is a copy of) the one Form of a table, every dog in the Form of a dog, and so on. Forms for Plato are perfect and unchanging, and the greatest Form is the Form of the Good, in which everything that exists participates. For Aristotle, forms (lower case 'f') only exist when they are instantiated, that is to say, when a particular body of matter is made to take on a particular form. For example, there is no 'sphere' apart from the spheres made out of brass or rock or wood and so on that exist in this world. For both Plato and Aristotle, forms really exist. Augustine holds that forms exist in the mind of God. Late medieval nominalism, in challenging the existence of universals, also sets itself against Forms. See also **universals**, **particulars**, **nominalism**.

fresco. A method of wall painting in which water-based pigments are applied to fresh plaster. The pigment soaks into the plaster as it dries, producing a rich and durable colour that is part of the wall itself. Notable examples include Michelangelo's Sistine Chapel and Raphael's *Stanze* in the Vatican (including the *School of Athens* in the *Stanza della Segnatura*).

fugue. A **polyphonic** musical form in which two or more equally dominant parts successively state and develop the same melody. The term comes from the Latin *fuga* (flight, escape), and each part chases after the preceding one. The fugue was a popular form of **Baroque** composition and was perfected by J.S. Bach.

GDP. Short for 'Gross Domestic Product'. The combined value of all the goods and services produced within a particular country in a given period.

globalisation. The process by which businesses source, produce or market their goods or services on a global scale. The term is applied by extension to aspects of culture (usually Western or, more specifically, North American culture) that become globally recognised and/or followed. See also **consumer society**, **postmodernity**.

Gothic. The term describes an architectural style popular in Europe from the twelfth to the sixteenth centuries. Pointed arches, **flying buttresses** and **ribbed vaults** are characteristic features of Gothic cathedrals. The first cathedral to be built in this style was the Abbey Church of Saint Denis (Paris), completed in 1144.

guild. In the **medieval** town, guilds were associations of craftsmen or merchants formed for mutual protection. Guilds would control the market and enforce quality standards for particular goods. The influence of the guilds fell with the rise of **capitalism**.

homophony. Music which has one predominant melody is homophonic. Homophony is characteristic of **Classical** era music, which largely abandoned earlier **Baroque** polyphony. See also **polyphony**.

humanism. A term to describe an important set of values prominent during the **Renaissance**. Renaissance humanists elaborated a picture of man (and yes, it usually was 'man' as opposed to 'woman') more heroic, noble and optimistic than the one they perceived in their **scholastic** predecessors, also replacing scholastic logic with rhetoric in the Renaissance curriculum. Prominent Renaissance humanists include Petrarch and Erasmus and, with qualifications, Montaigne.

hyperreality. In Jean Baudrillard's account of **postmodernity**, he describes hyperreality as a the state of a society in which the replication of images or ideas become more real (more immediate, more expressive, more intense, more experienced) than the reality those images reproduce. Baudrillard uses Disneyland as an example of hyperreality.

id. In Freud's second map of the human mind, the unconscious id is a reservoir of energy, including instinctive impulses which demand instant gratification (for sex, food and dominance). It is in conflict with the ego and superego, and usually kept in check by them. See also **ego**, **superego**.

Impressionism. In art, a movement originating in France in the 1860s that seeks to capture the momentary effect of light and colour on a landscape. Impressionists usually worked outside and employed a bright palette of colours. Major practitioners include Monet, Degas, Sisley, Pissarro and Renoir. In music, impressionism as pioneered by Claude Debussy moves away from the direct force of **Romantic** music and towards a smoother, less differentiated style.

incarnation. Literally meaning 'enfleshment', incarnation is a term in Christian theology that refers to God taking on human flesh in Jesus Christ. In the words of John's gospel, 'the word became flesh'. Orthodox theology holds that the incarnate Christ has two natures: he is fully God and fully human.

International Style. In twentieth-century architecture, the International Style was developed in the 1920s and 1930s and is characterised by its rejection of ornamentation in favour of functionality and by its use of steel and reinforced concrete in simple, orthogonal lines. Ludwig Mies van der Rohe and Le Corbusier are leading exponents.

khôra (Greek). In Plato's theory of the **Forms**, *khôra* is the place or 'receptacle' between the world of the Forms and the material world, where Forms materialise, and where they gain the imperfections they manifest in the material world.

logical positivism. Also known as logical **empiricism**. A movement in early twentieth-century philosophy according to which only empirical propositions are meaningful, and the only meaningful philosophical problems are those that can be solved through logical analysis. Important logical positivists include Gottlob Frege, Bertrand Russell and the early Wittgenstein.

logos (Greek: word, reason). For the **pre-Socratic** philosopher Heraclitus, *logos* is the cosmic principle that gives order to the world. For Plato, all

217

reality is reasonable, ordered according to *logos*. In the gospel of John in the Bible, the *logos* is identified with Jesus Christ. For Derrida, all Western thinking from Plato onward is logocentric because it assumes such an order-giving foundation. See also **logocentrism**.

logocentrism. In *Of Grammatology*, Derrida argues that throughout its history Western thinking has assumed the existence of one simple, stable principle of reason and identity. Thinking which makes such an assumption he calls logocentric. According to Derrida the assumption must be challenged. See also ***logos, différance***.

lyric. Ancient Greek lyric poetry was simply poetry sung to the lyre. Lyric poetry is a varied genre in the ancient world, and it is not written in any set metre. In the case of choral lyric (performed by a group of singers), the subject matter of lyric tended to be in praise of a god or goddess, and with monodic (solo) lyric the poem's themes were usually taken from the life of the poet. The dithyrambs, sung at the festivals where the first Greek **tragedies** were performed, were a development of lyric. Sappho is often considered the greatest Greek lyric poet, and Horace and Catullus are foremost among the Latin lyric poets. See also **elegiac.**

means of production. The land, factories, machines, labour and capital that are necessary for the production of goods and services in a society. For Marx, **capitalism** is characterised by the **bourgeoisie**'s ownership of the means of production, leaving the **proletariat** nothing to sell but their labour. See also **capitalism, bourgeoisie, proletariat**.

medieval period, see **Middle Ages**.

metanarrative. For Jean-François Lyotard, a metanarrative (French: 'grand récit') is a big story that is told about the historical progress of a society and which legitimates certain actions within that society. Examples include the **Enlightenment** narrative of the progress of the human race towards inevitable perfection and the Marxist narrative of the inevitable overthrow of the **bourgeoisie** by the **proletariat**. Lyotard considered metanarratives to be **totalising**, and defined **postmodernism** as an 'incredulity towards metanarratives'.

metaphysics. The branch of philosophy which deals with what is beyond the physical world. The word was invented to name books by Aristotle that came after his *Physics* in collected volumes. Metaphysics is often concerned with the first principles of reality: time and space as such, being and substance, and the nature of the universe. It has two branches: **ontology** (inquiry into being as such, as opposed to beings), and cosmology (inquiry into the structure of the universe). See also **ontology**.

metre. The regular rhythm of sound units in a line of poetry. In Greek and Latin poetry, a line is commonly divided into a groups of syllables called feet, and feet with different rhythms are given different names, each composed of short and long syllables, denoted by the signs $\cup$ and $-$ respectively. Common feet include the iamb ($\cup\,-$), trochee ($-\,\cup$), spondee ($-\,-$) and dactyl ($-\,\cup\,\cup$). The line 'shall I compare thee to a summers day' has five iambic feet, called an iambic pentameter. It would be written ∪ – ∪ – ∪ – ∪ – ∪ –.

Middle Ages. Commonly understood to denote the period from the fall of the Western Roman empire in 476 AD until the Florentine **Renaissance** in the fourteenth century. It can be split into three rough periods: the early Middle Ages, with its highpoint in the court of the Holy Roman Emperor Charlemagne, from the fifth to the tenth centuries, the high Middle Ages, characterised by **scholastic** philosophy and the building of cathedrals and universities, from the eleventh to the thirteenth centuries, and the late Middle Ages in the fourteenth century. The designations 'Middle Ages' and 'Dark Ages' both wear their negative value judgments on their sleeves, leading most scholars to avoid the latter term altogether.

mimesis, **mimetic** (Greek: imitation). In Aristotle's *Poetics*, works of art should imitate nature, reproducing within themselves a reality which is found outside them. Non-mimetic art has a long history in the West, with the stylised, other-worldly representations of **Byzantine** art as an example of early art with non-mimetic features. Twentieth-century movements such as **Cubism** and **modernism** reject mimetic principles.

moderate Enlightenment, see **Enlightenment**.

moderate realism, see **realism**.

modernism. The literary, artistic and cultural sensibility prevalent the early decades of the twentieth century, sharing many traits with **avant-garde** movements. A prominent characteristic of the modernist sensibility is **alienation**, particularly evident in the **novels** and short stories of Franz Kafka. The modernist architecture of Le Corbusier and Ludwig Mies van der Rohe is sparse and functional, and the modernist **Abstract Expressionist** painting of Jackson Pollock and Mark Rothko is highly abstract and expressive of deep artistic feeling. The modernist literature of James Joyce and Virginia Woolf is frequently dismissive of low culture and full of allusions and word plays, making great demands of its reader. In modernist music, Stravinsky experiments with **dissonant** rhythms and Schoenberg moves away from the **diatonic** scale in favour of **atonal** compositions. The **Pop Art** of the 1960s can be seen as a reaction against the austere seriousness of modernism. Modernism is not to be confused with modernity. See also **modernity**.

modernity. In the fifth century AD, the Latin term *modernus* was used to distinguish the modern Christian present from the Greco-Roman past, but it is most commonly taken to mean that period of Western history that follows the **Middle Ages**. The assertion of the **autonomy** of human knowledge with Descartes' *cogito* and Bacon's **empirical** method are often taken to be milestones in the development of the modern outlook. Some twentieth-century thinkers hold that modernity has now been superseded by **postmodernity**, others that the postmodern is in fact late modernity. Modernity is not to be confused with modernism. See also **modernism**.

monotheism. The belief that there is only one God. The belief becomes widespread in the West through the influence of Hebrew thought and culture. Christianity holds a complex **Trinitarian** monotheism, in which God the Father, God the Son and God the Holy Spirit are 'one God in three persons'. See also **pantheism**.

muse. In Greek myth, the nine muses are daughters of Zeus and Mnemosyne, and preside over the arts and sciences. They are: Calliope (**epic** poetry), Clio (history), Euterpe (flute playing and **elegiac** poetry), Terpsichore (choral dancing and song), Erato (lyre playing and **lyric** poetry), Melpomene (**tragedy**), Thalia (comedy and light verse), Polyhymnia (hymns, and later mime), and Urania (astronomy). Appeals to the muses for help are common at the beginning of ancient works of literature, for example in Homer's *Iliad* and *Odyssey*.

Neoclassicism. In late eighteenth- and nineteenth-century art, Neoclassicism revives ancient Greek and Roman ideals of form, proportion and line in a reaction against the ornate decoration of the **Rococo**. Its theory was provided by Winckelmann and the style is epitomised by Jacques-Louis David's *The Oath of the Horatii* and *Death of Socrates*.

Neoplatonism. A philosophical system based on the thought of Plotinus. It combines an interpretation of Plato's **Forms** with religious doctrines. All reality flows from the One, which is beyond all categories (neither large nor small, good nor evil ...). Out of the One comes intelligence (Greek: *nous*), and out of intelligence come souls, some of which take on material bodies. Just as everything comes from the One, everything will eventually return to the One. Boethius is influential in blending Neoplatonic teaching with elements of Christianity, and this Christianised form of Neoplatonism is prominent in **medieval** and **Renaissance** thought.

neurosis. In Freud's psychoanalysis, a relatively mild disorder of the nervous system that does not result in the sufferer losing touch with reality. Might include anxiety or depression. See also **psychosis**.

new novel, see **novel**.

nominalism. The late **medieval** philosophy according to which universals are nothing but 'empty breath' (Latin: *flatus vocis*), and particulars are all that exists. The greatest nominalist philosopher was William of Ockham, and the doctrine finds precursors in Abelard and Boethius. See also **particulars**, **realism**, **universal**s.

noumenon, **noumenal**. In Kant's critical philosophy, a noumenon is a 'thing in itself' (German: 'Ding an sich'), as distinct from a thing as it is known to the human mind. The Kantian noumenon, unlike the Platonic **Form**, cannot be known even through the intellect, and this unknowability leads the generation of idealists who follow Kant to dispense with the notion altogether. See also **phenomenon**.

novel, **novelist**. An extended narrative genre, usually in prose, originating in the modern era. More than other literary genres, the style, structure and subject matter of novels is varied and flexible. It is commonly accepted that Cervantes's *Don Quixote* is the first modern novel. The twentieth century saw innovations in novel form, notably in the **modernist** novels of James Joyce and Virginia Woolf employing the **stream of consciousness**, and in the French 'new novel' of Robbe-Grillet, Simon and Sarraute.

omnibus genre. A literary genre that incorporates fragments of other genres within it. Two salient examples in Western literature are the **epic** and the **novel**.

ontology. The branch of philosophy that considers Being as such, rather than particular beings. For Plato, the perfect and eternal 'Being' of the **Forms** is contrasted with the changing and decaying 'becoming' of **particular** objects in the world which we apprehend with our senses. In the wake of Nietzsche, Darwin and Freud, **postmodern** philosophy considers any notion of Being to be derivative of becoming. See also **aesthetics**, **epistemology**, **metaphysics**.

onto-theology. The position that understands God primarily or exclusively in terms of his Being, and seeks to know God through an exercise of reason. The approach is often ascribed to Anselm of Canterbury and the **scholastics**. This God of Being, sometimes disparagingly called the God of the philosophers, is widely critiqued in **postmodern** thought.

oratorio. A form of sacred musical composition for orchestra and voices, originally presented in the chapels (or oratories) of seventeenth-century Italy. The most famous oratorio is Handel's *Messiah*.

overture. An orchestral piece that begins an opera or play. Overtures often introduce melodies that will recur in the work they precede. In the **Classical** period, the overture developed into the symphony form.

pantheism. The belief and doctrine that the universe is identical with God, or with the gods. All life is divine. The most celebrated modern pantheist is Spinoza. See also **deism**, **monotheism**.

pantheon (Greek: 'all the gods'). The collective term for all the deities of a particular culture (for example: 'the pantheon of Greece'), or a temple dedicated to all the gods. The Pantheon, Rome's best preserved ancient building, was begun by the emperor Agrippa in 27 BC.

pantocrator, *pantokrator* (Greek: 'ruler of all'). In **Byzantine** iconography, pantocrator images of Christ show him glorified as the ruler of the universe, sometimes sitting on the globe and frequently holding a book.

parousia (Greek: 'presence, arrival'). In Christian theology, the term refers to the 'second coming' of Christ, his future return in glory to judge the world. It is the time when all secrets will be made known and all injustices righted. See also **eschatology**.

particular, **particularism**. In philosophy, a particular is a single thing (the white rectangular sheet of paper on my desk) as opposed to a universal (whiteness, or the form of a rectangle). Plato held that particulars participate in the **Forms** from which they are derived, whereas Aristotle held that forms only exist when they are instantiated in particulars. The late **medieval nominalists** held that only particulars exist, and that universals are mere words. See also **universal**.

pastiche. An artistic work that imitates a previous work, either in style or in content, or that combines obvious influences from two or more different styles. Pastiche is a mode of artistic production characteristic of **postmodernity**, a salient example being the AT&T Building (now the Sony Building) in Manhattan, New York.

patristic. In Christian church history, patristics is the study of the early 'church fathers', who were active from the first to between the fifth and eighth centuries AD (scholars differ on the end date), known as the patristic period. Prominent church fathers include Tertullian, Irenaeus, Ambrose and Augustine.

perspective. In art, a method for depicting three-dimensional objects on a two-dimensional surface. Following the theoretical work of Brunelleschi and Alberti, mathematical or linear perspective became popular among artists in **Renaissance** Florence. Traditional perspective begins to be questioned and then rejected in twentieth-century art.

phallocentrism. Phallocentric thought is focused on or obsessed with the male phallus (penis), as a symbol of male authority or domination. In **third-wave feminism**, the claim is made that **Aristotelian logic**, along with Western culture and language as a whole, are phallocentric, that is to say they reflect a male point of view that suppresses and excludes women.

phenomenon, **phenomenal**. In Kant's critical philosophy, a phenomenon is an object or event as we experience it or as it appears to us, in contrast to what Kant calls a '**noumenon**', an object or event as it is in itself. For Kant, the phenomenal world bends itself to the categories of my understanding (such as space and time), whereas most earlier pre-critical philosophers thought that human understanding bends itself to the world. This fundamental change is what Kant called his **Copernican Revolution**.

philology. The study of how languages develop over time.

philosophe. Name given to a loosely connected group of eighteenth-century French writers, politicians, scientists, thinkers and public intellectuals, broadly sympathetic to **Enlightenment** values. Prominent *philosophes* include Voltaire, Rousseau and Diderot.

polyphony. A term to describe music with two or more equally stressed **autonomous** melodies. Polyphony is characteristic of **Baroque** era music, and is perfected in the compositions of J.S. Bach. See also **fugue**, **homophony**.

Pop Art. A style of 1950s-1970s art that takes its inspiration from the images and objects of popular **consumer** culture, including food packaging, comic books and photographs of musical or Hollywood stars. Silk-screen printing allowed for the rapid reproduction of many thousands of copies. The movement flourished primarily in the USA and Britain, and notable exponents include Andy Warhol, Roy Lichtenstein and David Hockney.

positivism. A nineteenth-century philosophical movement based around the writing of Auguste Comte. A reworking of **empiricism**, positivism recognises as knowledge only that which can be scientifically verified or can be proven logically or mathematically. It is usually allied with an optimism about the scope and benefits of science. Positivism influenced the **realist** writing of Flaubert and Zola, and the realist artistic style of Courbet, but its popularity faded quickly after the First World War. See also **logical positivism**.

postmodernity, **postmodernism**. Many scholars describe the period of the late twentieth and twenty-first centuries in the West as one of postmodernity. It is often taken to indicate the prominence of **globalisation** and the **consumer society**, and the proliferation of images in what Baudrillard called **hyperreality**. Postmodernism is the philosophy prominent in the period of postmodernity, though in truth those grouped under the umbrella of 'postmodernism' often disagree with each other on important matters. Prominent moves in postmodernism include an incredulity toward **metanarratives** (Lyotard), the primacy of becoming over Being (Deleuze) and the **deconstruction** of the Western *logos* (Derrida).

pre-Socratic philosophers. Those philosophers from the sixth and fifth centuries BC in ancient Greece who are active before Socrates. The Milesians Thales, Anaximander and Anaximenes (named after the town of Miletus, on the Aegean coast), sought for the origin (Greek: *archê*) of all things. Pythagoras considered the world to be constructed according to deep harmonies and proportions which could be apprehended mathematically, as well as discerned in musical pitch and the rotating planetary spheres. Heraclitus of Ephesus gives us the first use of the *logos* in Western thought. Parmenides holds that reality is 'one', and that change is an illusion.

programme music. Music that expresses an extra-musical idea of some sort. It may seek to tell a story, paint a scene or evoke a mood. The idea is explained in the programme, a written preface intended to guide the listener's understanding of the music. Salient examples in include Beethoven's Sixth (Pastoral) Symphony and Berlioz's *Symphonie fantastique*.

proletariat. The working class. In ancient Rome, a *proletarius* was a person with no property to be taxed. Marx defines the proletariat as the class which, not owning the **means of production**, must sell its daily labour as its only source of income. In Marx's **dialectical materialism**, the proletariat would inevitably overthrow the factory-owning **bourgeoisie**.

providence. The Christian view that God is at work in the universe, ordering everything according to his ultimate plan. Providence is not to be confused with fate, according to which human destinies are fixed by an impersonal force. See also **fate**, **teleology**, **eschatology**.

psychosis. In Freud's psychoanalysis, a psychosis is an illness of the mind not of organic origin, and often accompanied by hallucinations, delusions and a loss of connection with external reality. See also **neurosis**.

Puritanism. An English Protestant movement of the late sixteenth and seventeenth centuries. Puritans considered that the **Reformation** in England had not gone far enough, and wished to see the Church of England take further steps to recover the purity of doctrine that characterised the New Testament documents themselves. It was a group of four hundred Puritans who, disillusioned with the slow pace of reform in England, sailed to found the Massachusetts Bay Colony in 1629.

Pyrrhonism, **Pyrrhonian scepticism**. Sometimes abbreviated to Pyrrhonism, Pyrrhonian scepticism is a tradition traced to the Greek philosopher Pyrrho of Elias as he is represented in the work of Sextus Empiricus. Given that the reasons in favour of believing a particular thing are never stronger than the reasons for not believing it, the best course of action is to suspend judgment and cultivate an attitude of untroubled calm. The influence of Pyrrhonism can be seen in Montaigne's *Essays*, and it is this position that Descartes tries to refute with his *cogito*.

quadrivium. The higher division of the seven liberal arts, those which are mathematically based. Arithmetic, music, geometry and astronomy. The quadrivium commonly comprised the advanced study in **medieval** universities, following on from the **trivium**.

radical Enlightenment, see **Enlightenment**

rationalism. Any philosophical position holding that knowledge is primarily acquired through the exercise of reason. Often accompanied by the belief that the mind is endowed from birth with innate categories that structure all knowledge. Plato is a rationalist when he takes the position that we can ascend to knowledge of the **Forms** through the use of our intellect, as is Descartes when he establishes the *cogito* as the basis of all 'clear and distinct' knowledge. See also **empiricism**.

realism. The term has different meanings in philosophy and in literature and art. In philosophy, realism is the position according to which **universals** have real existence, in opposition to **nominalism** which claims that they do not. Some realists hold that universals exist apart from **particulars** (Plato), others that universals exist only when instantiated in particulars (Aristotle). This latter position is called moderate realism. Aquinas' **scholastic** philosophy develops a form of Aristotelian realism. In literature and art, realism is a nineteenth-century movement influenced by Auguste Comte's **positivism**. It seeks to provide a faithful record of life, particularly those base or sordid elements usually ignored by earlier **romance**. Important realist authors include George Eliot, Honoré de Balzac and Gustave Flaubert, with Gustave Courbet prominent among realist artists.

redemption, **redeem**. In the Bible and in Christian theology, Christ's death on the cross redeems **sinners** from their slavery to sin (according to the teaching that 'everyone who sins is a slave to sin', John 8:34). The image evoked is that of paying a price to secure someone's freedom (Greek: *apolutrosis*, meaning 'ransom' or 'deliverance'). In the ancient world, slaves could be redeemed (released from slavery) in this way.

Reformation. The movement in sixteenth-century European church and society that first sought reform within, and then split from, the Roman Catholic church. The main leader of its first generation was Martin Luther, who attacked the corruption of the church and preached that people are saved by God's grace (free gift) alone, apart from good works they perform. Prominent among the second generation of reformers was John Calvin, who sought to govern the city of Geneva according to Reformation principles. The Reformation resulted in the development of two major religions in Europe: Protestantism and Catholicism, with Europe divided between the Protestant north (The Low Countries and England) and the Catholic South (France, Spain, Italy and Portugal). Partly in response to the Protestant Reformation, the Catholic church underwent its own reforms, many of which were formalised in the Council of Trent (1545-63).

Renaissance (French: rebirth). Refers to the rebirth of interest in ancient Greek and Roman artistic and literary forms in the fourteenth to sixteenth centuries. Humanism is characteristic of the philosophy of the time. We commonly distinguish between the early or Florentine Renaissance, which saw the increasing development of artistic naturalism and the birth of **capitalism** with the rise of the merchant class, and the high or Roman Renaissance, with the masterworks of the 'Roman Trinity' of Leonardo, Michelangelo and Raphael. See also **humanism**, *sprezzatura*, *virtù*.

revelation. In Christian theology, revelation is God's self-disclosure to the human knower. God reveals himself to a limited extent in the natural world, and more fully in the Bible and in the **incarnation** of Jesus Christ. The mystical tradition within Christianity holds that God reveals himself to the human soul through direct, ecstatic experience. Knowledge of ultimate reality through the gift of revelation is to be contrasted with **empiricism** and **rationalism**.

ribbed vault. A characteristic feature of **Gothic** cathedral design. A vault with an under-surface divided by stone ribs, allowing for the construction of higher arches and windows than was previously possible.

Rococo. A style of furniture, architecture and painting popular in eighteenth-century Europe after the **Baroque** and preceding **Neoclassicism**. It is known for its elegant playfulness and elaborate ornamentation, often with floral and shell-like themes. Rococo art has an air of lightness, some would say frivolity. Prominent artists include Fragonard and Boucher.

romance. A literary genre that came to prominence in the early **Middle**

Ages. Usually written in verse, romances frequently tell of heroic exploits and enchanted or magical creatures and events. Whereas **epic** dwells on the sensibility of a warrior's *aretê*, romance foregrounds the sensibility of **courtly love**. The most important medieval romance is the *Romance of the Rose*, and notable **Renaissance** examples include Ariosto's *Orlando Furioso* and Edmund Spenser's *The Faerie Queene*. Cervantes parodies the genre in *Don Quixote*.

Romanticism. In literature and the arts, a movement beginning in the late eighteenth century, with a focus on imagination and spontaneous creativity. Romanticism is often taken as a rebellion against the **epistemological** privilege accorded to reason in the **Enlightenment**, though the two share much in common. Characteristic of the Romantic sensibility is the **cult of feeling**. There is a substantial overlap between the Enlightenment and Romanticism, two important examples being the thought of Rousseau and Kant's theory of the **sublime** in his *Critique of the Power of Judgment*. Major figures associated with Romanticism include the Schlegel brothers, Schelling and Novalis in Germany, the English Romantic poets Shelley, Keats and Byron, and the artists Turner, Friedrich and Delacroix.

Romanesque. The architectural style dominant in Europe from the tenth to the twelfth centuries, when it is eclipsed by the lighter and higher **Gothic** style. Seeking inspiration in the semicircular arches of ancient Rome, Romanesque architecture is noted for its vaulted stone ceilings. Important examples of the Romanesque style include Durham Cathedral in England and the Abbey Church at Cluny.

scholasticism. The method of philosophical enquiry that became dominant in high **medieval** universities, or 'schools'. The scholastic method proceeds by analysing a philosophical text into a series of key propositions (*sententiae*) and then elaborating for each *sententia* a series of arguments for and against, before appealing to previous commentators and arriving at a conclusion. This method was most frequently used in relation to Aristotle, the Bible, and the early **church fathers**. Scholasticism could be either **realist** (Aquinas) or **nominalist** (Scotus), and scholastic philosophers are also known as schoolmen. The scholastic method was rejected by **Renaissance humanists** in favour of the study of rhetoric. Prominent exponents include Eriugena, Abelard, Anselm, Aquinas and Scotus.

Scientific Revolution. A term intended to group together a number of developments from Copernicus to Newton considered to be crucial in the rise of modern science, and including Bacon's elaboration of the scientific method, Descartes' mathematisation of space, Galileo's laws of motion and Newton's law of gravity. In broad terms, the revolution establishes scientific investigation on a rigorously mathematical base.

scientism. A belief that the methods of the natural sciences can adequately address all philosophical questions and problems, or that society should be based on scientific principles. The term is often used pejoratively. See also **positivism**.

second-wave feminism, see **feminism**.

secular. From the Latin *sæculum*, meaning a generation or an age. If something is secular it belongs to this age, not to the age to come. The opposite of sacred, hence non-religious.

shalom (Hebrew: 'peace'). The biblical notion of *shalom* is broader than 'peace' understood as a cessation of hostilities. It is a state of all-round personal and social flourishing.

simulacrum. In Plato's theory of **Forms**, a simulacrum is the copy of a copy. A bed built by a carpenter is a copy of the Form of a bed, but a bed painted by an artist is a copy of that copy. In twentieth-century thought, the term is taken up by Deleuze and Baudrillard. For Baudrillard, **postmodern** society is a society of the simulacrum with no original ideas or images but rather the endless circulation of copies of copies. Deleuze rejects Plato's privilege of Form over copy. For Deleuze himself, the simulacrum no longer resembles the form but serves as its destabilising foundation. In one of Deleuze's examples, Plato's myth of the cave grounds the difference between truth and myth.

sin, **sinner**. In Christian theology, the distinction is made between 'sin' – humankind's rebellion against God's rule that began when Adam and Eve ate from the tree of the knowledge of good and evil in Genesis 3 – and 'sins' – individual thoughts, words or actions that are symptoms of this rebellion. Sin provokes God's judgment, but human beings can be **redeemed** from sin through the death of Jesus Christ. Sin will end at the **parousia**.

sprezzatura. A characteristic sensibility of the **Renaissance** period, *sprezzatura* is a demeanour of restrained and studied ease, an appearance of effortlessness. It is portrayed most famously Castiglione's *Courtier* as the ideal attitude for a gentleman at court. In an age of growing urbanisation, *sprezzatura* replaced the earlier ideal of **courtly love**. Leonardo's *Mona Lisa* has been said to portray an attitude of *sprezzatura*.

stream of consciousness. A device characteristic of the **modernist novel** in which an interior monologue takes the form of the continuous flow of a character's thoughts, perceptions and memories. Important examples of the stream of consciousness can be found in Joyce's *Ulysses*, Woolf's *Mrs Dalloway* and Faulkner's *The Sound and the Fury*.

structuralism. The movement in twentieth-century philosophy and social thought that eclipsed **existentialism** in 1950s France and flourished in the 1960s. Structuralism approaches its objects of study as elements of an irreducible system or field, not as independent atoms. The structuralist approach to language is based on the linguistics of Ferdinand de Saussure, who argued that meaning is not a function of a correspondence between a single world and a concept, but emerges from a system of differences between the meaning of words. For example: the difference between 'river' and 'stream' in

English is that a river is larger that a stream, but the difference between 'fleuve' and 'rivière' in French is that a 'fleuve' flows into the sea, whereas a 'rivière' does not. The two languages construct reality in different ways, and English strictly has no word either for 'rivière' or for 'fleuve'. Prominent structuralists include Claude Lévi-Strauss, Roland Barthes and Jacques Lacan.

sublation. In Hegel's **dialectical idealism**, sublation is the process whereby two seemingly incompatible and contradictory categories (for example: 'being' and 'nonbeing') are superseded by a new category which includes and transforms them both (for example: 'becoming'). Hegel's German term (*Aufhebung*) carries meanings of raising up, negating and preserving. If the second category (nonbeing) negates the first (being), then sublation is the negation of a negation.

sublime. Prominent in eighteenth-century **aesthetics**, the sublime is an experience or thought that overwhelms the capacity of the human mind to comprehend it, apt to be described as ' breathtaking' or 'beyond words'. The sublime often provokes fear (a storm at sea) or wonder (the starry heavens). The most prominent theorist of the sublime in the modern period is Kant, and it is frequently evoked by **Romantic** poets and thinkers.

subversion. To subvert an idea, a movement or a truth is not to oppose or to argue against it, but to challenge the categories that make sense of it. For example, instead of merely opposing masculinist logic (which would itself conform to the logic of opposition that underpins masculinist thought) **third-wave feminists** disrupt its categories and oppositions through *écriture féminine*. The rejection of opposition in favour of subversion is a helpful way of understanding the difference between the early twentieth-century **avant-garde** and later **postmodernism**. Ironic subversion can be considered a characteristic sensibility of the postmodern **ethos**.

superego. In Freud's second map of the human mind, the superego is a censor, an internal policeman that adopts standards of behaviour dictated by society or by the father, and that constrains the id. See also **id**, **ego**.

suprasensory. The suprasensory is a term employed by Heidegger in 'Nietzsche's Word: God is Dead' to describe that domain of being which, after the **death of God**, ceases to be a meaningful category for our understanding of the world. It includes Plato's **Forms**, as well as any idea of God that places him beyond human experience.

Surrealism. A twentieth-century **avant-garde** artistic and literary movement that evolved out of **Dada**. Taking inspiration from Freud's account of the unconscious, Surrealists sought to give expression to the unconscious mind through surprising juxtapositions of objects and ideas, through trance, and sometimes through violence. Major figures include Breton, Aragon, Dalí, Magritte, Miró and Klee.

syllogism. The most basic and widespread form of philosophical argumentation, formalised by Aristotle. A syllogism contains two premises and a conclusion such that, if both the premises are true and the reasoning is valid, the conclusion is also true.

tabula rasa (Latin: 'blank slate'). Many **empiricist** philosophies hold that human beings enter the world as a blank slate, without any innate ideas, and that all knowledge is gained through sense experience. The term is used by the **scholastic realists** and is often applied to Locke's empiricism.

Tanach. The word refers to the Hebrew Scriptures or Christian Old Testament. Its three syllables indicate the three divisions of the law (*torah*), prophets (*nevi'im*) and writings (*kethuvim*).

teleology (from the Latin *telos*: end). The study of the purposes or ends of things. Aristotle's notion of **final causes** gives a teleological understanding of nature, according to which every substance is 'good for' a particular function. Many **Enlightenment** views of history are teleological, assuming incremental progress to a *telos* of human perfection. The notion of a determined teleology in nature is challenged by Francis Bacon, and by some interpretations of Darwinian evolution. Teleology is not to be confused with Christian **eschatology**.

thaumazein. For ancient Greek philosophers, *thuamazein* is the state of wonder and/or incomprehension at the world that gives rise to philosophical thought.

theism. The belief or doctrine that there exists one or more than one gods. See also **pantheism**, **monotheism**.

third-wave feminism, see **feminism**.

theogony. The creation of gods by other gods. Common to many cultures of the ancient Middle East, but opposed in the opening words of Genesis 1: 'In the beginning, God ...'. The word is also the title of a work by the Greek poet Hesiod that describes the genealogy of the gods.

þrym and *ellen*. The Anglo-Saxon **epic** *Beowulf* celebrates the *þrym* (glory) and *ellen* (valour) of the ancient Danish kings. The two terms encapsulate the **ethos** of the Anglo-Saxon warrior. Glory is seen primarily as praise from one's community and peers, and valour is shown supremely in battle.

timbre. The character or 'colour' of a musical sound that depends on the particular voice or instrument producing it. The 'piano-ness' of a piano or the 'flute-ness' of a flute.

totalisation. For much **postmodern** thought, the modern era is characterised by systems that seek exhaustively to encompass what they categorise, providing complete explanations of their objects. Such 'totalising' systems would include Hegel's **dialectical idealism** and Marx's **dialectical materialism**. These systems of knowledge are thought by many postmodern philosophers to lead to violence because they neglect or oppress exceptions or nuances to their generalising schemes.

tragedy. A theatrical genre, serious in tone, that represents the downfall of a notable or elevated character (the tragic hero) to a state of wretchedness or, frequently, death. The three great ancient Greek tragedians are Aeschylus, Sophocles and Euripides, and Seneca was the greatest ancient Roman tragedian (though some critics refuse to classify his plays as tragedies). Tragedy re-emerged in **Renaissance** England (with Shakespeare and Marlowe) where it was intermingled with comedy, and in seventeenth-century France (with Racine and Corneille), where it most certainly wasn't.

Trinity, **Trinitarian**. The Christian belief and doctrine that God is one God in three persons: God the Father, God the Son and God the Holy Spirit. Trinitarianism is a characteristic belief of orthodox Christianity. The word does not appear in the Bible, and became established at the Council of Nicaea (325 AD) as the orthodox understanding of the Bible's teaching on the relation of Father, Son and Spirit.

trivium. The lower division of the seven liberal arts, typically studied as an introductory course in the **medieval** university. The trivium comprised grammar, rhetoric and logic (also known as **dialectic**). See also **quadrivium**.

type, see **typology**.

typology. In the New Testament and the early church, typology is a way of interpreting the Old Testament according to which people, objects and rituals are understood to foreshadow Jesus Christ. For example: Noah's ark is understood to be a **type** of Christian baptism, and the sacrifices in the Old Testament temple are understood as types of Christ's sacrifice of himself on the cross. In each case, the Old Testament provides the type, and Christ is the **antitype**.

universals. In philosophy, universals are properties that can be instantiated in any number of particular objects. For example, the universal 'red' can be instantiated in the red mug on my desk, the red chair in my room and the red pen in my hand... Both Plato and Aristotle hold to the real existence of universals, though for Plato they exist independently of particulars in the world of **Forms**, whereas for Aristotle they only exist in particulars. Boethius takes a broadly Aristotelian approach, as does **medieval scholastic** realism, whereas nominalism denies the existence of universals. See also **nominalism**, **particulars**, **realism**.

vernacular. The language or dialect spoken by the majority of people in a country or region. In **medieval** and **Renaissance** Europe, vernacular languages are commonly contrasted with Latin, the language of learning. Notable early books in the vernacular include Dante's *Divine Comedy* (finished 1321), Wycliffe's translation of the Bible (1380s-90s) and Chaucer's *Canterbury Tales* (late fourteenth century).

virtù. In Machiavelli's writing, *virtù* is the quality desired of rulers, which could often contradict an understanding of virtue as moral goodness. It is derived from the Latin *virtus*, meaning manliness or excellence, and for Machiavelli the leader displaying *virtù* will show ruthlessness military prowess and use strategic violence to make himself feared.

Visigoths. One of the Germanic tribes that proliferated in Europe during the latter centuries of the western Roman empire. It was the Visigoths, under the leadership of Alaric, who invaded and sacked Rome in 410 AD. They were defeated by the Franks (ancestors of Charlemagne) in 507.

Yahweh. In the Hebrew of the Old Testament, Yahweh is the personal name that God reveals to Moses. From a Hebrew form of the verb 'to be', the Hebrew YHWH usually appears as 'the LORD' in modern translations.

Further Reading

This list of further reading is offered as a tasting menu, not as a full steak meal. It does not detail all the texts mentioned in this book, but instead offers extracts from select key primary texts relevant to each chapter. The aim is to provide the reader with a jumping-off point for acquiring or deepening a crucial first-hand acquaintance with some of the most influential and important writing in the Western tradition. References are given to print editions and, where the texts are in the public domain, also to URLs, and the excerpts and selections have been kept to an average of no more than 30 pages each. Selected secondary histories and commentaries are also listed for each chapter.

In addition to these extracts and secondary texts, readers may wish to pursue further reading in volumes that draw together themes that overarch the history of Western philosophy, literature and art. Two of the most helpful of these synthesizing books are Mortimer J. Adler's hefty and now somewhat dated *The Syntopicon: An Index to the Great Ideas* (2 vols, Chicago; London: Encyclopaedia Britannica, 1952), and Bernard Williams' more manageable and less dated *Keywords* (now revised and updated by Tony Bennett, Lawrence Grossberg and Meaghan Morris and re-issued as *New Keywords: A Revised Vocabulary of Culture and Society*, Oxford: Blackwell, 2005). For nineteenth- and twentieth-century critical and literary theory, David Macey's *The Penguin Dictionary of Critical Theory* (London; New York: Penguin Books, 2001) is a welcome machete enabling the reader to cut a path through the thick undergrowth of theoretical jargon. Finally, Sister Wendy Beckett's beautifully produced *The Story of Painting* (London; New York: Dorling Kindersley, 1994) provides a host of high quality full colour reproductions illustrating the development of Western art from the Greeks to the late twentieth century.

1. The Roots of Western Culture: Greece and Rome

Primary reading

Homer, *The Odyssey,* translated by E.V. Rieu; revised translation by D.C.H. Rieu; introduction by Peter Jones. London; New York: Penguin Books, 2003, chapter 5, 'Calypso', 63-75. Also available at http://classics.mit.edu/Homer/odyssey.5.v.html. Last accessed July 2011.

Plato, *The Republic*, edited by G.R.F. Ferrari, translated by Tom Griffith. Cambridge: Cambridge University Press, 2001, book 7, 514a-541b (pp.

220-51). Also available at http://classics.mit.edu/Plato/republic.8.vii. html. Last accessed July 2011.

Secondary reading

The Cambridge Companion to Aristotle, edited by Jonathan Barnes. Cambridge: Cambridge University Press, 1995.

The Cambridge Companion to Plato, edited by Richard Kraut. Cambridge: Cambridge University Press, 1992.

Noble, Thomas F.X., *Western Civilization: Beyond Boundaries,* 6th edn. Belmont, CA.: Wadsworth, 2011, chapters 3-7.

Tarnas, Richard, *The Passion of the Western Mind: Understanding the Ideas that have Shaped Our World View.* London: Pimlico, 1991, chapters I and II.

2. The Roots of Western Culture: Christianity

Primary reading

Holy Bible, English Standard Version. London: Collins, 2002, Genesis chapters 1-12 (pp. 1-11); 'The Gospel According to Mark' (pp. 1008-29). Also available at http://www.gnpcb.org/esv/. Last accessed July 2011.

Secondary reading

Noble, Thomas F.X., *Western Civilization: Beyond Boundaries*, 6th edn. Belmont, CA: Wadsworth, 2011, chapter 7.

Prickett, Stephen, and Robert Barnes, *The Bible: Landmarks of World Literature.* Cambridge: Cambridge University Press, 1991.

The Cambridge Companion to Augustine, edited by Eleonore Stump and Norman Kretzmann. Cambridge: Cambridge University Press, 2001.

The Cambridge Companion to the Age of Constantine, edited by Noel Emmanuel Lenski. Cambridge: Cambridge University Press, 2006.

Tarnas, Richard, *The Passion of the Western Mind: Understanding the Ideas that have Shaped Our World View.* London: Pimlico, 1991, chapter III.

3. From Catacombs to Cathedrals: The Middle Ages

Primary reading

Dante, *The Divine Comedy*, vol. I: *Inferno*, translated by Mark Musa, Cantos 1-3 (pp. 67-96). Also available at http://www.gutenberg.org/ files/1001/1001-h/1001-h.htm. Last accessed July 2011.

Kreeft, Peter, *A Summa of the Summa: The Essential Philosophical Passages of St Thomas Aquinas' Summa Theologica.* San Francisco: Ignatius Press, 1990, 'Proofs for the Existence of God', 51-70. Also available at http://www.ccel.org/ccel/aquinas/summa.FP_Q2.html. Last accessed July 2011.

Secondary reading

Clark, Kenneth, *Civilization: A Personal View*. London: British Broadcasting Corporation and John Murray, 1969, chapters 1-3.

The Cambridge Companion to Dante, 2nd edn, edited by Rachel Jacoff. Cambridge: Cambridge University Press, 2007.

Noble, Thomas F.X., *Western Civilization: Beyond Boundaries*, 6th edn, Belmont, CA: Wadsworth, 2011, chapters 8-11.

Tarnas, Richard, *The Passion of the Western Mind: Understanding the Ideas that have Shaped Our World View*. London: Pimlico, 1991, chapter IV.

4. Man the Measure of All Things: The Renaissance

Primary reading

Montaigne, Michel Eyquem de, *Essays*. London; New York: Penguin Books, 1993, book 3, chapter 2: 'Of Repentance', pp. 235-50. Also available at http://www.gutenberg.org/files/3600/3600-h/3600-h.htm. Last accessed July 2011.

Pico Della Mirandola, Giovanni, *Oration on the Dignity of Man*, translated by Aloysius Robert Caponigri. South Bend, Indiana: Gateway Editions, 1996. Also available at http://cscs.umich.edu/~crshalizi/Mirandola/. Last accessed July 2011.

Secondary reading

The Cambridge Companion to English Renaissance Drama, edited by A.R. Braunmuller and Michael Hattaway. Cambridge: Cambridge University Press, 1990.

Clark, Kenneth, *Civilization: A Personal View*. London: British Broadcasting Corporation and John Murray, 1969, chapters 4-6.

The Cambridge Companion to Renaissance Humanism, edited by Jill Kraye. Cambridge: Cambridge University Press, 1996.

The Cambridge Companion to Montaigne, edited by Ullrich Langer. Cambridge: Cambridge University Press, 2005.

Noble, Thomas F.X., *Western Civilization: Beyond Boundaries*, 6th edn. Belmont, CA: Wadsworth, 2011, chapters 12-13.

Tarnas, Richard, *The Passion of the Western Mind: Understanding the Ideas that have Shaped Our World View*. London: Pimlico, 1991, chapter V.

5. Into the Modern Age: Religious Reformation and Scientific Revolution

Primary reading

Descartes, René, 'A Discourse of a Method for the well guiding of Reason and the Discovery of Truth in the Sciences', in *Descartes: Selected Philosophical Writings*, edited by John Cottingham. Cambridge: Cambridge University Press, 1988, pp. 20-56. Also available at http://www.gutenberg.org/files/59/59-h/59-h.htm. Last accessed July 2011.

Luther, Martin, 'Preface to the Letter of St Paul to the Romans, 1522', in *Martin Luther: Selections from his Writings*, edited with an introduction by John Dillenberger. New York: Doubleday, 1961, pp. 19-34. Also available at http://www.ccel.org/l/luther/romans/pref_romans.html. Last accessed July 2011.

Secondary reading

The Cambridge Companion to Reformation Theology, edited by David V.N. Bagchi and David Curtis Steinmetz. Cambridge: Cambridge University Press, 2004.

Clark, Kenneth, *Civilization: A Personal View*. London: British Broadcasting Corporation and John Murray, 1969, chapters 7-9.

The Cambridge Companion to Descartes, edited by John Cottingham. Cambridge: Cambridge University Press, 1992.

The Cambridge Companion to Martin Luther, edited by Donald K. McKim. Cambridge; New York: Cambridge University Press, 2003.

Noble, Thomas F.X., *Western Civilization: Beyond Boundaries*, 6th edn. Belmont, CA: Wadsworth, 2011, chapters 14-17.

The Cambridge Companion to Bacon, edited by Markku Peltonen. Cambridge: Cambridge University Press, 1996.

Tarnas, Richard, *The Passion of the Western Mind: Understanding the Ideas that have Shaped Our World View*. London: Pimlico, 1991, chapter V.

6. Reason and its Limits: The Enlightenment and Romanticism

Primary reading

Kant, Immanuel, *An Answer to the Question 'What is enlightenment?'*, translated by H.B. Nisbet. London; New York: Penguin, 2009, pp. 1-11. Also available at http://www.english.upenn.edu/~mgamer/Etexts/kant.html. Last accessed July 2011.

Wordsworth, William, 'The Prelude', in *The Major Works*, edited with an introduction and notes by Stephen Gill. Oxford: Oxford University Press, 2000, book X (lines 693-1038; pp. 550-8). Also available at http://

www.gutenberg.org/files/12383/12383-h/Wordsworth3c.html (though in a different version). Last accessed July 2011.

Secondary reading

Clark, Kenneth, *Civilization: A Personal View*. London: British Broadcasting Corporation and John Murray, 1969, chapters 10-12.

The Cambridge Companion to Voltaire, edited by Nicholas Cronk. Cambridge: Cambridge University Press, 2009.

The Cambridge Companion to British Romanticism, edited by Stuart Curran, 2nd edn. Cambridge: Cambridge University Press, 2010.

The Cambridge Companion to Kant, edited by Paul Guyer. Cambridge: Cambridge University Press, 1992.

Noble, Thomas F.X., *Western Civilization: Beyond Boundaries*, 6th edn. Belmont, CA.: Wadsworth, 2011, chapters 18-23.

The Cambridge Companion to Rousseau, edited by Patrick Riley. Cambridge: Cambridge University Press, 2001.

Tarnas, Richard, *The Passion of the Western Mind: Understanding the Ideas that have Shaped Our World View*. London: Pimlico, 1991, chapter VI.

7. Old Certainties, New Crises: The Death of God, Modernism and Existentialism

Primary reading

Nietzsche, Friedrich Wilhelm, *The Gay Science: With a Prelude in German Rhymes and an Appendix of Songs*, edited by Bernard Williams; translated by Josefine Nauckhoff; poems translated by Adrian Del Caro. Cambridge: Cambridge University Press, 2001, 'Parable of the Madman', §125, 119-20. Also available at http://www.fordham.edu/halsall/mod/nietzsche-madman.html. Last accessed July 2011.

Kafka, Franz, *The Metamorphosis and Other Stories*, translated by Joyce Crick, with an introduction and notes by Ritchie Robertson. Oxford: Oxford University Press, 2009, 'The Metamorphosis', pp. 29-74. Also available at http://www.gutenberg.org/files/5200/5200-h/5200-h.htm. Last accessed July 2011.

Sartre, Jean-Paul, *Jean-Paul Sartre: Basic Writings*, edited by Stephen Priest. London: Routledge, 2000, 'Existentialism and Humanism', pp. 25-46. Also available at http://www.marxists.org/reference/archive/sartre/works/exist/sartre.htm. Last accessed July 2011.

Secondary reading

Clark, Kenneth, *Civilization: A Personal View*, London: British Broadcasting Corporation and John Murray, 1969, chapter 13.

The Cambridge Companion to Sartre, edited by Christina Howells. Cambridge: Cambridge University Press, 1992.

Further Reading

The Cambridge Companion to Camus, edited by Edward J. Hughes. Cambridge: Cambridge University Press, 2007.

The Cambridge Companion to Modernism, edited by Michael H. Levenson. Cambridge: Cambridge University Press, 1999.

The Cambridge Companion to Nietzsche, edited by Bernd Magnus and Kathleen M. Higgins. Cambridge: Cambridge University Press, 1996.

Noble, Thomas F.X., *Western Civilization: Beyond Boundaries*, 6th edn. Belmont, CA: Wadsworth, 2011, chapters 24-8.

Tarnas, Richard, *The Passion of the Western Mind: Understanding the Ideas that have Shaped Our World View*. London: Pimlico, 1991, chapter VI.

8. Evolving Ideas of Humanity: Darwin, Marx, Freud and Feminism

Primary reading

Darwin, Charles, *The Descent of Man, And Selection in Relation to Sex*, with an introduction by John Tyler Bonner and Robert M. May. Princeton, NJ: Princeton University Press, 1981, Introduction, pp. 1-5. Also available at http://www.literature.org/authors/darwin-harles/the-descent-of-man/introduction.html. Last accessed July 2011.

Freud, Sigmund, 'Some psychical consequences of the anatomical distinction between the sexes', in *The Standard Edition of the Complete Psychological Works of Sigmund Freud*, edited by James Strachey and Anna Freud. London: Hogarth, 1961, vol. 19, pp. 248-58. Also available at https://www.college.columbia.edu/core/students/cc/optitexts/freudsex.pdf. Last accessed July 2011.

Kristeva, Julia, 'About Chinese Women', in *The Kristeva Reader*, edited by Toril Moy. London: Blackwell, 1986, pp. 138-59.

Marx, Karl, and Friedrich Engels, *The Communist Manifesto*, edited with an introduction by David McLellan. Oxford: Oxford University Press, 2008. Also available at http://www.marxists.org/archive/marx/works/1848/communist-manifesto/. Last accessed July 2011.

Secondary reading

The Cambridge Companion to Marx, edited by Terrell Carver. Cambridge: Cambridge University Press, 1991.

Clark, Kenneth, *Civilization: A Personal View*. London: British Broadcasting Corporation and John Murray, 1969, chapter 13.

The Cambridge Companion to Darwin, edited by M.J.S. Hodge and Gregory Radick, 2nd edn. Cambridge: Cambridge University Press, 2009.

The Cambridge Companion to Feminism in Philosophy, edited by Jennifer Hornsby and Miranda Fricker. Cambridge: Cambridge University Press, 2000.

The Cambridge Companion to Freud, edited by Jerome Neu. Cambridge: Cambridge University Press, 1992.

Noble, Thomas F.X., *Western Civilization: Beyond Boundaries*, 6th edn. Belmont, CA: Wadsworth, 2011, chapters 24-8.
Tarnas, Richard, *The Passion of the Western Mind: Understanding the Ideas that have Shaped Our World View*. London: Pimlico, 1991, chapter VI.

9. What Comes After the New? Postmodernism and Postmodernity

Primary reading

Barthes, Roland, 'The Death of the Author', in *Modern Criticism and Theory: A Reader*. London: Longman, 1988, pp. 313-16.
Calvino, Italo, *If on a Winter's Night a Traveller*, translated by William Weaver. London: Vintage Books, 1998. See in particular chapters entitled '1' and 'If on a Winter's Night a Traveller', pp. 3-24.

Secondary reading

The Cambridge Companion to Postmodernism, edited by Steven Connor. Cambridge: Cambridge University Press, 2004.
Eagleton, Terry, *Literary Theory: An Introduction*, 2nd edn. Oxford: Blackwell, 2008.
Culler, Jonathan D., *Literary Theory: A Very Short Introduction*, Oxford: Oxford University Press, 1997.
Noble, Thomas F.X., *Western Civilization: Beyond Boundaries*, 6th edn. Belmont, CA: Wadsworth, 2011, chapters 29-30.
Tarnas, Richard, *The Passion of the Western Mind: Understanding the Ideas that have Shaped Our World View*. London: Pimlico, 1991, chapter VI.

Index